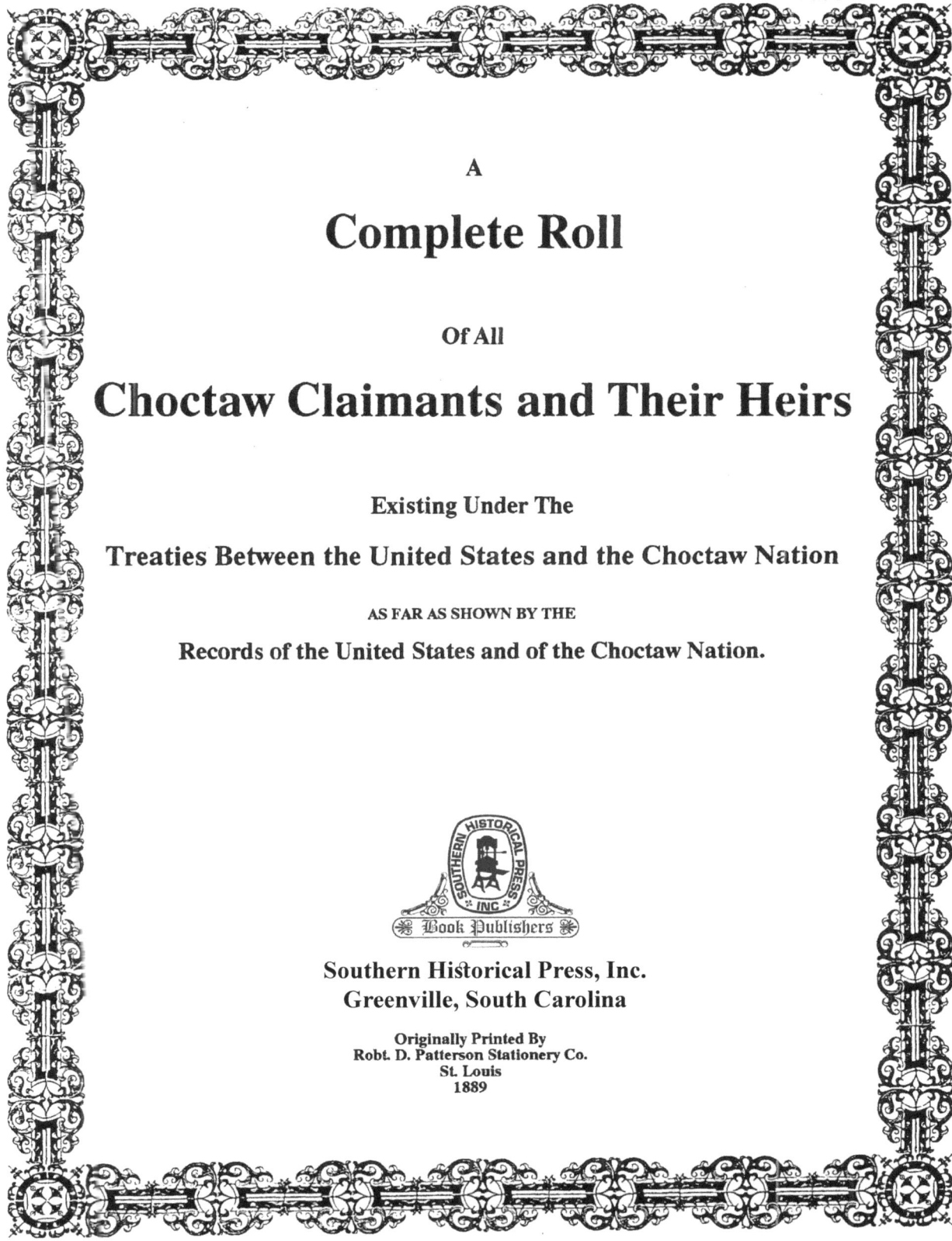

A

Complete Roll

Of All

Choctaw Claimants and Their Heirs

Existing Under The

Treaties Between the United States and the Choctaw Nation

AS FAR AS SHOWN BY THE

Records of the United States and of the Choctaw Nation.

Southern Historical Press, Inc.
Greenville, South Carolina

Originally Printed By
Robt. D. Patterson Stationery Co.
St. Louis
1889

Please direct all correspondence and book orders to:
SOUTHERN HISTORICAL PRESS, Inc.
PO Box 1267
Greenville, SC   29602-1267

Originally printed St. Louis, 1889
ISBN #978-1-63914-254-5
Printed in the United States of America

Table of Contents

Introduction.. i

Treaties Between the U.S.
and the Choctaw Nation.................................. iii

Selected Bibliography... v

Choctaw Claimant's.. 1

Key to Symbols found in List......................... 193

Introduction

To be Read

This work was originally published in 1889 by the Patterson Stationary Company, St. Louis, Missouri. Indications are that this was an official Choctaw document, however we are not certain of that. The work is an alphabetical listing of all known Choctaw Claimants against the United States government. These claims were based upon treaties that had been made between the United States and the Choctaw Nation. A listing of all treaties between these parties is included in this work.

The source for this listing is some what in question. However, there are indications that not only were official United States documents used, but that records of the Choctaw Nation were also searched. Most of the official government documents have been microfilmed and are available from the National Archives. Locating these records will present a challenge to the most experienced researcher.

In the National Archives, Record Group 75, are located the Records of the Claims Commission connected with the 1830 Treaty of Dancing Rabbit Creek. Article 14 of the treaty allowed Indians who chose to remain in the East and not emigrate to the Indian Territory to claim special allotments. Much of these allotments were in the form of land, but some were for scrip. The United States appointed several commissions to rule on these various claims. The time period covered is around 1837 to 1854. These dates may vary as some of the documents have information in them that was added much later, some as late as 1906. Many of the names included in this work are located within Record Group 75.

Located within the Records of the Bureau of Land Management, Record Group 49, are copies of scrip certificates surrendered for land. These records primarily cover the period 1843 to 1849. These certificates were given to Choctaw Indians who could not be given their allotments from the treaty of 1830, commonly called The Treaty of Dancing Rabbit Creek. A special act of Congress (dated August 23, 1842) provided for the issuance of this scrip. What this entitled the bearer to was selected public lands located in Mississippi, Louisiana, Alabama, or Arkansas. Two certificates were needed to make the claim. The second certificate was not presented unless the Indian moved to the Indian Territory. On March 3, 1845 it was enacted that instead of

giving the scrip certificates to the Choctaw, the value of the scrip would be determined and that amount as well as interest on it would be paid to the Indians. These records should be checked if one feels the person or persons being researched remained in the East.

Also connected with the 1830 Treaty of Dancing Rabbit Creek are the Choctaw Net Proceeds Case. These were claims by individual Choctaw Indians that came about due to their removal to Indian Territory. Lands that had been ceded by the Choctaw Nation in the East were sold. After "expenses" had been deducted the monies were set aside to settle the above mentioned claims. Beside the value of their land some Choctaw made claims for the value of improvements to the land, emigration expenses, and other loses. For many, many years the United States made no payment to the Choctaw in regards to these claims. The legal arguments connected with these claims ran from June 22, 1855, when congress wanted the Senate to set a gross sum to cover all the claims of both the Choctaw Nation and individual Choctaw, to 1898 when a commission appointed by the Choctaw Council took up the issue of any claims remaining unpaid up to that time. Beside the National Archives Record Group 75 mentioned above, many of the records connected with these claims are located in the Records of the U.S. Court of Claims, Record Group 123, Case File 12742.

Information on these Record Groups can be had by contacting the National Archives - NNRC, Washington, DC 20408. Please be specific in your letter, and do not expect a very rapid response to your inquiry.

Information might also be had by writing the Oklahoma Historical Society, 2100 North Lincoln Blvd., Oklahoma City, Oklahoma 73105

As stated earlier, the research is challenging, but I think we would all agree the results are often times so very, very sweet.

Treaties Between the United States and the Choctaw Nation

January 3, 1786..Treaty of Hopewell

December 17, 1801..Treaty of Ft. Adams

October 17, 1802..Treaty of Ft. Confederation

August 31, 1803...Treaty of Hoe Buckintoopa

November 16, 1805...Treaty of Mount Dexter

October 24, 1816..Treaty of Fort St. Stephens

October 18, 1820..Treaty of Doak's Stand

January 20, 1825..Treaty of Washington City

September 15, 1830...Treaty of Dancing Rabbit Creek

NOTE: Most treaties super cede the one before them, thus most of the claims referenced in this work will fall under the jurisdiction of The Treaty of Dancing Rabbit Creek. Some may also apply to The Treaty of Doak's Stand, however, their numbers should be very few. If you are interested in the detail of the above treaties I would suggest going to one of the works listed in the bibliography.

Selected Bibliography

Baird, E. Daniel 1972 *Peter Pitchlynn: Chief of the Choctaws*. Norman: University of Oklahoma Press.

---------- 1973 *The Choctaw People*. Phoenix: Indian Tribal Series.

Benson, Henry C. 1860 *Life Among the Choctaw Indians and Sketches of the South-West*. Cincinnati: Swormstedt & Poe.

Bounds, Thelma V. 1961 *An Indian Tribe of the Mississippi: Meet Our Choctaw Friends*. New York: Exposition Press.

Coleman, Michael C. 1985 *Presbyterian Missionary Attitudes Toward American Indians*. Jackson: University of Mississippi Press.

Conklin, Paul 1975 *Choctaw Boys*. New York: Dodd, Mead, & Company.

Cotterill, Robert S. 1954 *The Southern Indians: The Story of the Civilized Tribes Before Removal*. Norman: University of Oklahoma Press.

Cushman, Horatio B. 1899 *History of the Choctaw, Chickasaw, and Natchez Indians*. Greenville, Texas: Highlight Printing House.

---------- 1962 *History of the Choctaw, Chickasaw, and Natchez Indians*. Norman: University of Oklahoma Press.

Debo, Angie 1934 *The Rise and Fall of the Choctaw Republic*. Norman: University of Oklahoma Press.

---------- 1940 *And Still the Waters Run*. Princeton: University Press.

---------- 1949 *Oklahoma: Foot-Loose and Fancy-Free*. Norman: University of Oklahoma Press.

De Rosier, Arthur H. 1970 *The Removal of the Choctaw Indians*. Knoxville: University of Tennessee Press.

Goss, Joe R. 1992 *The Choctaw Academy, Official Correspondence 1825 - 1841*. Conway, Arkansas: Oldbuck Press.

Kidwell, Clara Sue, and Charles Roberts 1980 *The Choctaw: A Critical Bibliography*. Bloomington: Published for the Newberry Library by Indiana University Press.

McKee, Jesse O., and Jon A. Schlenker 1980 *The Choctaw*. Jackson: University Press of Mississippi.

Peterson, John 1985 *A Choctaw Source Book*. New York: Garland Publishing.

Reeves, Carolyn Keller 1985 *The Choctaw Before Removal*. Jackson: University Press of Mississippi.

Smith, Allene DeShazo 1951 *Greenwood LeFlore and the Choctaw Indians of The Mississippi Valley*. Memphis: C.A. Davis Printing Co., Inc.

Swanton, John R. 1931 *Source Material for the Social and Ceremonial Life of the Choctaw Indians*. Bulletin No. 103. Washington, D.C.: Government Printing Office.

Tubbee, Okah 1848 *A Sketch of the Life of Okah Tubbee, Alias William Chubbee, Son of the Head Chief, Mosholeh Tubbee, of the Choctaw Nation of Indians*. Springfield, Mass.: H.S. Taylor.

Washburn, Wilcomb E. 1975 *The American Indians*. New York: Harper and Row Publishers, Inc.

Wells, Samuel J., and Roseanna Tubby 1986 *After Removal: The Choctaw in Mississippi*. Jackson: University Press of Mississippi.

Young, Mary Elizabeth 1961 *Redskins, Ruffleshirts, and Rednecks*. Norman: University of Oklahoma Press.

Aaihtahubbi, 50

A al bee, 95

A al ber, 145

Aaoubbee, 1041

Aba, 190

Aba cha hona, 194

Aba che hona, 191

A ba chub bee, 148

A ba chuf fa, 475

A ba ha la ta, 169

A bah ka tubbee, 394

Ab a ho ca, 797

Aba hona, 223

*Aba hotima, 288

Ab ah we le, 377

A ba la ho ka, 148, 243

A ba la tubbee, 26

Aba na la, 162

A-ba-nan-tub-bee, 146, 221

A-ban-a-tub-bee, 147, 190

Abanintubbe, 275

Abatemah, 515

Abatiya, alias Hobateia, 275

Abatekala, 169

Ab a took a loo, 806

Abatuja, alias Hobateia, 320

Abawala, 157, 219

Abba ho nah, 400

R.C. Ab-ba-wa-la-ho-yo, 658

Abbe, or Ahmahbe, 512

Abbe cheffah, 491, 825

Abbechiffah, 572

Abbe-chuf-fah, 386

Ab-bee-ho-nah, 141

Ab-bee-toak-cha-ah, 137

Abbee took che-ah, 114

Abbeetook chiah, 88

Abbe ho chiah, 509

Abbe hoka, 525, 538

Ab be hom ah, 894

Abbe honah, 531

Abbe ho yo, 568, 689

Ab be ish ti yah, 525

Ab be ish to nah, 504

Ab be na chubbee, 1063

Ab be neen tubbe, 516

Ab-be-tiah, 377, 442, 554

Abbe-ti-yah, 376, 388, 484, 540

Ab-be-took-chi-ah, 382, 457, 515, 816, 827, 979

Abbetook chiah, or Hopiah, 600

R.C. Ab-be-took-chi-ah, or Hopiat ska te na, 655

Ab bitonah, 530

Abbitookcheah, or Hopiaskatena, 465

R.C.*A-be-che-ho-na, 661, *136

Abe haya, 274

Abehona, 264

A-be-nin-tub-bee, 146

Abe tisteia, 243

Ab e ti yah, 814, 825

Abe ti yea, 116

Abe tona, 265

Ab-e-too-nah, alias Amy, 796

Abetya, 212

Abichehona, 226

Ab-il-ish-ti-ah, 384

*Abistiayo, Jincy, 180

A-bit-au-you, 147

A-bit-coo-cha, 148

Ab-it-ik-ah-no-wah, 386, 475, 519

Ab-it-ik-O. no-wa, 825

Abit ish te ah, 561

Ab it ish ti ah, 504, 582

A-bi-ti-yea, 138

*Abitiyoh, 96

*Abi tok chaya, 228

Abit ti yah, 499

Ab le honah, 548

Abo chahona, 197

Abo wa tubbee, 192, 196

Abow watonah, 404

Abruika, 196

A cha, 406

Achaba, 192, 242

Achabah, 199

*Achafala, 12

*Achafantubbe, 312

Achaf-fah, 102, 145

*Achaffahonah, 58

Achaffola, 192

R.C. Achafola, 198, 204, 229, 318 [R.C. 664] 1027

A cha ho ma, 178

R.C.*Achahona, 50, 911, [R.C. 666] *12

*Achahpahtubbe, 32

*Achahtonabe, 194

*Achahube, Sampson, 248

Achaia, 158, 205, 225, 330, 838

Achaiatubbee, 235

Achain, 408

*Achakanle, 6

*Acharfona, 164

*Acharfar, 200

*Acharkamle, 28

Acha-tu-nub-bee, 139

Acha ya, 163

*Achaya hona, 194

*Achayahumne, 212

Achea, 1013

A-che-ab-bee, 139

A-che-ah, 148, 817

A. che-at-ub-bee, 144

A-che-ba, 145, 277, R.c. 645, 193

*A-che-bah, 100, 147, 435, *58

Ache hona, 250

*Ache hopia, Cap't, 202

Acheia, 201

A-che-le-tah, 139

A-che-mil-e-tub-bee, 139

*Acheta, 14

*Achetambe, 220

Ache tema, 265

A che to ho na, 930

*Achetona, 44

Ache-ubbee, 99, 139

*Acheyahona, 272

Achi ah, 419, 454, 457, 828

A-chick-e-ma-he-quo, 111

Achick-e-ma-hoy-no, 137

Achick-ma-hi-ah, 144

*Achiletta, Cap't. 126

*A china tubbee, 310

*Achintubbee, 50

*A chofahona, 126

*A chof atona, 304

*Achokmantima, 210

A-cho-mun-tubbee, 141

R.C. A. Cho-nes, 661

Achoon a tubbee, 198

*Achuckamah, 64

A-chun-ant-ub-bee, 143, 463

Achuse, 1005

R.C. Adam, 250, R. c. 665

*Adam, Elizah, 38

*Adam, Possey, 104

Afahmo var, 781, 789

*Afaliahoka, 227, 330, 408, *82

Afalopa, 213

*Afamatubbe, 242, * 224, 320

A-fan-A. che, 143

Afapolubbe, 256

R.C. A-fa-po-lubbee, [R. c. 642,] 915

Afapotubbi, 50

A far mo yar, 761

Af-fam-mo, 143

A-fol-lia, 142

Afolbapah, 317

A folo ble chubbee, 92

A folo blee chub bee, 142

A fo loo pa, 817, 825

Afoloopah, 274

Afolopa, 211

Agonohona, 1042

*Aha tatubi, 146

Aha cacha, Cap't,

A haic, chubbee, 910

Ahashtubbe, 535

Ahathla, 272

*Ahatubbee, 224, 244, 250

*Ahayutubbee, 6

Ah ba che, 500

Ahbah katubbee, and Cunne chunah, 440

Ahbah lah ho nubbee, 547

Ahbahnah tubbe, 531

R.C. Ah-ba-ho-ca, 619

Ah bah pil a bakah, 505

Ah bah wala hoyo, 590, 989

Ahbahwela, 690

Ah ban non tubbe, 514

Ah ba no tubbee, 378, 455, 533

Ah be chunk ta, 423

Ah be che ho nah, 1008

Ah be chunk tah, 396, 422

Ah be coo chah, 389, 485, 503

Ah be hah tah, 398

Ah be hah tubbe, 508

Ah be hattah, 551

Ah be ho chi ah, 579

Ah be ho ka, 501

Ah be ho nah, 504

Ah be lah, 798

Ah be nah tubbe, 544

R.C. Ah be nela, 592, R. c. 649

Ah be netubbe, 549

Ah be tah tah, 507

Ah be tiah, 440

Ah be tiah hoka, 512

R.C. Ah be tiyah, 459, 600, [R. c. 650], 964

R.C. Ah be too nah, alias Amy, 617

*Ah bi ti gah, 150

Ah bote shubbe, 509

*Ah bo tonah, 38

Ah bow we la, or Uhah wela, 569

Ah car neubbee, 734

Ah cha cun tubbe, 608

Ah cha fah ho, 387

AH cha fahona, 478

Ah cha fa honah, 522, 814, 827

Ah cha fa tubbee, 474

Ah chaf fah ho nah, 377, 442, 502

Ah chaf fa tubbee, 463

Ah chafo tubbe, 532

Ah chafo tubbee, 387, 814, 826

Ah chah ah tubbe, 551

Ah chah fah te mah, 405

Ah chah fah tubbee, 404

Ah chah fou tubbee, 403

*Ah chah kah hona, 98

Ah chah kan tubbe, 607

Ah chah le honah, 545

AH chah pa tubbee, 399

Ah cha kah hoonah, 517

Ah cha le tah, 521

Ah cha pa ho nah, 387, 474, 524, 579, 814, 826

*Ah cha pa howah, 120

Ah cha po tubbe, alias Elah po chubbe, 522

*Ah chayah tubbee, 50

R.c. Ah che ah, 384, 407, 440, 462, 521, 535, [R.c. 671,] 824

Ah cheah, 1064, 1065

Ah che ah ho ka, 584

R.c. Ah che ah honah, 405, 515, 557, [613 R. c.]

Ah che ah tubbe, 507, 579

Ah che ah tubbee, 381, 398

Ah che ba, 935, 936

Ah che bah, 376, 381, 436, 448, 502, 507, 531, 579

Ah che bah tam be, 597

Ah che ho nah, 579

Ah che la ta, 386

Ah che la tah, 469, 827

Ah che le tah, 530, 817

Ah che le tubbe, 540

Ah che te mah, 540

Ah che to mah, 504

Ah che to nah, 521, 543

Ah che too na, 579

Ah che too nah, 382

Ah che tubbe, 507

Ah che tubbee, 491, 572

Ah chia, 568

Ah chiah, 379, 383, 557, 689

R.c. Ah chick a ma ho nah, alias Ah ha chi o man, 619

Ah chick a maho nah, alias Ar ha chi o mah, 789

R.c. Ah chick e mah ho na, [R. c. 621], 788, 138

Ah chick mah ho nah, 537

Ah chick ma ho yo, 457

Ah chin tubbee, 375, 389, 468, 567, 639, 690

Ah cho ah, 54

Ah cho ah ho ka, 382, 505

*Ah choah hoke, 108

Ah chock a lin tubbee, 389

Ah chock mul a tubbee, 387

Ah cho fo la, 1026, 1027

Ah chok e mah, 179

Ah chok mulle tubbee, 478

Ah cho mah kah, 385, 471, 530

Ah cho mok ka, 826

Ah cho nan tubbe, 525

Ah chooch chah tubbe, 577

Ah chook e mah, 778

Ah chuck ma, 500

Ah chuck ah mah, 493, 565

Ah chuck mah, 455

Ah chuck mah hamah, 976

Ah chuck ma ho yo, 382

Ah chuck mah te ka tubbee, 379, 455

Ah chuck mah tubbee, 566, 689

Ah chuck mish stubbee, 690

Ah chuck mish tubbee, 564

Ah chuffah take ubbe, 560

Ah chukala, 514

Ah chuk mah, 389

Ah chuk mah heah, 509

Ah chuk ma hoka, 492, 562

Ah chuk ma ho yo, 516, 816, 827

Ah chuk mah ta ka tubbe, 533

Ah chuk mah tubbe, 538

Ah chuk ma tubbe, 529

Ah chuk mul la tubbee, 814, 827

Ah chuk multe tubbee, 570

Ah chu nau tubbee, 405

Ah chu non tubbe, 547

Ah chu wah, or chi no ka, 522

Ah cun e hub bee, 143

Ah cun ne ubbe, 579

A he ah tubbee, 405, 464

*Ah eh la homa, 144

*Ah eh la tona, 224

*Ah elhah ona, 62, 192

Ah e min tubbe, 522

Ah e nah, 510

Ah e ka timah, 556

Ah fab moon tubbe, 506

Ah fah mah, 395, 529

R.C. Ah fah mah ho nah, 601, 979 [R. C. 655]

Ah fah moah, 391, 395, 417, 418

Ah fah moon tubbee, 451

Ah fah moon tubbee, or Fal ah mo tubbee, 378

R.C. Ah fah ma yah, 380, [R. C. 617]

Ah fa ko ma, 383, 530

Ah fa ko ma tonah, 529

Ah fa ko me, 459, 520, 813, 826

Ah fa ko me honah, 507

Ah fa ma ho ka, 519

*Ah famah toklo, 78

Ah fam mah took a li, 474

Ah fa moon tubbe, 535

Ah fa moon tubbee, 389

Ah fa mo tubbe, 522

Ah fa nah, 579

Ah fanah tona, 1115

Ah fo ho lo ble chubbe, 445

Ah fo kah tubbe, 530

Ah fumah took alo, 452

Ah fum a took lo, 813

Ah fum e took a lo, 386

Ah fum ma took a lo, 826

Ah fum me, 389, 557

Ah ha cah cha, 480

R.C. Ah ha chi o man, alias Ah chick a ma ho nah, 619

Ah hah ka tubbe, 504

R.C. Ah ha ka tubbee, 623

Ah halth la, 497

Ah halth lah, 379

R.C. Ah ham ba, [R. c. 618,] 788

R.C. Ah han, 615

Ah ha tam be, 528

Ah ha tona, or Ahn tonah, 464

Ah ha to nah, 378, 448, 457, 783

R.C. Ah ha tonah, alias He i on to nah [R.C. 623,] 723, 724

Ah he kah ho nah, 507

Ah he oke, 507

Ah him ah, 921

R.C. Ah hi o chubbee, 420, 1041, [R.C. 681]

Ah hi o tubbe, 510

Ah hi o tubbe, or Hio tubbe, 580

Ah hi o tubbee, 389

Ah hock lin tubbee, 141

*Ah hog lacha, 403, 451, 464, *118

R.C. Ah ho gle cha, 1122, 1123, [R. c. 682]

Ah hog tichee, 420

Ah ho ka, 384, 561

Ah ho la ta mah, 398

Ah ho la tim ah, or Ha o le tim ah, 508

Ah ho le che, 381

R.C. Ah ho le tubbe, 579, [R. c. 679]

Ah ho le tubbee, 1106

Ah hom bah, 381, 512, 579

Ah ho nah, 387, 388, 395, 483, 500, 509, 541, 568, 690, 814, 826

Ah hook lin tubbe, 505, 507, 579

Ah hook li n tubbee, 388

Ah hook tubbe, 515

Ah ho temah, 551

*Ah ho ton ah, 50

Ah ho tu nah, 498

Ah ho yo, 390, 445, 492, 563

Ah ho yo tubbee, 391

R.C. Ah i ko te mah, 616

*Ah io chabbe, 232

R.C. A hi o chubbee, 178, 250, 319, 1117, 1119, [R. c. 666]

Ahio tubbee, 1038

Ah ish tim ah, 388, 504, 579

Ah is tubbe, 581

R.C. Ah is tubbee, 143, 806, [R. c. 677]

Ah ka che honah, 531

Ah kah na la tubbe, 514

Ah kah ne ah, 579

Ah kah ne ubbe, 445, 502

Ah kah ne ubbee, 377

Ah kah ne yubbe, 562

Ah kah ne yubbee, 492

*Ah kah noubbee, 58

Ah kah po tubbe, 522, 539

Ah kah puletubbe, 510

Ah ka ko kubbe, 509

Ah ka lam bee, 894

Ah ka ne ah, alias Nok ah neah, 508

Ah ka ne yubbee, 389

Ah ka oe ah, or Nok ha ne ah, 382

Ah kas te me tubbe, 505

Ah ko le tubbe, or Chah kloo a, 579

Ah ko moon tubbe, 509

Ah koo chaw tubbee, 462, 824

Ah koo chun tubbe, 530

Ah koo chum tubbe, 384

Ah la chubbee, 396

Ah lah chim ah, 509

Ah lah hoka, 587

Ah lah ho nubbe, 509

Ah lah ho te mah, 407

*Ah la ho ke, 126

*Ah la honah, 216

Ah lah tamah, 60½

Ah la kotub bee, 396

Ah la mah honah, 394, 569, 690

Ah la matubbee, 932

Ah la mo tubbe, 538

Ah la mo tubbee, 379

Ah le ha min tubbee, 95

Ah le ho ca, 88, 140

Ah le ho ka, 149, 388, 505

Ah le ho ka, or E lah ho ka, 579

Ah le ho tonah, 542

R.C. Ah le lah, 803, [R. c. 617]

Ah le mah tubbee, 141

*Ahle moon tubbe, 518, *70

*Ah li hona, 188

Ah lock ka cha, 396, 419

Ah lock ka cha, or Kachah, 417, 418

Ah loh ma, 507

Ah lo ko tubbee, 508

*Ah loma, 68

Ah lomah, 383, 459, 531, 813, 826

Ah lo mah honah, 515

Ah lo mah tubbe, 507, 531

Ah lo mah tubbee, 386, 474, 826

R.C. Ah lo ma tubbee, [R. c. 632] 860

R.C. Ah lo mut che, 626

Ah lo mutchey, 761

Ah lo nim chubbee, 497

Ah losho motubbee, 552

*Ah losh otubbee, 280

Ah lo wa tubbe, 552

R.C. Ahlubbee, [R. c. 619, 641], 906, 907

Ah lumme, 553

*Ah luttay cha, 26

Ah mah be, or Abbe, 512

Ah mah tu na, 89

Ah man to nah, 512

Ah man ton ah, 377

Ah man tubbee, 569, 690

Aa ma tuna, 140

R.C. Ah me ah che, [R. c 679,] 1106

Ah me ah tubbe, 801

R.C. Ah me ah tubbee, [R. c. 620,] 681

Ah miah, 1083

Ah min tubbe, 606

R.C. Ah min tubbee, [R. c. 647,] 396

Ah mi yah, 446, 478, 564, 492, 914, 827

R.C. Ah mo gla tubbe, 597, [R. c. 658]

Ah mo gla tubbee, 398, 987, 988

Ah moi ah, 382

Ah mok le tubbe, 507

Ah mook lah, 386, 474, 531, 826, 813

Ah mo te ah, 378, 448, 533

Ah na bo la, 386, 873

Ah na chubbee, 400, 451

Ah nah hotenah, 601

R.C. Ah nah tubbee, 804, [R. c. 617]

Ah naintubbee, 949

Ah na ko ah honah, 498

Ah na la hoyo, 451

Ah nan tubbee, 690

*Ah na ta ya, 2

Ah na tim ah, 500

Ah neal to nah, 976

Ah ne he mah, 545

Ah ne honah, 544

Ah ne hoon tubbe, 521

Ah ne ho te mah, 561

*Ah ne le honah, 62

*Ah ne tam bi, 136

Ah ne te mah, 517

Ah ne to bi, 190

Ah ne tubbee, 949

R.C. Ah nin tubbee, [R. c. 682], 1124, 1125

*Ahni Ochubbe, 136

*Ahnitubbee, Charles, 262

Ah no ah chubbe, 531

Ah no ah ha cubbee, 389, 498

Ah no ah hambee, 536

R.C. Ah no ah hubbee, 678

Ah no ah ka, 394

Ah no ah ta cubbe, 556

Ah no ah tam be, 559

Ah no ah tam bee, 384

Ah no ah tubbee, 1103, 1104

Ah no ba, 394

Ah nock ko wah tubbee, 139

Ah noc phe lah, 148

Ah no fa nubbee, 400

Ah no ha, 440, 569, 690

Ah no ho tim, 497

Ah no la, 383, 395, 459, 813, 826, 866

Ah no la che mah, 395, 570, 690

Ah nola ham bee, 573

R.C. Ah no la ho nah, 530, 796, 866, [R. c. 620]

Ah no la tubbe, 515

Ah no la ho yo, 405

Ah no le chubbe, 501

R.C. Ah no le ho nah, 381, 505, 579, [R c. 623,] *54, 64

Ah no le ho ner, 723, 724

Ah no le tah, 435

Ah no le te mah, 1110

R.C. Ah no le te nah, 681

Ah non tubbee, 786

Ah nook cha mah honah, 518

Ah nook che to, 573, 817, 825

Ah nook chin to, 389, 493, 565

Ah nook chi to, 420

Ah nook falah, 376, 585

Ah nook fil e ho ka, 386, 474, 813, 826

Ah nook fil e tubbee, 825

Ah nook filla, 515

Ah nook fille, 532

Ah nook fille ho ka, 522

Ah nook homah, 515

Ah nook ne abbee, 478

*Ah nook sota, 184

Ah nook tah lubbee, 400

Ah nook wah ah, 554

Ah nook we abbee, 827

Ah nook we ah, 522

Ah nook we ah che, 531

Ah nook we ubbe, 552

Ah nook we ubbee, 387, 814

R.C. Ah noon cha, 400, 451, 861, 975, 976, [R. c. 632]

Ah noon pis sah cha, 452

Ah noon pis ah cha, or He tock looah, 401

Ah noon ti yah, 533

Ah noon to nah, 375, 689*

Ah noon tubbe, 516

Ah noon tubbe, or An un tubbe, 579

Ah noo se honah, 505

Ah nootombe, 554

*Ah no pasubbe, 33

Ah no po lubbee, sometimes Po lah, 377

Ah no po tubbe, 531

R.C. Ah no que ah ho ka, 597, 987, 988, [R.C. 658]

Ah nosa, 548

Ah no sa cubbe, or nosacubbe, 587

Ah no sa cubbee, 550

Ah no sa kah, 468

Ah no skooh nah, 498

Ah no si, 514, 518

Ah no sooo nah, 579

Ah no so tubbe, 523

R.C. Ah no ti mah, 1122, 1124, [R. c. 685]

Ah no ubbee, 1041

Ah no wah cha, 939, 940

Ah no wa ha cubbe, 449

Ah no wah tubbe, 540

R.C. Ah no wah tubbee, alias At chi o tubbee, 623

Ah no yo ka, 405

Ah nu ah, or Ok lah mi ah, 479

Ah nubbe, 505

*Ah nubbee, 320

Ah nuk fille, 382, 508

Ah nuk ham ubbee, 497

Ah num pola, 379, 569, 690

Ah num polah, 449

Ah nu sa, 395

Ah nu sa cubbee, 397

Ah nu sku nah, 384

Aho bah tubbee, 89, 140, 149

*Ah o bo tima, 184

*Ah ogle cha, 178

Aholata, 236

*Ahona, 176

*A hook lin tub bee, 143, *120

A hoon tam bee, 449, 528

A ho pah, 147

Ahotema, 223

*Ahotubbe, 12

Ah ouk tim ah, 527

Ah oust tubbee, 137

A how a chubbee, 179

Ahoya, 191, 193, 197

Ahoya, or hoya, 222, 316

Ahoy ochubbi, 50, 78

Ah pa ha, 27

Ah pa ha, alias Johny Walk, 593

Ah pa hah, 85, 376

Ah pan hah, 148

*Ah pan hah, or Billy Halloway, 36

Ah pah lah honah, 526

Ah pah la honah, 559

Ah pah ma, 448

Ah pah mo ah, 141

Ah pah po tubbee, 915

Ah pah ta tubbee, 522

Ah pah tubee, 397

*Ah pais autubbe, 20

Ah pa kah tubbe, 530

Ah pa lah honah, 396, 581, 593

Ah palah hoonah, 389

R.C. Ah pa la ho nah, 510, [R. C. 673]

Ah pa lah ton ah, 388, 552

Ah pa le honah, 387

Ah pa li ah, 140

Ah pa nam tim, 559

R.C. Ah pan sa tubbe, 659

Ah pa sah, 395, 440

Ah pa sah hoka, 510, 519

Ah pa sah honah, 514

Ah pa sa ho ka, 138, 383, 457, 824, 828

Ah pa sa ho nah, 137

Ah pa sah te mah, 397

Ah pa sah too nah, 547

Ah pa sah tubbe, 440

Ah pa sa ka, 574

Ah pa sam ba, 400

Ah pa sam bee, 605, 972

Ah pa sam bee, or Pa sam bee, 464

Ah pa san tubbe, 520, 592

Ah pa san tubbee, 401, 994, 995, 996

Ah pa sa tam ba, 382, 457, 816

Ah pa sa tam bee, 827

*Ah pa sa ttubbe, 36, 38

R.C. Ah pa sum bee, 652

R.C. Ah pat tah, alias Es te ah ho ka, 616

Ah pausat ubbe, 585

Ah pe ah tubbee, 690

Ah pe hah tubbe, 569

Ah pe hat i yubbe, 525

Ah pe hat ti yah, 868

Ah pe hat ti yubbe, 869

R.C. Ah pe hat ti yubbee, 634

Ah pe lah tubbe, 507

R.C. Ah pe le hubbee, 677

Ah pe sah, 509, 521

Ah pe sah ho ka, 381, 579

Ah pe sah tubbee, 497

*Ah pe satimah, 561, *96

Ah pe ut i ah, 867

Ah pisahla, 445

Ah pis ah te mah, 598

Ah pis ah tubbe, or Ta nah pis no wah, 579

*Ah pis alley, 14

*Ah pissaha, 84

Ah pis sah lah, 389

Ah pis salla, 492, 562

Ah pis ta ka tubbe, 571

*Ah pi tah, 388, 483, 814, 827, *60

Ah pock ahmo, 424

Ah pock ah na tubbee, 393, 439

Ah pock ah naw tubbee, 395

Ah pok ah mo, 423

Ah poka mah, 512

*Ah po karmah, 100

Ah pok hah mah, 390, 445

Ah pola, 389, 445

Ah pola, or Big BILLY, 493, 565

Ah pola chubbe, 540

Ah pola chubbee, 388

Ah polah chubbee, 484

Ah pole tubbee, 436, 556

Ah po sa tam be, alias Pis ah tubbe, 525

Ah po ta, 138

Ah po to la, 375, 814, 827, 831

Ah po to lah, 387

Ah po to le, 523, 569, 690, 896

AH PO TO LEE, 478

Ah po to tubbe, 514

Ah po to tubbee, 405, 464

*Ah pu hah, 52

Ah puk yo hubbe, 525

Ah pul e chubbe, 384

Ah pul e chubbee, 384

Ah sah cha, 422

Ah san ti yah, 579

Ah see tah honnah, 388

Ah se ta ho nah, or I ath le pah, 583

Ah sha chim ah, 384, 561

Ah shah che honah, 1106

Ah shah ho ka, 579

Ah sha hoka, 381, 505

Ah shah, la tubbee, 399

Ah shal in tubbe, 381, 508

Ah shal in tubbe, or Shal in tubbe, 579

R.C. Ah shal in tubbe, [R. c. 681,] 1116

Ah shal ish chah, 588

Ah she ap pi a, 377, 442

Ah she ap piah, 501

Ah she bah, 524

Ah she ho ka, 579

Ah sho letah, 415

Ah sho mah, or Ash so mah, 579

Ah sho mah to nah, 958

Ah sho me honah, 388, 509, 579

Ah sho me ta, 465

Ah sho me tekah, 378, 536

Ah sti cubbee, alias Billy Mackey, 796

R.C. Ah sti lubbee, alias Billy Mackey, [R. c. 620,] 717

Ah sto ne ha jo, 1066

*Ah ta ha, 182

Ah ta hah, 404

Ah tah be le honah, 554

Ah tah chubbee, 392

Ah tah hah, or, Ah ta ha, 465

Ah tah honah, 507, 535, 377

Ah tah hubbee, 199

*Ah tah le honah, 448, 552, *58

Ah tah nah, 579

Ah tah sho nah, alias Hush ta sho nan, 574

Ah ta hubbee, 393, 439

Ah tash leah, 555

Ahte ble cha, 833

Ahteah honah, 561, 689

Ahteah lo hona, 393

Ahte ko fubbe, 505

R.C. Ah te mas, [617, R. C.]

Ah te meas, 797

Ah ter hon no chubbe, 727

R.C. Ah te ubbee, 391, 465, 604, [R. C.—; M.], 971

Ah the honah, 517

Ah the o hubbe, 502

Ahthle eppoke chiah, 388, 509, 579

Ah tim ah, 498

Ah ti ye, 389

Ah to ba, 387, 474, 532, 814, 827

R.C. Ah to bah, LOG, [R. C. 627, 657,] 769, 796

R.C. Ah to bah he mah, 626

Ah to bah tim ah, 378

Ah to bah tubbe, 542

Ah to bah tubee, 452

Ah to bate mah, 551

Ah to be, 449

Ah to be tubbee, 569, 690

Ah to ber hemah, 758

Ah tob le cha, 669, 375, 442, 552, 566, 689

Ah to ble tubbee, 557

Ah to bo hubbe, 509

Ah to butcha, 379, 555

Ah to chubbe, 505

Ah to go temah, 542

R.C. Ah to hon ah chubbe, 623

Ah to hon no chubbee, 726

Ahtokah, 390, 571, 579

Ah tok ah ho nah, 579

Ah to ka hoo mah, 388

Ah toke ah te mah, 507

Ah toke ah hon ah, 381

Ah toke ah tema, 382

Ah toke ah temah, 571

Ah toke co la, alias Ware, Andrew, 503
Weir, "

Ah toko ah, 574

Ah to ko tubbe, 504

Ah to man ka, 400

Ah to ma tubbee, 400

Ah to me che, 945

Ah to me tom be, 525

R.C. Ah to min tubbee, 678

Ah to na Jo, 825.

Ah to na ho Jo, 137

Ah to ne, or Sto na, 388

Ah tone, or Stane, 484

Ah tone chubbe, 763, 780, 783

R.C. Ah to ne chubbee, 380, [R. c. 3, 626,] 761

Ah tone chubbey, 760

Ah tonee, 538

*Ah tono chube, 322

Ah to no ham be, or To ni ah, 579

Ah to no ham bee, 381, 497

Ah to no ho mah, 492, 559

Ah to nubbee, 397

Ah to mum bee, 862

Ah toog la he mah, 542

Ah tooh ah low tubbe, 448

*Ah tooka, 106

Ah tookah, 445

Ah took ah lah, 375, 497, 570, 690

Ah took ah lah himah, 596

Ah took ah lan tubbe, 449, 544

Ah took ah lan tubbee, 568, 690

Ah took ah liah, 506

Ah took ah te nah, 579

Ah took al hi ah, 381

Ah took al i ah, 579

Ah took ba, 397

*Ah took ko, 405, *74

*Ah tooko, Simeon, *74

*Ah took o tubbe, 16

Ah took lah, alias Ah took la tubbee, 376

Ah took lah ha ko, 508

*Ah took lah himah, 76

Ah took lah honah, 538

Ah took la homah, 529

Ah took lah tubbe, 531

Ah took lah tubbee, 895

Ah took lan tubbe, 509, 516

*R.c.Ah took lan tubbee, 1103, 1104, [R. c. 678,] *288

Ah took la tubbee, 442

Ah took la tubbee, alias Aht ok lah, 376

Ah took lish, 515

Ah tosh otubbee, 587

Ah to sho tubbee, 376

Ah to sho ubbee, 396

R.c. Ah to sha wah ho nah, 605, 971, [R. c. 652]

Ah tubbe, 505

Ah tuck a lamah, 442

Ah tuckolo, 468

Ah tuk la me honah, 528

Ah tun ah, 144

Ah tush e nul tha, 113

Ah tush e nulth la, 137

Ah tuth le ah, 378

Ah uain tubbee, 278

Ah ubbee, 198

*Ah uichabe, Isel, 298

Ah um ba, 143

Ah unk falah, 381, 556

*Ah uoka, 94

Ah us hubbee, 141

Ahu tah, 398

R.c. Ahu to nah, 403, 861, [R. c. 632]

Ah wa che honah, 525, 573

Ah wah che, alias Ah wah che ho nah, 573

Ah wah che ho nah, alias Ahe wak che, 573

Ah wah te ah, 557

Ah wah teo nah, 386, 476, 825

Ah wan ton ah, 567, 689

Ah wan tubbe, 569

Ah wan tubbee, 375

Ah wa tunah, 537

Ah we ah tubbee, 717

Ah we che hona, 1084, 1085

R.c. Ah we che ho nah, 675

*Ah we chiha, 22

Ah woon to ner, 566

Ah ya ha, 140

Ah yah honah, 512

Ah yo mah te kah, 507

Ah yo mah tubbe, 561

Ah yo mah tubbee, 384

Ah yo pun nu ho yo, 924, 925

Aia hona, 251

Aim moc enny tockeenlubbee, 196

Ai nain ta, 156, 191, 218

Ainaintubbee, 179, 251, 319

*Ainintubbee, *44, 230

Aio watchee, 205

A-ish im-mah, 144

Aispunnehovo, 319

Aish la tona, 969

*Aiyimmitubbee, 274

*Aiyuka tubbee, 294

Akahcheah, 417

*Akames, 214

*Akanabbee, 22

Akanaubbee, 236

*Akchemahka, 94

Ake-Ne-ah, 92

A-ki-ne-ah, 142, 144

Akomotubbee, 235

Akastemtubbee, 275

A-ko-tah, 147

A-kuck-at-ub-bee, 143

Ak wat o cubbee, alias ⎫
Hush to mubbee, alias ⎬ 275
Tis humus tubbee, alias ⎪
Ogleisteia, ⎭

Ala a chones, 1005

Ala ba che, 18

Ala ba ho na, 139

Alae min tabbee, 95

A la e min tub bee, 144

Ala hama, 236

A lah c ta ha, or Al tahl ta ah, 26

A lah nubbee, 1005

Al a ho ka, 388

Ala ho na, 934

Ala ho timah, 273

*Alam ahoky, Auston, 136

R.C. A la mon a tubbee, [R. c. 668], 932

A la mon tubbe, 253, 223

Alan ubbe, 225

R.C. A la nubbee, 661

A lan tubbee, 147, 921

Al ata hona, 276

Ala tema, 242

Alaw, 148

Al ba che, 525

R.C. Al ba ho nah, 603, [R. c. 651], 895, 967

Al bain ta, 191, 196, 236, 319

*Al bama ha cho, 194

Al bin tah, 419

Al che hoka, 237

R.C. Al chee, 615

Al chey, 803

Ale he mah, 501

*Alele hona, 82

*Ale lewah, 148

Alexander, or Alick, 406

Aley, 50

Alfred, 50

*Alh toba, 12, 14

Ali ah tubbe, 584

Alick, or Alexander, 406

*Alimoh tona, 184

*Aliobi, 184

Alis, 401

R.C. Al la hoo nah, 616

Alla hoo nan, 801

Allah ho tema,

*Allamah, 42

*Allas a hubbee, David, 248

Alla tah hoyo, 544

A

All bain ta, 169

Allen, Samuel, 171

*Allen, John, 58

*Allen, Benj., 132

Allen, 1073

Allice, 565, 493

Allison, 406

Allo mutch ah, 380

Allo mutchey, 780, 783

Ally James, or Hock e lo tubbee, 382, 493

Ally, James, or Hoke lo tubbe, 564

*Al me ho yo, 146, 97, 102, 377, 501, *76

Almioka, 190

Al mon to nah, 535

Al moon to nah, 503

Al moon tubbe, or Oon an cha hubbe, 512, 579

*Al moon tubbee, 380, 501, 516, *122

Al mo tubbe, 508

Al ne go, 1032, 1033

*Alo ba homa, 208

*Alo ba tema, 148

*Alobi tana, 180

Aloc ca cha, 192

*Aloh matubbee, 272

*Aloh me tubbee, 250

Alo ma, 138, 169

Alo ma cha, 378, 449, 569, 690

*Aloniache, 58

Alo ma chee, 140

A lo mah, 140

Alome che, 277

R.C. Al o min che, 646, 946, 947

Aln min tubbee, 1097, 1098

*Alomo hta, 222

*Alon oah, 116

Alonsa, 223

Alosa, 967

Alow a ho nah, 401

A low a tah, 148

A low wa tub bee, 147

Al tahl ta ah, or A lah c ta ha, 26

Alth po tah, 825

Alth to ba ho nah, 514

Alubbee, 255, 806

*Alukahooma, 28

Amah, 242, 507

R.C. A mah ho nat, [R. c. 681,] 1115

R.C. A ma ho ta na, 668

Am a ho tona, 252

A mah to nah, 149

Amaia, 197

A man che hubbee, 385, 469, 871, 872

A math la chubbee, 148

Amaya, 192

Am ba, 139

*Am ba la tubbe, alias [hookahoma, 4

Am be honah, 509

Amey, 709

Amich tonah, 436

R.C. Am ish e ho na, 643

Am ish he ho na, 917, 913

A mi yah, 113, 137

A mi yah, or E mi yah, 543

Am mi ah, 143

A mon na hoo na, 140

A moon te ah, 148

Amos, 405, 569, [R. c. 631,] 690, 859

*Amos, Silas, 38

*Amos, 38

*Amugla cho, 286

*Amy, 50, *132

R.C. Amy, alias Ah be too nah, 617

Amy, alias Ab e too nah, 796

Anah chemah, 689

Anah chubbi, 50

Anahoka, 319

*Anahoka, 292

* Anainba, 178

Anainta, 316

Anaintubbee, 221, 223

A nan to nah, 141

An an tubbee, 143

Anatambe, 233

Ana wa tubbee, 1063

Anaw che ho yo, 1061

An cha lah, 147

An cha tonah, 514

An che ha ba, 137

An che to na 1061

An chie a mah, 734

An chin tubbee, 568

Anch'oah, 515

An chock to nubba, 382

An chock to nubbee, 816, 827

An chok to nubbe, 517

An chok to nubbee, 457

An chubbee, 137

An cubbee, 86, 91, 139

An cubbee, alias Oon cubbee, 317

An cubbee, or Oon he kub bee, 825

*Anderson, 591, *29

*Anderson Adam, 292

*Anderson, Andel, 220

*Anderson, Daniel, 316

*Anderson, Ed., 318

*Anderson, Edmond, 318

*Anderson, Gains, 182

*Anderson, Jincy, 194

*Anderson, Jno., 316

*Anderson, Joseph, 316

*Anderson, Reason, 292

*Anderson, Reson, 300

*Anderson, Reuben, 316

R.C. Andrew, 50, R.c. 629

A ne ah, 140

A ner ta ker, 791

R.C. Angelina, or Chillico, 665

An ha timah, 509

R.C. A nia, 392, [R. c. 631,] 857

*Anim tubbee, 302

*Anin chubbee, 8

An it im ah, 507

R.C. An na bo la, 469, 540, [R. c. 635,] 817, 827, 874

Annachi, 50

R.C. An na wa tubbee, 671

An no arch ka, 141

An no himtubbi, 77

An nok tac hubbee, 82

An no la tah, 422

An no sa tubbee, 404

An no tubbee, 250

Anno wa go go, 143

An no wah tubbee, alias Atchi o tubbee, 721, 722

Annowatubbee, 281, 320

Ann se ho nah, 143

Anny, 280

An noachi, 77

Ano ba ta, 199

*Anobola, 156

Anock chato, 213

A nock che to, 139

Anoc waatonah, 235

Anoha, 199

Anohuntubbi, 50

Anokadubbee, 18

Anok cha ta, 179

Anok cha to, 158, 163, 211

Anokcha tubbee, 141

Anok cheto, 219, 271, 317

*Anok felle hoke, 98

Anok filla tubbee, 212

Anok filla tubbee, alias Filla tubbee, 272

*Anoksita, 4

*Anok wihli, 294

Anola, 18

*Anolachobi, 128

Anolahona, alias Yimmanola, 272

Anolahona, 1031

A no la ho yo, 255, R. c. 668

Anolata, 316, 193, 243

*Anole, 302

Ano le hoyo, 252

Ano letah, 439

*Anole hona, 292

*Anoli tima, *176

Ano lohoya, 926, 927

*Anonachabe, 194

Anone tamba, 191

Anone tam ba, alias Ano toia ubbee, 167

Anone taniba, 195

Anonetema, 273

Anon tama, 219

Anon tamba, 194

Anontamba, alias Anotaionbbee, 234, 316

Anontona, 235

Aneokche to, 91

Anook i mah, 504

Anook palah, alias Nook falah, 548

An oon tam bee, 379

*Anosaka, 168

*Anoseka, 222

Ano taia ubbee, alias Anone tamba, 169

Anotaion bbee, alias Anontamba, 234, 316

An o tam ba, 107

Ano teta, 192,

R.C. An o ti yah, 622

Ano ti yah cham ney, 807

An o tiyer, 379, 717

Anotizer, 785

Ano tombey, 785

Ano wa, 145

Ano wa ab bee, 145

R.C. A no wa cha, [R. c. 645,] 939

Anowah ho nah, 1008

Anowa ho ne ubbee, 1003

Ano wah tah, 388

Ano wahte, 976

*Anowatcha, 319, *322

Anowatche, 179

Anowatchee, 172, 179, 203, 258

*Anowatubi, 4

Anow tam ba, 839

*Anoyimee, 120

R.C. An ta bee, alias Nock o nah hah cho, 615

An ta bi, alias Nock o iah hab cho, 803

An ta cubbee, 139, 891

An ta ha mah, 571

An tah cubbe, 528

An tah cubbee, 891, 892

An tah hobbee, 1041

An tah honah, 493, 515

R.C. An ta hubbee, ——, 666

An ta nabbee, 179

An ta tubbee, alias I an ta tubbee, 643

An ta tubbee, alias I an ta tubbee, 928

*Ant hi kubbee, or Bancy, 28

*Anthla honah, 80

An tic cubbee, 211

*An ti kubbee, 271, 317, 817, 825, *270

*Anto lubi, 134

An to nah, 142, 148

An to no ho mah, 384

*An tubbee, 137, 387, 473, 552, 814, 827, *116, 308, 314

An tu nah, 523

*Anutbe, 236

Anuhoka, 50, 77, 78

An uk fil e tim ah, 384

Anum bulla, 224

*Anum pe subbee, 120

An un te mah, 512

An un tim ah, 500

An un tubbe, 505

An un tubbe, or Ah noon tubbe, 579

An un tubbee, 388

An u tam bee, 145

A o na nonah, 402

Aoola, 910

Ao poctn la, 92

*A pa hah, 26, *26

Apal aheko, 269

A pa liah oka, 406

Apa li hoka, 207

A pol i o ho ka, 204

A polla tubbee, 163

A pol yo, 198

*Ap arm ayer, 140

A pa sa, 197

A pasa ho ka, 106, 138, 461

A pasa honah, 113

A pa sam bee, 1005

A pa tio ka, 190

A pa tubbee, 317, 211, 214, 272

*Apa tubby, 98

A pela tubbee, alias Stona ho je, 281

R.C. A pel a tubbee, alias Sto na ha jo, 671

*Apela tubee, Reuben, 300

Apell a tubbee, alias Stonahje, 320

A pe sa ha, 144

R.C. A pe sam ba, 225, [R. c. 661]

*Apes an tobi, Hudgon, 174

*Apesa tema, 112

*Apisa, 170

Api sa ho ge, 143

A pis am bee, 1005

A pis a tub bee, 144, 147

*Apis satona, 130

Apoc cona, 197

A pock ah mah, 404

Apol atubbee, 221

Apo le tubbee, 158

A pol li a, 110

Apota, 114

Ap pah la ho nah, 388

R.C. Ap pa lah, 625

Ap pa moon tub bee, 148

*Ap'paso, 160

Ap pa tub bee, 825

Ap pe la hon na, 146

Ap pi la, 139

Ap pis ah yah, 579

Ap pi tub bee, 139

Ap po to tubbee, 442

A pul le tubbee, 144

*Arch a a ho ya, 322

Arfomo yar, 707, 708

Ar ha chi o man, alias Ah chick a ma ho nah, 789

Ar ha chi o man honer, 715

Ar hair, 803

Ar ha ka tubbee, 734

Ar ha ka tubbey, 732

*Ar hak in tubbee, 254

Ar ha ma tubbee, 733

Arhan, 697

*Ar he tubbee, 288

Ar iko timer, 704, 803

Ar leemer tooner, 707

Ar luck ala tubba, 83

*Aama hoky, 270

wrmstrong, Col., 171

*Armstrong, Martha, 302

Armstrong, Wm., 171

*Arnuk hama, 274

*Ar pal er tubbee, Reuben, 254

*Ar pa ta, 126

Ar patter, 705

Ar patter, alias Is te ah ho ca, 789

*Ar sho tata, 178

*Art ah li hona, 152

*Ar tomicy, 64

Artone chubey, 708

Ar yer honar, 705

Asaga, 167

Asarche, 235, 316

A sha cha, 169

As ha he ma, 275

Ash a ho gee, 144

Asha homa, 223

A shak ta, Widow, or A sha ta, 28

*Ash a lin tobi, 186

Asha ta, Widow, or A shak ta, 28

*Ash atima, 278

*Ashelin chi, 44

Ash ha cambee, 536

Ash ho la ta, 218

*Ashier, 30

Ash ka ma, 575

Ash lubbi, 50

Ash o lata, 318, 157, 162, 191, 197

Ash o le ta, 194

Ash o le tah, 118, 420

*As ho mata, 288

As ho mo ta, 169, 166, 196

Ash o mote, 235

*Ash polah, 118

Ash so mah, or h Asha mah, 579

Ash tah oka, 50

Ash te mah, 579

Ash tubbe, 522, 523

*Ash tubbee, 387, 474, 827, *106

Ash wa chubbe, 600

Ash wah, 378

Ash wah chubbee, 402

Ash wah tubbee, 1008, 1009

Ash wa tubbe, 540

R.C. *Ash wa tubbee, 472, 226, 385, 826, [R. c. 661,] *94

As noley honer, 722

As shal cut abbee, 143

A ta ha, 26

A tah hah le ho nah, 376

*Ata hona, 314

Ata hubbee, 191

Ataia hona, 235

*At ane pabi, 132

At an ah a jo, 316

A ta nubbee, 903

*A tatambi, 182

Ata tubbee, 147

*At chewah, 55

At chey, 697

R.C. At chi o tubbee, alias, Ah no wah tubbee, 623

Atchi o tubbee, alias An no wah tubbee, 722, 722

Atchio Tubbey, 720

At cle wah, 780, 787, 790, 806

R.C. At cle war, 617

Ath ka la, 384

Ath ko la, 462, 574, 824

Ath later, 1064

Ath la tona, 968

*Ath la tonah, 26

Ath la yo hubbe, 507

Ath le chubbe, 604

R.C. Ath le chubbee, 652

Ath le ho ka, or Is ho ka, 505

Ath leo hah, 1027

Ath po ta, 317, 211, 214, 283

Ath ta lam ba, 516

Ath thle lah, 148

Ath thle wah, 147

Ath to ba hoka, 276

Ath tubbee, 397

At leth ler, 715

*Atoba, 186, *164

At oba, or Immat e boh ona, 229

At o ba cha, 148

Atoba hema, 272

*Atoba hona, 144

*A to ba tona, 1037, *196

A to bli jah, 146

A to bo tema, 265

A tof a mah, 147

*Atoh no tema, 316

*Atoh not ima, 284

*Atoka, 914, *308

A to kah, 142

Atok alan tubbee, 275

At oke it im mah, 144

Atoko, 176, 198

A to ko la ya, 1010

Atokolia, alias Osh he homa, 925

Atok otubbee, 276

*Atolubi, 162

R.C. A to na, 628

*Atonabe, 302

Ato na hajoe, 112, 113

Aton ah a jo, 261

Atona mus tubbee, 181, 182

At oni cubbee, 235

At ono, 233, 834

*Aton o chubbe, 28

Atoobee, 96

A took a lan tub bee, 140

A took al iah, 143

A took a lun tubbee, 85

A took a law tub bee, 149

A took lan tub bee, 95

A to po lick ah, 147

A touk a lan tub bee, 147

At ta hay, 148

At tah le ah, 442

Attah tam bee, 435

At ta la hon nah, 148

*Atta ta ah, 228

At ta tam ba, 316

At ta taw ba, 243

At te tam bee, 436

At to bah, 98, 451, 983, 986

Atto ba tubbee, 377

*Attok lan tubbee, 262

At took a lah, 148

Atuk lam bee, 525

A tusk ha chick a mah, 140

Atu te mah, 146

Auch a too a, 905

Au che ha ba, 114

Auck fillat ubbee, 212

Au cubbee, 109

Au cubbee, or One cubbee, 212

Aueu bbee, alias Oon cubbee, 276

A uk la, 144

Aunah chemah, 566

Au no ti yea, 780

Aun te tubee, 375, 566, 689

Aun tu tubbee, 83

Aus coon la tubbee, 276

Aush tubbee, 569, 814

Au ta cubba, 115

Au ta honah, 565

Au tam ba, 264

Au ta te mak, 516

Authle ho nah, 501, 527

Au ti cubbee, 213

Au ti kubbee, 242

Au tubbee, 106, 515

Au uk fil etemah, 561

Au wa che, 421

A wat am bee, 144, 145

Awa tea, 198

A wat te nah, 146

A ya con tu wah, 147

Ay a ha, 159

Ayaha or Iaha, 220, 316

R.C. Ay a he ma, 667

Ay a ho na, 921

*Ay ahon ubbe, 30

A yak le hah, 146

*Ayan ta hubbee, 1041, *232

*Ay ash tobi, 120

Ay a tona, 271

Ay ella, 229

*Ay lip, 28

Ay nair ta, 162

A yo ah ho nah, 95

A yoh a hon na, 105

A yok a ho nah, 145

*A yok oma, 200

R.C. A yo wa, [R. c. 629,] 845, *28

A yella, 1033

Ay yo ha, 899

Ay yah ha, 157

R.C. Ay yo pun ne ho yo, 643, *254

Ba a ba la tubbee, 1032

R.C. Ba cha, [R. c. 640], 906

Ba for chubbee, 140

Ba fun ka, 143

Bah-ah nubbe, 528

Ba ha ka, 249

Bah chah la, 378, 542

Bah fa chub bee, 139

Bah fo cubbee, 404, 424

Bah fon cubbee, 115

Bah funk ah, 381, 506

Bah funk kah, 579

Bah ho tenah, 514

Bah ka tubbe, 595

Bah ka tubbee, 376

Bah lah hoo nah, 499

Bah lutta, 118

Bah nah tubbee, 1022, 1023, *64, *80

Bah na tubbe, 528

Bah na tubbee, 399, 401, 451, 528, 996

Bah ne tubbe, 539

Bah ni ah, or Ub ah ni ah, 579

Bah nubbe, 596

Bah nubbee, 463

Bahonah, 514

R.C. Bah pa sah, 450, 603, [R. c. 651,] 969

Bah pa so, 132

Bah pi pa, 139

Bah pissa, 115, 140

Bah-pissah, 405, 424

Bah sa, 399

R.C. Bah tah ho-yo, 593, [R. c. 648,] 954

Bah te mah, 528

Bah tom-bee, 139

Bah tubbe, 500

Bah tuk lo, 422

Bak-a-tubbee, 89, 140, 149

*Baker, Heaston, *108

*Baker, Samuel, *168

Bama ha, 270

Ba na che, 516

Ban-ah-tu-nah, 386, 475

Ba nan cha hoka, 505

*Banan tima, *64

Ba-nan-tubbee, 100

R.C. Banatubbee, 239, 319, R. c. 663

*Ban chah, *144

Ban-cha-lah, 148

*Bancy, or Ant hi kubbe, *28

*Banetubbee, *162

Bani-timer, 705

*Ban nah tema, *146

*Bannah temah, 140, *148

R.C. Ba nubbee, 398, [R. c. 631,] 857

*Barnett, *298

*Barnit, *298

*Bascum, Cornelius, *120

*Basey, *170

Bash-pah-ho-mah, 807

*Bash po homma, 180

Bash-ta-bu-no-na, 26

*Basin, *72

*Basy, *74

Bat-cha-at-u-nah, 143

Batis, 238, 319

R.C. Batteese, R. c. 625

Battees-favver, 379

*Batteste, Nicholis, *160

*Batteste, Winny, *160

*Battice, *270

*Battiece, Capt. Benj., *230

*Battiece, Norman, *294

Vol. II—2.

*Battiece, Sarah, *212

Battiese, 748, 749

*Battiest, 132, *134

*Battiest, McKinzie, *188

*Battiest, Turner, *188

R.C. Bat-tise, [R. C. 662,] 843, 1012

Bat tus farver, 785

*Bay, *276

*Beam, Jesse, *4

Beames, Amy, 610

Beames, Betsey, 610

Beames, Kitty, 610

Beames, Vicey, 610

Beams, Amy, 599

Beams, Betsey, 599

Beams, Betsy, 75, 142

Beams, Betsy,

*Beams, Hettie, *4

*Beams, Isom, *88

Beams, Jesse, 82, 142

Beams, Kitty, 599

Beams, Vicey, 599

*Beams, Widow, *88

Beck-a, 376, 395, 566, 689

Becky, 220, 279

Bee-ling-go-nah, 148

Beemes, Betsey, 18

Been-an-tubbee, 803

Be-le-at-ab-bee, 144

*Belinda, *282

Belingalia, 203

Belingatubbe, 270

Belingelia, 207

Belingona, Jim, 440

Be lin go nah, 395, 464

Belingonah, John, 421, 422, 436

B

Be lin kat tah, 504

Bell, Alexander, 227

*Bell, Anoyatima, *4

*Bell, David, 140, 203, 207, 228, 330, 407, 408, 1029, *82

Bell, James, 227

Bell, Lila, 228

Bell, Martha, 227

Bell, Rachel, 227

Bell, Robert, 140, 204, 205, 207, 208 223, 316

*Bell, Sallen, *76

Bell, Winna, 228

*Belvin, Billy, *250

*Belvin, Jesse, *250

*Belvin, Selina, *228, 256

R.C. Ben, 560, [R. C. 683,] 912, 1127, 1128

*Ben, John, *198

*Ben, Lincy, *184

Be-nah, 389, 419, 504

Be-nah-cha, 442

Be nah tam be, 531

Ben-ah-tubbe, 792, 385

R.C. Be-nah-tubbee, [R. C. 619,] 717, 781, 786, 790

Benanche, 542

Ben-an-tub-bee, 147

Benintubbe, 595

*Benton, Jacob, *172

*Benton, Robt., *64

Beo tubbee, 141

Bessy, 569, 690

*Betcey, *296

Betchey, 707

R.C.*Betsey, 243, 250, [R. c. 616, 623, 625, 665,] 735, 736, 789, 1023, *80

*Betsy, 407, 747, *166, 196, 230, 236

Betty, 746

R.C. Bi a la tubbee, 392, [R. c. 631,] 857

*Biata, 234, 316, *176

Big Ax, 578

*Big Cloud, Capt., *172

Big Jacob, or Ish-ta-tubbee, 382

Big Jacob, or Ish-tah-tubbe, 563

*Big Pumpkin, *290

*Big Shol make, *196

*Billey, Ellen, *286

*Billey, Susan, *312

Billy, or Wahli, 520

Billy, Big, or Ah po la, 493, 565

*Billy, Big, *100

Billy, Bob, alias, Nock ah tubbee, 952

Billy, John, or Kan-sho-non-che hubbe, 564

*Billy, Ellison, 268

*Billy, Jackaway, *52

*Billy, John, *70

*Billy, Lewis, *308

*Billy, Lucy, *104, 106

*Billy Thomas, *142

Billy, Tom, or Lah ta kah, 492, 562

Bina, 141

*Bing, *174

*Bingord, or Buyard, *168

Binia, 265

Binna, 201, 205

Bin-nah, 141

Bi o glah, 402

Bise, 255

*Black, Wm., *86

Bl-na, 185

Blue, James, 139

Blue, Jim, 104

B nan tubbee, 803

B nan Tubbe, 725

B nan tubbee, 721, 723

Bo-at kon cho, 144

*Boat man, Eblam, *320

R.C. Bob, 144, 279, [R. c. 29,] 845

*Bob Captain, 574, 583, 584, *222

Bob, Captain, alias Min go ho nah, 382, 508, 576, 579, 581

*Bob Wesley, *82

Bob la ba kah, 579

Boffa cubbee, 423, 424

*Bohannan, Ellis, *316

*Bohannan, Jessee, *154

*Bohannan, William, *316

Boh la honah, 541

R.C. Boh-la-hoo-nah, [R. c. 635,] 877, 878

Bohole, 266

*Boh li hona, *314

Boh tubbe, 518

*Boh tubbee, *190

Boky-hon-nah, 98

Bola, 190, 196, 393, 419

Bole henah, 550

Bole hona, alias Tabolehona, 272

Bo-le-ho-nah, 377

Boley, 81

Bo-ley-hon-nah, 102

Bol-la-ho-nah, 442

Bo-ly-hun-na, 145

Bon-a-tub-bee, 141

Bon cha, 780

Bon-chah, 385, 786, 797

*Bond, James, *98, 102, 104, 106, 118

*Bond, Tiah, *106

*Bond, T. J., *304

*Bone, Deer, *214

Bonetubbee, 1029

*Bonham, Joe, *144

Boo-nah, 143

Booth, Sarah, 388

Boothe, Richard, 86

Boothe, Sarah, 86

Bo-tah-ho-yo, 595

Bou cha, 717

R.C. Bou-chah, R. c. 621

R.C. Bowatubbee, 239, 319, [R. c. 665]

Bow e tubbee, 1029

Bow-ka (Bow-o-ka), 579

Bow-o-ka, (Bow-ka), 579

Bowonubbe, 587

*Bowotobbe, *132

*Boyer, Robert M., *182

Brandy, or Po-tubby, 385

*Brandy, James, *112

Brashears, Alexander, 18, 75

*Brashears, Benjamin, 28, *200

Brashears, Delilah, 18

*Brashears, Lewis, *196

Brashears, Rachel, 18

*Brashears, Turner, 18, *32, 266

*Brashears, Vaughn, *32

*Brashears, William, *200, 266

Brashears, Zadoc, 18

Brashears, Zedoc, 75

Brown, 254

*Brown, James, 190

Brown, Joshua T., 202

Brown, Lewis, or Ock-li-yah-cubbee, 382

*Brown, Morris, *12

Bryant, Lewis, 18

Buchah ho no, 569

Buckannon, Charles, 18

R.C. Buf-fa, [R. c. 663,] 1016

Bulle, 95

Bul-lee, 145

*Bully, Isbell, *210

*Bully, Wilburn, *206

Bum ah tah ka, or Tik be ubbe, 515

Bun ah ta nah, 523

Bun-ah-tu-nah, 825

R.C. Bun-an-tub-bee, R. c. 615

Bun nah, 537

Bun nah chubbee, 397

Bun na hona, 242, 243

R.C. Bun-nah-te-mah, [R. c. 616,] 801

Bun-na-tu-ma-her, 94

Bun-na-tuna, 116. 138

Bur-ma-tu-na, 91

*Burris, Benj., *274

*Burris, Gabrial, *218

*Burris, Mrs. Kasey, *218

*Burris, Widow, *218

*Burris, Wm., *274

Bush-ke, 141

R.C. Bush-pah-ho-mah, 436, R. c. 627

Bush-pah-ho-nah, 783

Bush-par-ho-mer, 779

Bushperhomar, 785

Bush-per-homer, 778, 780, 785

Bush-per-ho-nah, 778

Bush-per-ho-ner, 379

*Bush po hooma, *288

Butah, 265

*Buyard, or Bingord, *168

Byana, 218

Byata, 167, 191

*Byington, Anna, *242

*Byington, Henry, *210

*Byington, James, *162

*Byington, Mary, *184

*Byington, Samuel, 18, *156

*Byington, T. H., *126, 156

Byoto, 196

R.C. By-sa, [R. c. 641,] 908

Bysa, 910

By-ya-ta, 169

*Cabbage, Ellis, *32

*Cady, Patsy, *164

*Caffrey, John, *240

*Caffrey, Sally, *240

Cah la ho nah, 417, 418, 419

Cah la tubbee, 402, 404

*Cahle, *272

Cah lo ho nah, 394

*Cah noon tan tah, *284

Cah nulle, 544

Cah po la, 395, 419

R.C. Cah-sho-nah, 389, 590, [R. c. 658,] 989

Cah-shun-ah, 147

Cah tah polah, 422

Cah te mah, 586

Cah to nah, 392, 405, 419

Cah tonah, or Eah cah to nah, 545

Cah tubbee, 422

Cain, Andrew, 140

Cain, Robinson, 140

R.C. Cal-a-vam, 662

Caleb, 470

Caleb, John, 524

Ca lo ka, 1005

*Cam, Milly, *306

Cam-ba-lubbee, 138

Ca moon ta chubbee, 917

R.C. Cam-pa-lubbee, R. c. 674

*Campbell, James, 26, *208

*Campbell, Margarett, *208

*Campbell, Peggie, *280, 282, 284, 324

*Campbell, Piakey, *252

*Campbell, Wm., *252

R.C. Cam-pel-la-ho-ka, [R. c 616,] 801

Campelli-hoka, 705

Cam-pil-ab-bee, 143

Cam-pil-la, 143

*Cams, Harris, *218

*Cams, Capt. Jas., *218

Canacha, 190, 196

Cana ho chubbee, 198

*Cana hoyo, 220, 316, *178

Can-ant-ab-bee, 143

Ca nan tubbee, 145, 910

Can au tubbee, 145

R.C. Ca-nau-tubbee, alias James Patterson, 641

Cancha, 211

Can chah onah, or Tan cha honah, 589

Canchatir, 744

Can chatona, 270, 671

Can-che-ter, or Can-chi-tiah, 783

Can-chi-tiah, or Can-che-ter, 783

Can cho tonah, 1061

Can e o tim ah, 1081, 1082

Canetambee, 536

Can-it-am-be, 105

Can-it-am-bee, 145

Can-jah, 148

Can ne la ha ma, 905

*Can nis tonah, *274

*Can noh tubbee, *274

Can nu ta mah, 504

Canohetubbee, 109

Can one taba, 274

Can one ta shubbee, 917

Can one tubbee, 197

Can on tubbee, 190

R.C. Ca-noon-ta-shubbee, R. c. 642

Can oon te mah, 973

Ca noon-tubbee, 158

C

Can shat tubbee, 191

*Can shatubbee, *300

Can she tema, 274

Can un tah bee, 504

Can-un-tubbee, 105

Ca o cho, 224

Cap-a-sa, alias Pash-am-ba, 718, 719

Cap a sah, 760

Cap a sha, 699, 701

Capha-sa ah, 708

Cap per sey, 710

Car ho na hok ta, 911

R.C. Carnes, Peggy, 142, 451, 606, [R. c. 654,] 975, 976

*Carnes, Roberson, *190

R.C. Carnes, Robinson, 103, 451, 466, 606, [R. c. 653,] 861, 974, 975, 976

Carnes, Tokiah, 398

*Carnes, Willis, 974, *172, 190

Carney, A., 142

*Carney, Allen, *156

Carney, Arthur, 18

Carney, Charles, 463

*Carney, Cornelius, *236

*Carney, Jeremiah, 282, 330, 403, 408, 452, *238

*Carney, Susan, *156

Carpola, 190, 196

*Carr, Henry, *90

Carr, Henry L., 26

*Carr, John, *90

Carsh on tubbe, 750, 780, 783

R.C. Carsh-on-tubbee, 380, [R. c. 625,] 750

Carsh on tubbey, 750

Carsome ta ma, 1051

Carson, or Kachien, 226

Carson, 392, 404

Cars-on-tubbey, 750

Cartchey, 730

*Casey, Solomon, *252

*Casha, Ellis, *140, 144

R.C. Cash-ah, [R. c. 622,] 793

*Cash one bubbee, *148

Cash on tubbee, 761

*Casley, Winney, *266

*Cass, Lewis, *2, 26

*Cass, M., *68

Ca to na, 167, 196

Ca-to-nah, 384

Caupalaubbee, 273

Causin, 568

*Cealy, *146

Celia, 395

Cha-chubbee, 140

Cha conubbee, 219

Cha cubbe, 604

R.C. Cha cubbee, 450, [R. c. 652,] 969

*Cha cubi, *174

Cha-fa-hee-nah, 148

Cha fa hona, 930

Chafahnutonoh, 587

Chafahonah, 242

Chafahutonah, 587

*Chaffah, *80

R.C. Chaffahona, 253, [R. c. 668]

*Chaf-fa-ho-nah, 143, *230

Chaf fah toke ubbe, 502

Chaf fah to nubbee, 885

*Chaf fah tubbee, *96

Chaffa-to-ka-cheia, 389

R.C. Chaf fa-to-ke-che-a, R. c. 683

Chaf fa to ke chia, 1127, 1128

Chaffa to no la, 1027

Chaf-fa-to-no-lah, 147

Chaffa to nubbe, 507

Cheffa to nubbee, 884, 885, 886

Chaf-fa-tubbee, 88, 825

Cha-fol-ah, 147

*Chafotambi, *178

*Chafotikobi, *160

Chaf ubbe, 531

Cha fubbee, 459, 813, 826

Chah-ah-tubbee, 379

Cha hamba, 191

Chaha tub-bee, 146

Chah be, 561

Chah e temah, 540

Chah hubbe, 509, 579

R.C. Chah-le, [R. c. 673,] 1074

Chah e honah, 530

Chah-look-a, or Ah ko-le-tubbe, 579

R.C. Cha hoka, 525, [R. c. 634,] 865, 866

R.C. Chah-pah-ho-nah, 616

*Chah tahomma, *122

Cha-hub-bee, 143, 381

Chaia hoka, 275

Chak-al-e-che, 380, 509, 584

R.C. Chak-lan-tubbee, 616

Chak-lin-tubby, 803

Chak-tah-ho-mah, 827

Chak-tah-ho-mah, or Pis-it-ti-yah, 827

Cha-lan-tah, 520

Cha-lan-tak, 138, 817

Cha lan tok, 383, 828

Cha-la-ste-ta-ha, 28

Cha-lau-tah, 114

Chalin tubbey, 704

Chal le, 508

R.C. Chal-lo-ke, [R. c. 676,] 1091

*Chambe, *248

Cha mis, 394

Cham nay, or Cham ney, 692, 693

Cham ne, 387

R.C. Cam-ney, 379, [R. c. 614,] 692, 775

Cham-ney, or Cham nay, 692, 693

Cham-pah, 716

Cham pah ya, 162

Cham paya, or Shampia, 219

Chanahajo, 212, 213, 265, 268, 319

Chanahajo, alias Oakchanahajo, 317

Chan-e, 384, 560

Chapah ho nah, 801

Cha paho mo, 61

Chap a honer, 705

Cha pa ka, 211

*Charbee, Liza, *122

*Charf fortubbe, *154

Char-fo-la, 141

Charity, 251

*Charity, Logan, *42

R.C. *Charles, 393, 525, [R. c. 625,] 748, 749, *150

*Charles, Eastman, *10

*Charles on, *320

*Charley, 397, 399, *268

*Charley, Willis, *280

*Charlman, *34

*Charlman, Mrs. *34

Charlotte, 50

Chas pohonah, 516

Cha-ta-ho-ma, 138

*Chatamattaha, Widow, *206

c

Chatam ba, 218

Cha tam tok, 457

*Chate, *302

Chat-tu-homa, 91

Chatub bee, 384, 462

Chaw-e-ha-jo, 825

Che-a-cha, 142

Che ah, 396

Che-a-jah, 97

Che-at-un-ah, 144

Che cah ta, 463

Che cah tah, 404

Che can ta, 690

Che-caugh-ta, 377

Che caughta, or Che cauta, 570

Che cauta, or Che caughta, 570

Che co tubbe, 531

Che cubbee, 968

Chee-a-kee, 144

Chee-a-tha, 95

Chef-am-ba, 848

Che-fa-tub-bee, 139

Chef-fa-he-lubbee, 864

Chef fah lim lubbe, 512

Chef fa hoka, 517, 826

Chef fah too nub bee, 875

Chef fa ti yah, 525

Chef fa to me wah, 520

Chef fa tonah, 525

R.C. Chef-fa-too-nubbee, [R. c. 635,] 876

Chef-fa-tub-bee, 138, 824

Chef-fo-te-yah, 138

Chef fo tiah, 491

Chef-fo-ti-yah, 103, 521

Chef fo to nubbe, 512

Che-fubbee, 383

Che hom bee, 392, 421, 440

Chehonah, 551

Cheho temah, 553

Che-ho-yuo, 138

*Che-ka, 144, *156

Che-kach-you, 80

Che kah, 507

Che lak kee, 475

Chelle, 507

Che-lok-ka, 112, 138

Che-lok-kee, 386, 542, 825

Che ma, 1016

Chemah, 474

Che mah ho ka, 507

*Chemahowah, *116

Che mah yoka, 550

Chemalehoka, 540

Che-mal-ley, 146

Che-man-te, 140

Chemaya, 195

Che milahoka, 592

Che-mi-o-ca, 442

Che-mi-o-ka, 377, 403

Chemona, 223

Che-my-o-ga, 146

Che-na, 138, 826

*Che-nah, 387, 523, 814, *112

Che no la, 965

*Chenubbee, *254

Che-pah-ka, 142

Che-pa-ka, 91, 137, 213, 817, 825

Che-par-ka, 141

Che poka, 274, 319

Che po lah, 508

Che-sha-ho-ma, alias Red Post Oak, 137

Ches-ha-Homah, or Capt. Post Oak, 111

Chesh ah ho mah, alias Capt. Red Post Oak, 818

Cheshombee, 421

Cheta, 190, 197

Chetah, 590

R.C. Che-tub-bee, 138, [R. c. 681,] 824, 1117, 1119

*Chewahoye, *120

Che-way, or She-way, 28

*Cheway, *154

Che-yah, 146

Chiahoka, 317

Chiaptonola, 1032

Chieasa, 223

Chieka-a-sah-ho-ka, 383

Chickah shamo, 421

*Chickaontubbee, *106

Chick a sah ho ka, 459

Chic-ka-saw, 148

Chickasaw, or E lah nubbee, 397

Chick a-saw-ho-ac-ta, 140

Chick-a-saw-ho-ka, 813

Chick-a-saw-ho-nah, 144

Chickasha, 190, 197

Chick a shamo, 185

Chick-a-sho-tub-bee, 142

Chick-a-shu-no, 141

Chick-a-tha, 144

Chick-e-saw-ho-ka, 139, 826

Chick e sha, 404

Chick-ma, 865

Chick-oon-tubbee, 384, 462

Chie-fe-tubbee, 84

*Chiffe, Mary, *268, 286

Chif fe te yah, 572

*Chi hona, *216

*Chika, *184

Chik a sah hoka, 520

Chik e mah, 520

Chik emah hoyo, 542

Chik mah em ah tubbe, 521

Chik oon tubbe, 518

Chik-oon-tub-bee, 824

Chileta, 184, 216

Chile tah, 418

Chil-e-tom-ba, 813

Chil-e-tom-bee, 826

Chil i ta, 941

Chilleta, 249

Chille tah, 400, 417, 419

Chille tam ba, 271, 317, 459

*Chille tam be, 516, *68

Chil-le-tam-bee, 383

Chil-le-tom-ba, senior, 138

Chil-le-tom-ba, junior, 138

Chillico, 250

R.C. Chillico, or Angelina, 665

Chil-lota, 80

*Chillotah, *26

Chilota, 50

R.C. Chim, 676

*Chime, *130

Chim mah la tubbee, 401

Chim male, 1089, 1090

R.C. Chim-pe-ya, 657

Chim peyah, 599

Chim pi ya, 983

China, 86

Chin al le, 507

Chinni, 229

*Chin upacha, *10

Chin sah, 394

*Chinubbe, *22

Chip-pah-che, 139

Chisa homah, 446

Chis ha homa, 182, 936

Chish a homah, alias Captain Red Post Oak,
    809

Chishahomah, alias Red Post Oak, 810

Chishehoma, 260, 261, 262

Chishehoma, Capt., 282, 287

Chis he homa, alias Captain Red Post Oak,
    263, 316

*Chitokaya, *152

Chit o kubbe, 525

*Chitto, Billy, *14

Choak ah tal lee, 474

*Choate, Betsey, *262, 266, 272

*Choate, James, *268, 270, 272

Chock-tah-ho-mah, or Pis-it-yah, 387

Cho-cle-ho-mo, 388

Choffa, 889

Choffa tubbee, 203

*Chof fotanoli, Sila, *136

*Chofotambi, *178

Cho-ho-ka, 866

*Chokabe, or Chokabi, *208

*Chokabi, or Chokabe, *208

Chok ema hema, 274

Chok-ma-bee, or Nok-chuk-ma-bee, 27

Chok-tah-homah, 814

Chok-tah-homah, or Pas it te yah, 515

Chok-tah-ho-mah, or Pis-it-ti-yah, 814

Chom-pa, 140

Chompah, 203, 207, 223, 316

Chonnis, 270

Cho no ka, or Ah chu wah, 522

Chook ab tal lee, 387

Chook-ah-tal-bee, 814

Chook-ah-tal-he, 139

Chook ah talle, 517

Chook-ah-tallee, 117, 827

Chookma, 264

Chook mam be, 529

Chook tah ho mah, 478

Choo-lah, 147

Choom pa, 275, 537

Choom-pah, 387, 478, 814, 827

Choonkcho, 264, 817, 825

Choonkchoo, 316

R.C. Christa, Josa, 617

Christey, Josa, 710, 762

*Christie, Jane, *22

*Christy, Bicy, *158

*Christy, Isom, *236

Christy, Iosa, 380

*Christy, Jackson, *142

Christy, Josa, 709, 780, 796

*Christy, Joseph, *142

*Christy, Michael, *150

*Christy, William, 18, 116, *158

R.C. Chub-bee, 145, 396, [R. c. 627,] 778, 779, 929

*Chubbee, John, *84, 100, 104, 116

Chubbee, Stilla, 401

Chubbee, Polla, 786

Chuf ah tam be, 557

Chu-fa-tubbee, 85

R.C. Chuf-fa-am-bee, 629

R.C. Chuf fah, 615

R.C. Chuf-fah-ho-mah, 619, 761

Chuf-fah-ho-nah, 379

Chuf-fa-ho-ka, 385, 471, 499

Chuf fah tam bee, 396

Chuf fah tiil, 468

Chuf-fah-tub-bee, 868

Chuffa tanola, 229, 406

*Chuf fatok chiya, *286

Chuf fatona, 270

Chuf fa to no la, 401

Chuffa to nubbe, 561

R.c. Chuf-fa-to-nubbee, 636

Chuf fa tubbe, 269, 512, 525, 868

R.c. Chuf-fa-tub-bee, 141, 212, 213, 256, 317, 319,
        397, 404, 462, [R.c. 634, 643,] 867, 868,
        919, 920

Chuf fa tu nubbe, 515

Chuffer ho mer, 781

Chuffe tubbe, 509

Chuff-fa-tubbee, 384

Chuf-fur, 803

*Chuk a humma, *238, 248

Chuk fy noo sa, 515

Chuk-la-ho-na, 141

R.c. Chuk mah, 524, [R. c. 634,] 866

*Chukmubbee, Winey, *266

*Chular, *180

Chul-leh, 148

Chulle, 535

*Chumpa, *142

Chum-pah, 143, 146, 381, 445, 498, 579

Chum pah, or I um pah, 565

Chum pah hoka, 537

*Chum pa homah, *42

Chum pah te mah, 533, 542, 551

Chump ulaka, or Shum pa la ka, 535

Chunc-cho, 88

Chun-cho, 137

Chu no la, 402, 436

Chush potubbee, 272

*Chustin, *88

Chu wah te ah, 520

Chu-wah-te-you, 386, 475

Chu-wa-te-yo, 825

Ci-es-unna, 97

Cim oon tambe, 553

Clarasey, 764

Clarisey, 757

R.c. Clarissa, R. c. 626, 756

*Clark, George, *212

*Clarke, Lucy, *278

*Clarke, Mrs., *240

Clasey, 708

*Clay, Patsey, *166

Clearesey, 708

Clearsey, 709

Cleasey, 709

Clements, Jessee, 390

*Cley, Belin, *246

*Clover, Wm. M., *184

Co ah ho mah, 504

Co-a-ho-mah, 381, 579

Cobb, 162

Cobb, Capt., 282, 296, 297, 298

Cobb, Amy, 404

Cobb, Betsey, Bat-se, 184, 186

Cobb, Betsy, 192, 198

Cobb, Buckey, 141

*Cobb, Eliza, *154

Cobb, Molly, 404

Cobb, Pickens, 404

Cobb, Sam., 411, 412, 413

*Cobb, Samuel, 18, 156, 160, 214, 215, 336,
        337, 410, 434, 467, *236

C

Cobb, Capt. Samuel, 295, 581, 582

*Cobb, Silas, *116

Cochabbee, 437

Coch ah tubbee, 417, 418, 440, 441

Cocha tamba, 221.

Co cha tubbee, 169, 393

Cochubbe, 597

*Co-chub-bee, 148, 389, 396, 422, *74

Coh tah, 508

Col-a-jah, 147

Col a yam, 238, 1010

*Colbert, 137, *88

Colbert, or Col-la-chubbee, 376

R.c. Colbert, alias Collashubbe, 598, [R. c. 649]

Colbert, or Collashubbee, 960, 961

*Colbert, Abel, *112

*Colbert, Ben, *318

*Colbert, Emily, *210

*Colbert, James, *262

*Colbert, Orilla, *306

Colbert, Samuel, *258

*Colbert, Silas, *26

*Colbert, Susan, 388, *258

Cole, Adam, 1035

Cole, Angelica, 1035

Cole, Augustin, 247

Cole, Betsy, 1035

Cole, Bob, 179

R.c.*Cole, Charles, 257, 319, [R. c. 644,] 934, 1035, *256

Cole, Colbert, 247

*Cole, Coleman, 78, 137, 170, 174, 176, 177, 245, 247, 319, 844, *198

*Cole, Edmond, *256

Cole, Forbus, 1035

Cole, Jenny, 1035, 1036

Cole, John, 247

Cole, Malinda, 1035, 1036

Cole, Molley, 1035

*Cole, Molsey, *252

*Cole, Nicholas, *256

Cole, Peter, 1035, 1036

Cole, R., 10, 12

R.c.*Cole, Robert, 141, 175, 177, 245, [R. c. 665,] 844, 1035, *198

Cole, Col. Robert, 250, 319

Cole, Sampson, 1035, 1036

*Cole, Selina, *264

*Cole, Sika, *32

*Cole, Stephen, *254, 316

Cole, Susey, 1035

*Colegie, *306

*Colemann, John, *110

Colick, 402

Col-la-chubbee, or Colbert, 376

R.c. Colla shubbe, alias Colbert, 598, 649

Colla shubbee, or Colbert, 960, 961

*Collen, Charles, *156

*Collen, Lyman, P., *156

*Collins, G. B., *234

*Collins, Gilbert, *230

Collins, Gilbert B., 29

*Collins, Joseph, *230, 234

Collins, L., 142

Collins, Lyman C., 18

*Collins, Polly, *266

Coller, Tick, 694

*Colstin, *202

Colt, Patsey, 419

*Comes, Wilburn, *186

Commedore, 50

Com pah lubbe, 598

Com pah lubbee, 405

Com pa lubbee, 403, 1076, 1077

Com-pil-lah, or Kom-pil-lah, 579

Comte, Jno. R., 76

Comtee, John R., 58

Con ah la cha, 690

Con ah la chubbee, 551

R.C. Con-ah-le-ho-yo, [R. c. 679,] 1107, 1108

R.C. Con-ah-man-tah, alias Yock-o-te-mah, R. c. 623

Con-a-lah, 147

Conamonubbee, 234

*Conamonubi, *134

Concha, 214

R.C. Con-chah-tah, alias Con-che-ti-ah, 624

Con-char-tubbi, 81

Con cha ter, 780, 785

Conchater, alias Conchitiah, 744

Con cha ter, alias Con-che-te-ah, 745

Con-cha-tir, 379

Con cha to nah, 978

R.C. Con-cha-too-nah, [R. c. 679,] 1107, 1108

Con chator, 785

Con cha tubbee, 196, 422

R.C. Con-cha [R. c. 626,] 763, 764

Con che ha tubbe, 539

Con-che-ha tubbee, 377

Con che ho ka, 492, 559

R.C. Con-che-ho-nah, [R. c. 616,] 800

Con che lo nah, 770

Con che ta nah, 771

Con-che-te-ah, alias Con cha ter, 745

Con che te mah, 398

R.C. Con-che-ti-ah, alias Con chah tah, 624

R.C. Con che tonah, 509, [R. c. 627]

Con-che-ton-nah, 388, 527

Con chitiah, alias Conchater, 744

Con ea hona, 170

Cone mah, 845

Conemoon tubbee, 570, 690

Con ex chubbee, 169

Congeah, 436

*Congo, Lewis, *276

Con na ho te mah, 544

Con-nar-ho-chubbi, 80

Conner manter, 720

Conner manter, alias Yock o tee mah, 721

Conner manter, alias Yock o te mah, 722

Con non te mah, 799

Conohemah, 588

Con on tam bee, 598

R.C. Con on te mah, 618

Con-onu-tub-bee, 147

Conoon tam be, 547

Con oon temah onah, 566

*Consaw, Peter, *76

Con sha hoka, 570, 690

Con sha honah, 590

Con sha la, 569

Con sha lah, 690

Conshatubbee, 316

Con-shaw-e-put-tubbee, 148

Con she ho ka, 381, 384, 507, 579

Con she ho yo, 493, 564

Con-she-ti-ah, 96

Coon oontah te mah, 552

Coon oontan tamah, 548

Coon oon te ma honah, 689

*Cooper, Eliza, *110

*Cooper, John, *16, 216

*Cooper, Rhody, *16

C

R.C. Co-pah-sha, alias Pa sham ba, 617

*Co-pah-sha, 619

Cop-a-sa, alias Pas-ham-ba, 720, 806

Cop a sah, 762

Copa sah, alias Pa sham ba, 791

Cop a sha, 702, 714

Co pa sha (alias Pa sham ba) 798, 803

Cop a she, 714

Copersy, 705

Cop hah sah, 712

Coph a saha, 710

Coph a sha, 713

Cop-pah-sah, 380, 710

Copp ah seah, 716

Copp a sha, 718

Cop Per sey, 710, 711

Coppesah, 763

Copt a sha, 713

*Cornelius, Wm., *134, 144

*Cornelius, Wm. A., *164

*Corroll, Sofina, *210

*Corson, *178

*Coss on an chi hubbee, *146

Cos te nubbee, 501

Co-tah, 148

*Cotton, Eliza Jane, *182

Coushatubbe, 234

Cow-ah-ho-yo, 158

Co-wan-ney, 100

Cow-taw-po-lah, 148

*Cravat, John, *234

*Cravat, Peter, *234

*Cravatt, Cassy, *138

*Cravatt, William, *246

Creesey, 398

Crevat, John, 179

Cristey, Josa, 709

Crockett, Davy, 972

*Crossley, Alfeus, *164

*Crouch, Basil, *220

*Crouch, H. B., *202

*Crowder, Eli W., 77, 102, 279, 320, 425, 428, 429, 432, *230

*Crowder, Nancy, *230

Cu a sin, 689

Cuf fah ka, 593

Cuffer ho mer, 789

Cuh tah ho chubbee, 396

Cul e yum, 1009

Culs-ah-po-la, 378

Cum-ah-le, 378

Cum-e-ah, 389

Cum e man tubbee, 886

Cumoon te mah, 605

Cun ah ha mah, 502

Cun ah he mah, 405

Cu nah ho cah, 926

Cun ah la, 452, 982

Cun ah min chubbe, 559

Cun-a-mah, 146

Cun a mo nubbee, 172

R.C. Cun-e-a, 662

*Cun e ah, 579, *60, 92

Cun e ah he nah, 689

Cun e ah hok ta, 689

Cun e ah hok tah, 566

Cun e ah homah, 566

Cun-e-ah-ho-na, 138

Cun-e-ah-ho-nah, 379

Cun e ah ho timah, 1011

Cun e ahstonah, 569, 690

Cun-e-ah-to-nah, 377, 454, 455

Cune-at-im-mah, 96, 101, 146

Cu ne au tubbee, 111

Cun e ish tu nah, 509

Cun e mah, 505

Cun e mah hona, 507

Cun e mah tim ah, 492, 502, 559

Cun e mah tubbe, 527

Cun e mah tubbee, 569, 690

Cun e mam ba, 502

Cun e man tubbee, 825, 885

Cun e me timah, 497, 561

Cun e me tonah, 533

Cun e me yubbe, 504

Cun e mo nubbe, 560

Cun e mo nubbee, 571

Cun e moon tubbee, 567, 689

*Cun e ohuah *58

Cun e o te kah, 506

Cun e o te mah, 535

R.C. Cun-e-o-tim-ah, 675

Cun e o tonah, 533

Cun-esh-to-nah, 579

Cun-e-stu-nah, 148

*Cun e ambe, *240

Cun e te mah, 508

Cun e ubbe, 504, 579

Cun e ubbee, 75, 380, 381

Cun i mam be, 504

Cun na cha, 392

Cun na che, 439

*Cun nahh ha, *144

Cun nah ho yo, 593, 610

Cun nah la tubbee, 610

Cun-na-ho-tub-bee, 148

Cun na i ah to nah, 395

Cunnallee tubbee, 137

Cun-nal-le-tub-bee, 113

Cunna-ma, 845

R.C. Cun-na-na-ho-na, 629

Cunna mam bee, 401

Cunnamantubbe, 269

Cunnamantubbee, 317

Cun na ma tubbe, 250

R.C. Cun nam a tubbee, 245, 319, [R. c. 666.] 1038, 1039

*Cun na mayat, *256

R.C. Cun-na-mo-nubbee, alias Mo-nubbee, 668

Cun na mo nubbee, 931

R.C. Cun-na-moon-tubbee, [R. C. 664,] 1024, 1025

Cun na see, 396

Cun na tam bee, 399

Cunna tan tubbee, 919

Cun na te mah, 391

Cun na tubbee, 212, 213, 947, 948

Cunnea, 238

Cun-ne-ab-bee, 144

Cunneah, 114

Cunneah chubbe, or Oak lahoma, 597

Cun-ne-ah-chubbee, or Oak-lah-ho-mah, 376

Cun-ne-ah-ho-chub-bi, 141

Cun ne ah ho na, 1009

Cun ne ah hon ah, 533

Cun neah lubbee, 423

R.C. Cunnea ho ka, 203 [R. c. 668]

Cun-ne-a-homa, 190

Cunne a hona, 196, 233, 316

Cun nea hoyo, 190

Cun-ne-ah-tub-bee, 137, 404, 424

Cun-ne-an-che-ha-bee, 139

Cunne-an-tubbee, 88, 137

Cun-ne-at-ab-bee, 143

Cunneatubbee, 233, 274

Cun ne cha na, 394

Cun ne chubbee, 393, 402, 451

Cun ne ho chubbee, 396, 419

Cunnehochubbee, alias Tom chito, 417

Cunnehochubbee, alias Tom chitto, 418

Cun ne ho yo, 420

Cun ne ich tonah, 420

Cun ne ish to nah, 394

R.C. Cunne mah, 594, [R. c. 649,] 955, 956, 957

Cunne mah chubbee, 555

Cunnemahona, 279

Cun-ne-man-tub-bee, 814

Cun-ne-ma-tub-bee, 141

Cun ne me ubbee, 395

Cunne mone tubbee, 197

Cun ne montubbee, 190

Cun ne mo nubbee, 395

Cun ne mo nubbi, 930

Cun ne moon tubbee, 414, 421

Cun-ne-mo-tah, 145

Cunne mubbee, 568, 689

Cunne mut tubbee, 203

*Cun neohuah, *56

Cun ne o nah, 404

R.C. Cunneotah, 599, 657

Cun ne o tonah, 405, 982

Cunne-o-tubbee, 113, 138

Cun ne tam be, 545

Cun-ne-tam-bee, 147, 398

Cun ne tam bu, 451

R.C. Cun-ne-tan-tubbee, [R. c. 640,] 905, 906

Cun-ne-tom-bee, 142

Cun ne tubbee, 398

Cun ne ubbee, 395, 404, 424, 434

Cun ne ya, 946

Cun-nin-tub-bee, 142

Cunn la tubbee, 593

Cun no ma tubbe, 597

Cun no ma tubbee, 398

Cun noon tah chubbee, 401

Cun noon tah cubbee, 397

Cun noon ta mah ho nah, 395

Cun noon tambee, 405

Cunn oon te mah la hoka, 549

Cun-noon-tubbee, 139

R.C Cun nuhl la, 599, [R. c. 657,] 982

Cunnuntubbee, 420

Cun ome tubbe, 542

Cun oon tah bee, 603

Cun oon ta kah, 596

Cun oon tamah, 601

Cun oon tam bee, 690

R.C. Cun-oon-te-nah, 653

Cun oon tick cah, 589

Cun ount ambe, 569

Cun-su-moon-tah, 147

Cunubbee, 556

Cun-ula-che, 145

Cun uta cubbe, 561

Cun-we-ah-tub-bee, 99

*Curtis, Edward, *216

*Curtis, Nancy, *216

R.C Cush-ah-nan-che-hub-bee, 616

Cush-ananah hubbee, 380

Cus ha nanhy hublhy, 703

Cus haw man cey hubby, 703

Cus-haw-maney-hubey, 703

Cush on ah, 544

Cush o nau chy hubbee, 761

R.C. Cush-o-ne-lubbee, [R. c. 620,] 781, 799, 800

Cus-hoo-in-che-habee, 106

Cush-oonacke-hake, 112

Cush-oon-a-in-che-pa-bee, 138

R.C. Cush-oon-lubbee, 616

Cush-o-ve-lubbee, 717

Cus-how-naney huby, 703

Cush-shoo-na-che-pa-ha, 137

Cus so nan che hubbee, 781, 789

Cus so nan che kubbee, 761

Cus to na chee, 781

Cus-to-na-chey, 379, 762

Cus to nachy, 791

R.C. Cus-to-nah, 615

Cus to natchey, 697

Cut-ah-po-la, 390, 448

Cut ap ola, 534

Cut teotonah, 594

Cyrus, 50

Dah-bah-tubbee, 376

*Daney, Louiza, *250.

Daniel, 403

Dannels, Jacob, 18

*Darnail, James, *6

*Davenport, Barnett, *172

*Davenport, Bonnett, *128

*Davenport, James, *128

David, 398

Davis, 569, 690

*Davis, Geo., *154

*Davis, Money, *172

Davis, Racel, 76

Davis, Rachael, 47, 49, 171, 172

*Davis, Rache, *318

Davis, Rachel, 46, 50, 140, 142

Davis, Willie, 153

*Davy, Poor, *166

Debrell, Charles, 140

Debril, Charles, 83

Delk, Baldwin, 423

R.C. Dennis, 236, 607, R. C. 654

Dibbrell, Charles, 282

Dibrell, Alzira, 389

Dicey, 50

R.C. Dixon, 400, [R. C. 663], 1016

*Doaty, John, *318

Donnelly, John, 27

*Doughty, John, *318

*Drew, Elcy, *260

*Drew, Wicey, *268

Durant, 423, 970

*Durant, Charles, 78, 278, 320, 422, 425, 426, 428, 431, 451, 970, *218

Durant, Ellen, 972

*Durant, Fisher, 142, 395, 422, *214

Durant, Francis, 972

Durant, George, 407,

*Durant, Harriet, 975, *136

Durant, Isham, 407

Durant, Jefferson, 407, 972

Durant, July, 972

Durant, Justine, 972

Durant, Leman, 198

Durant, Lewe, 432

Durant, Lewis, 422, 425, 428, 429

Durant, Linen, 19

R.C. Durant, Louis, R. c. 653, 673

Durant, Melissa, 972

Durant, Mina, 1126

R.C. Durant, Molly, 451, 609, [R. c. 656,] 981

*Durant, Nancy, alias Hopakinhona, 2

Durant, Peter, 972

Durant, Pier, 79

*Durant, Pierre, 407, 422, 425, 451, *214

Durant, Rasease, 425

Durant, Risseze, 317

Durant, Rissezo, 279

Durant, Roseau, 142

Durant, Silvester, 407

*Durant, Siny, *26

Durant, Sophia, 407

Durant, Stephen, 1126

Durant, Susan, 142

Durant, Susey, 972

R.C. Durant, Swaney, 451, 605, [R. c. 653]

Durant, Swansy, 972

*Durant, Swany, *136

*Durant, Sylvester, *214

*Durant, Taylor, 972, *218

Vol. IV—2.

D

Ea-ah-puh, 142

Ea-cho-ho-pia, 172, 174

Ea-chub-bee, 144, 167, 169, 191, 196, 234, 273, 318

Ea-ham-be, 218

Eah-an-tubbee, 556

*Eah-attubbee, *72

Eahau tubbee, 273

Eah cah tim ma, 554

Eah cah to nah, or Cah to nah, 545

Eah che hubbe, 561

Eah chubbee, 417, 418, 397, 452

Eah-ha cubbee, 498, 950

Eah hah te mah, 548

*E ah hah tubbee, 376, *52

Eah hal poh ho nah, 1104

E-ah ham be, 579

E-ah-ham-bee, 378, 381, 508, 531, 569, 690, 829

Eah ha tubbe, 558, 581, 582, 583

E-ah-ha-tubbee, 384

Eah he tubbe, 548

*Eahhetubbee, *82

E ah-ho che, 763, 764

E ah-ho chubbe, 503

E-ah-ho-chubbee, 380

E-ah-ho-ka, 377, 508, 569, 671, 690

E ah ho kah tubbe, 507

E ah ho ka te mah, 511

E ah ho ka tubbe, 507

E ah hoke ta, 451

E ah hok ta, 401

E ah hone, 504

*E ah ho nah, 396, *68

E ah ho nubbe, 521, 523, 535

E ah ho nubbee, 395

E ah ho nubee, 601

E ah ho te mah, 542

E ah ho tim ah,

E ah is tiya, 211

E ahistya, 213

*E ah kah timah, *60

E ah kah tubbe, 592

R.C. E-ah-kah-tubbee, [R. c. 681,] 1115

E ah ka tubbee, 491

*E ah kaya, *40

E ah kiah hoka, 504

E ah kiah tonah, 595

E ah la ho nah, 392, 393

E ah le honah, 983

E ah le ho tim ah, 492, 559

E ah mock in tubbee, 406

R.C. E-a-ho-che-mah, 626

Ea-ho-chub-bee, 143

*Eahoka, 191, 195, 407, 843, 1065 *110, 136

E a ho ka chubbee, 218

*E a hok atonah, *82

E a hona, 224

*E ahotubbee, *146

Ea hotubbee, 97

Ea hoyo, 191, 194, 197

R.C. E-ah-pah-tubbee, 397, [R. c. 615,] 761, 781

E ah pah tubby, 788

E ah peh tubbey, 700

E-ah-pel-ah, 378

Eah pel lah, 568, 689

R.C. Eah sha tubbee, 399, 465, [R. c. 633,] 862

Eah tahn tubbee, 595

E ah tal ah homah, 508

*E ah tal ah hona, *104

E-ah-tal-ah-ho-nah, 579

E ah te mah, 533

*E ahtimah, *82

Eah-to-chubbe, 577, 579, 583, 584

Eah-to-chubbee, 89, 149

E ah to cubbe, 507

E ah to mah, 556

E ah tom bee, 382, 518

E-ah-to-nah, 382, 388, 509, 584

*E ahtubbe, *40

R.c.*E ah tubbee, 396, 554, [R. c. 673], 761, 1072, *40, 54

E aish tubbe, 269

E aistya, 275, 317

Ea-ka-lubbee, 85

Ea-ka-tub-bee, 140, 149

Eakitubbee, 561

*Eak ka tubbee, *54

Ea maa honubbee, 234

Ea min tu hoka, 252

E-an-la-tub-bee, 146

*E ap ah tubbe, *180

*E apalaka, *184

E as-ta-abbee, 383, 457

Eas-ta-ho-la, 90, 91, 138

Easta-ho-lubba, 115

Eas ta-ho-lub-bee,

Eas ta honah, 531

Easta-ma-la, 112, 138

Easta-mi-yah, 116, 138

Easta ubbe, 521

Easta ubbee, 106, 138, 386, 817, 825, 828, 475, 557

*Eastman, *280

*Eastmancha, *282

Ea-tam-ba, 156, 162

Eatamba, Charles, 198, 316

Eatambee, Charly, 220

Eath la pah, 1102

Ea-to-chub-bee, 140

Ea tona, 268

Ea-tub-bee, 148

Eat-un-ah, 144

E ba catubbee, 212, 213

E-ba-che-homa, 107

E baha luta, 236, 319

E ba ha lutta, 167, 196

*E baheka, *168

E bah fo quah, 391

E bah ho lettah, 419

E bah le honah, 508

R.c. E bah ma ah hoka, 596, [R. c. 659]

E bahnoah ho nah, 569, 690

E bah non tubbee, 978

E bah oyotama, 234

E bah pa lubbe, 528

E-bah-pa-lubbee, 388

E bah pis ubbe, 533

E bah tah, 560

E-bah-took-a-lah, 814, 827

E bah took e lah, 387, 478

E bah took lah, 387, 478, 521, 814, 827

E bak ah hubbe, 520

*E bak ah tubbee, *56

R.c. E bak a tubbee, 276, 320, 670

E ba ma ah ho ka, 997, 999

E bana tubbee, 194, 196

*E banetubbee, *310

*E banetubbee, Simon, *310

*E banoah, *122

*E banonatubbe, *320

*E bark a tubbee, *300

E ba tocolo, 196

E ba to ke la, 167

E ba took ela, 233

*E bat ookla, *182

E-ba-we-cha, 377

E ba we che, 505

E bia tubbe, 256

R.C. E-bi-a-tubbee, 643

E bok-ah-tubbe, 90

E-bok-ah-tub-bee, 814, 825

E bok a tubbee, 1053, 1054

E-boo-nah, 803

Echa hona, 1029

E-chah-pah, 377, 383, 448, 501, 531

E chah pah honah, 493, 564

*Ech-a-pa, 93, 110, 137, 139, *146

E-cha-pah, 459, 813, 826

E cha-pah hona, 110, 139

E cha pa hoyo, 273

*E chapat abbe, *226

E cha pat ubbe, 163

E cha pat ubbee, 406

*E chapohona, *158

E chapohoyo, 317

E cha po tubbe, 514, 525, 531

R.C *E cha po tubbee,   108, 138, 225, 383, 457,
    [R. c. 646,] 817, 828, 942 *66

E-che-ho-nah, 143

E cle po tubbee, 789

R.C. E co no, 451, 466, 607, [R. c. 654,] 977

*Edge, John, *168

R.C. Edmond, [R. c. 664,] 1027, 1028, 1058, 1059

R.C. Edmond, Eliza, alias Hi-to-wat-cha, 281,
    R. c. 670

R.C. Edmund, 227, 256, 567, [R. c. 642,] 689, 916,
    917

Edward, 748, 749

*Edward, Goste, *322

Edwards, John, 139

*Edwards, Lucity, *264

Ee a tubbee, 185

Een lah tubbe, 598

R.C. Een-lah-tubee, 649

Een pak a nubbee, 273

R.C. Een-shul-la-tubbee, 641

Een ta hoka, 271

Een to nubbee, 250

Eg bar ah ga, 198

Eg len ah tubbe, or E klen ah tah, 509

E glen ah tubbe, or E klem ah tah, 579

E-glen-ah-tub-bee, 144

E-glen-al-tah, 381

*E glen nubbee, *242

E glen ubbe, 507

E ha-chubbee, 111

E haia tubbee, 925

E-ha-ley, 96, 146

E-ham-bee, 147, 537

E-ha-tam-bee, 142

R.C. E hema, 228, [R. c. 669,]

E hemah, 1051, 1052

R.C. Eh-lah-cha-te-mah, 617

E ho ah tubbee, 566, 689

E ho a tam be, 568

E ho a tam bee, 690

E ho a tonah, 553

E ho yo, 402

E hue le tubbe, 544

E hu la tonah, 548

Eia, 269

Eia-ho-tub-bee, 146

E

Eian ta ubbee, 250

Ei-ham-bee, 147

Ei kona, 184

Ei-tom-ub-bee, 139

E kah tubbee, 498

E ki o nubbe, 509

E-klem-ah-tah, or E-glen-ah-tubbe, 579

E klen ah tah, or E glen ah tubbe, 509

R.C. Ek-le-po-tubbee, 616

E la a nahona, 271

E-la-a-shub-bee, 148

E-la-ba-chub-bee, 140, 149

E la ba cubbe, 512

E-la-ba-cubbee, 89, 377

E la ba tubbe, 546

*E laba tubbee, *308

E-la-be-ka, 137

E la bo tiah, or Nulthla, 523

E-la-bo-ti-yah, 386, 825

E labo tubbe, 522

E la botubbee, 212, 213, 272, 317, 387, 814, 825, 826

E la cha, 275

E la che, 767

R.C. E-la-che-ho-nah, [R. C. 680,] 1113

*E la che howa, *120

E lafata, 191, 199

E-laf-fe-ton-ah, 382

E-la-fish-tu-na, 143

E la ha cubbee, alias E lah he kah, 552

R.C. E-la-ha-ka-tubbee, 274, [R. C. 630]

E-la-ha-ki-tubbee, 854

E la hala, 236

*E la ha tonah, *4, 46

E lah bo ti yah, 476

E lah bo tubbee, 474

E lah cha temah, 548, 804

E lah cha tubbee, 484

*E lah che hamba, *46

E lah che honah, 512

E lah che te mah, 521, 767

E-lah-chin-tubbee, 442

E la-he-gah, 144

E lah em ah, 540

*Elahennubbee, *48

E lah e shubbe, 502

*E lah fat ubbee, *302

E lah fe tunah, 556, 584

E lah ha cubbe, 594

E lah ha cubbe, or Il la he cah, 509

E-lah-ha-cubbee, or Il-ah-he-kah, 381

Elah he kah, alias Ela ha cubbee, 552

E lah he mah, 523

E lah he nubbee, 567, 689

R.C. E lah ho chee, [R. c. 617,] 789

E lah ho ka, 506

E-lah-ho-ka, or Ah-le-ho-ka, 579

R.C. E-lah-hok-ta, 680

Elah holah, 436

R.C. E-lah-ho-nah, [R. c. 621,] 788

E lah hook ta, 1112, 1113

E-lah-ho-ta-ka, 389

E lah ho teah, 523

E lah ho te mah, 391

E lah ho tim ah, 504

E lah ho to nah, 497

E lah hoyo, 517, 816, 827

E lah ho yo ho nah, 396

E lah hoyubbe, 530, 564

E lah ho yubbee, 493

*E lah ima, 168

E lah in im ah, 505

E lah lo matubbe, 531

E lah ma tubbee, 591

E lah ne ho nah, 507

E lah no an tubbe, 512

E lah no hubbee, 395

E lah nola, 593, 610

E lah-nook-fil-le-ho-you, 388

E-lah-nook-pil-ah, 579

E lah noon tubbee, 404

E la noka, 236

*E lahoke, *32

R.C. E lahola, 191, 319, [R. C. 629]

E lah olo, 236, 843

E la hon ah, 548

E lah onehoka, 277

E la ho ne hona, 944, 945

E la-hook-tah, 146

E-la-ho-te ka, 388

E lah otema, 235

E la ho te mah, 550

E la ho to ka, 503

*E la ho onah, *50

E lah o tubbe, 503

R.C. E-la-ho-we-ho-ka, 646

E lah pa ah, 540

*E lah pa hah, *98

E lah pan ne, 529

E lah pah nubbee, 491, 558

E lah pam ba, 497

E lah pam bee, 379

R.C.*E-lah-pe-ah, [R. C. 638,] *302

E lah pe ah honah, 493, 565·

E lah pe ba, 895

E lah pe bah, 459, 531, 813, 891, 895

E lah pe kah, 383

R.C. E lah pe mah, 516, [R. C. 634,] 868

E lah pe tim ah, 579

R.C. E-lah-pin-le-ho-nah, 1103, 1104, [R. C. 678]

E la pis an, 147

E lah pish ah, 569, 690

E lah pish no wah, 480

E lah-pish-ti-ah, 381, 579

E-lah-pish-ti-yah, 388, 483

E lah pis tiah, 505

E lah pis ti yah, 515

E-lah-pis-tu-na, 579

E lah pis ubbe, 530

E lah po chubbe, alias Ah cha po tubbe, 522

R.C. E-lah-po-nah, [R. C. 674,] 1078, 1079

E lah po tubbe, 516

E lah pun ah hoyo, 502

E lah pun te mah, 492, 563

E-lah-put-tun-nah, 147

E lah shubbee, 445

E lah shubbee, or Billy Naconsha, 492

E-lah-tah-to-nah, 385, 471, 530, 826

E lah tah tubbee, 556

E lah tam be, 507, 579, 1074

*E-lah-tam-bee, 382, * 84

E lah te che ma, alias E lea teha timer, 737

R.C. E-lah-te-che-mah, alias E-le-a-te-ha-te-mah, 624

E lah te che mah, alias O nah ho ca, 738

E lah te kah, 445

R.C. E-lah-te-mah, 594, [R. C. 649], 955, 956, 957

E lah te nah, 570

E lah te ubbe, 516

E lah timah, 561

R.C. E-lah-to-nah, 379, [R. C. 616], 690, 761, 781, 800

E

*E lah took ambee, *78

E lah tubbe, 531, 533

E-lah-tubbee, 375, 442

E lah ubbee, or Chickasaw, 397

E lah u kah, 505, 508

E lah u ka tubbe, 510

*E lah wartubbee, *164

E lah we tubbee, 497

E lah yo kah to nah, 568, 690

E lah yo kah tubbe, 502

E lais tema, 269

E la-it-umah, 95

E la-it-un-nah, 146

E-lak-cha-tubbee, 388

*E lakika *166

E la le homa, 448

E la lutta, 191

*E lam, Wilson, *158

E lambe, 217

*E lambe, John, *14, 42

*E lambe, Sina, *42

E lambe, Siney, *14

E-lam-bee, 141, 395, 417, 418, 419, 420

*E lambee, John, *64

E lan ain tubbee, 242

E lanoauche, 76

E lanoauchi, 50

E lan o nubbee, 394

E-la-no-wa, 817

E-la-no-wah, 825

*E lanowubbe, *32

E lan tonah, 532

E lan tubbee, 526

R.C. E lantubbee, 235, 251, [R. C. 667, R. C. 671,] 921, 1064, 1065

E lan-tub-bee, alias Tis-ho-pia, 141, 313

E lantubbee, or Tis ho peia, 224

E la pahoka, 263

E la pam bee, 502

*E lapanubbee, Billy, *18

*E lapanubbee, Elsy, *18

E lapanubbee, 229

E la pa subbe, 536

*E lapatubbe, *34

E lapea, 1024

E-la-pe-ah, 377, 378, 502

E la pe sa hoka, 502

E lapewah ho nah, 554

*E lapiah, *184

E lap ik e bah, 521

E lap in tubbe, 560

R.C. E-lap-in-tu-nah, [R. c. 677,] 1096

E-lap-ish-ti-yah, 817

E-lap-ish-ti-yea, 828

E-lap-ish-to-nah, 388

E la pissa, 218

E-lap-it-te-ab-bee, 92, 138

E lap no wah, 510

E lap oka, 174

E la polo, 194, 196

E-la-po-nah-ho-ka, 378

E la po tim ah, 504

E-lap-o-tubbee, 91, 138

E-lap-pe-ha, 826

E lap pe mah, 525, 867, 869

E-lappish-nowah-me-hah, 442

E-lap-pis-no-wah, 376

E-lap-tah-hok ta, 736

*E lar bar, tubbee, *258

E la shubbe, or Billy Nakon sha, 563

*E a-shubbee, 94, *68

E-la-shul-bee, 141

E lataia hona, 235

E a-ta-ka, 94, 141

E la tal lawahonah, 253

E-La-tam-bee, 143

*E latema, *14

*E latima, *8, 310, 312

*E latohnubby, *318

E latonubbee, 235

E la took, am be, 502

E lat to nah, 701, 761

E-la-tubbee, 260, 261, 262, 266, 476, 617, 825

E la um bee, 185, 186

E la-un-nah, 146

E lawa tubbee, 222

E law tubbee, 201

E le ah honah, 502

E le a hona, 941

E leah tubbe, 548

E le-a-min-tub-bee, 145

R.C. E-le-a-te-ha-te-mah, alias E-lah-te-che-mah, 624

E lea te ha temer, 738

E lea teha timer, alias E lah te che ma, 737

E lea tich a timer, 716

*E le chubbee, *78

E le-ho-gub-bee, 144

E-le-hon-nah, 145

*E le hopan, *252

E le hoyo, 503

E-le-lo-me-tubbee, 377

E le mah hona, or La mah hona, 508

*E le moon tubbee, *82

E le no ah chubbe, 508, 584

E-le-no-ah-chubbee, 381

E-le-no-wa-cha, 143

E le oka te mah, 567, 689

E le onah, 530

*Elesebe, *320

E le tubbee, 806

E le-u-meu-tubbee, 105

E lexander, 694

Eli, 150

E liah, 65

E liah chubbe, 538

E liahona, 259

E li an ne honah, 528

E lias, 470, 875, 876, 877, 878

E lias and Caleb, 469

E-lia-subbee, 389

E lice, 512

E li cha tubbe, 540

E li cheta, 138, 211, 214

E li-che-tah, 113, 825

E li che to, 273, 317

E li che tubbe, 524

E li-che-tubbee, 383, 387, 461, 824

E-li-chin-tubbee, 388, 484, 575

E li chuf ubbe, 524

E liemah, 574

E-li-e-qua-tub-bee, 148

E li-ge-ho-nah, 146

E li-he-nubbe, 575

E li-hic-cah, alias E li-hic-cubbee, 375, 442

E li-hic-cubbee, alias Eli-hic-cah, 375, 442

E li-hi-quah, 26

*E lihiyah, *170

Eli ho ka, 943

Eli ho kubbe, 531

Eli-hon-na, 105

Eli-hoyno, 90

Eli-ho-yuo, 137

E-li-ish-shubbe, 541

R.C. E-li-ish-shubbee, [R. c. 636,] 879, 880, 881

E-li-ish-te-mah, 579

E lijah, 242

E lik-hon-nah, 388, 527

E lilubbee, 274, 317

E li-met-abbee, 95

E-lim-met-ab-bee, 146

E li o cubbe, 571

E li-oner, 710

E lionubbee, 588

E li oon ah, 521

E li-o-te-ka, 381, 508, 579

E lio temah, 509, 536

E lio tubbee, 553

E-lip-ah-tubbe, 579

E li-pi-o-ca, 142

E lip ipa, 557

E-li-piss-sub-bee, 869

E li pis subbe, 512

E-li-pis-sub-bee, 871

R.C. E-li-pis-ubbee, [R. c. 634], 870

E lisa, 501

E li shubbe, 565

E li-tah-tic-na, 85

E li-tah-tu-na, 139

E li-te-chubbee, 457

E li-to-nah, 788

E li tonubbe, 516

E li-tubba, 90

E litubbe, 540

E li-tub-bee, 139, 211, 456, 458, 482, 483, 825

E li-tub-bee, alias Tom Gibson, 863

E li-ya-tub-bee, 146

E li yubbe, 521, 535

R.C. E liza, 218, 228, 234, 393, 406, 537, 544, 557, [683, R. c.]

E lizabeth, or Lizy, 109

R.C.*Ellen, 279, [R. c. 626], 756, *92, 132, 136, 168, 298, 302

Ellin, 757, 764

R.C.*Ellis, [R. c. 620], 756, 796, 971, *136, 176

Ellis, John, 332, 411, 433, 435, 437, *226

E lam bee, 393

E loch-phe-ho-na, 107

E loffe tubbee, 498

E-lok-ah-tub-bee, 138

E lom a chubbee, 229

E-lo-mah-to-cubbe, 448

E-lo-mah-to-cubbee, 378

R.C. E-lo-mah-to-nah, 627

E lo mah toon ah, 777

E lo mon to cubbe, 547

E lo na chubbee, 406

E lo nah, 502, 569, 570, 690

E lo na him mah, 531

E lonah too nah, 776

E lo-ne-ab-bee, 144

E-lo-ni, 141

E lonia, 203

E loniah, 249, 319

E lo-ni-ho-ya, 88

E-lo-nubbe, 579

E-lo-nubbe, or Oon-nub-be, 579

E-look-cha, 387, 478, 814, 827

E-look-chi-ah, 385, 469, 499, 817, 827

E loomah ho kah, 573

R.C. E-loo-nah, 617

E lopen Tubby, 710

E lotuno, 269

E low e te mah, 397

E-low-ner, 798

E loyah tubbe, 541

*E lsey, *242, 276

E lsey, fry, 977

*E lsie, *320

E lu nah tubbe, 498, 507

E lu nubbe, 504

*E ma, *118

E ma amba, 191

E ma ambee, 194

E ma cha tubbe, 540

E ma che ah honah, 554

E ma chubbee, *78

E mah, 541, 570, 690

E mah a lubbe, 530

E ma hata, 223

E-ma-ha-to-nah, 147

E-ma-ha-tub-bee, (Bob), 146

E-mah-cha-tubbee, 388

E-mah-che tubbee, 484

R.C. E mah ho bah, 609, [R. c. 656,] 981

R.C.*E-mah-ho-ka, 389, 402, 465, 482, 585, [R.C. 656,] 994, 995, 996, *306

E mah ho nah, 474

E mah ho nah, alias E mah le honah, 515

E mah ho tonah, 499, 538

R.C. E mah la, 604, [R. c. 652]

E mah la tubbe, 561

R.C. E-mah-la-tubbee, [R. c. 636,] 884, 885, 886

Emahlee, 971

Emah-le-ho-nah, 383, 459, 813, 826

E mah le honah, alias E mah honah, 515

E mah lubbe, 564, 601

E mah lubbee, 417, 418, 419, 421, 493, 996

E-mah-min-che, 387

*E mah ninche, 478, 542, 827, *98

E-mah-nin-chee, 814

E-mah-nu-wah, 387, 478, 814, 827

E-ma-ho-bee-tubbee, 148

E ma ho go, 178

E mah om be, 492, 564

E ma ho na, 178, 269

E mahotona, 197

R.C. E ma hoyo, 180, 257, 319, [R. c. 644,] 934

E mah sha, 478, 524

E-mah-shah, 579

E mah shah chubbe, 502

E-mah-shah-chubbee, 377

R.C. E-mah-spa-subbee, 626

E-mah-tall-ah, 386, 475, 524, 825

E mah tam bee, 515

*E mah toka, 549, *50

E-mah-tom-bee, 387, 825

E mah yah ste mah, 502

E maia he ku ta, 191

*E maichi, *186

E ma itch a tubbe, 169

E ma itch a tubbee, 191, 196, 235, 316

E makcha hub bee, 114

E mak ko nubbee, 497

E makona, 270

E mala, 221

*E mala habe, *260

E ma la ho nah, 406

E mal-be, 584

E mal la tubbee, 886

E mal le, 505

E mal-le (for Ok-chah) 381

E mal spa lubbe, 755

E mal spa subbe, 754

E

E mal spa subbee, 754, 755

E malth pis lubby, 754

E malth pis subby, 754

E ma lubbee, 163, 186, 201, 205, 221, 331, 408, 902

*E malubi, *176

E mam be, 570, 690

E mam bee, 422

E man cha, 192, 571

E-man-cha-ha-ba, senior, 139

E manchahubbee, 213

E man che, 542

E-man-che-a-tubbee, 390

E-man-che-ha-ba, 942

E-man-che-ha-be, 817

E-man-che-ha-bee, 825

E man che hubbe, 499

R.C. E man che hub-bee, 139, 211, [R. c. 635, 646], 817, 827, 872

*E man chi, *186

E manoa tona, 242

E manoa tubbee, 220

E man ta hocah, 922

E ma number, 169

E-mar-char-cha, 141

*E marhobarchubbe, *202

*E-ma-sha, 387, 814, 827, *98

E-mash-a-chub-bee, 148

*E mash oky, *150

E math la cubbee, 502

E-math-la-cubbee, 375, 442

E math toba, 271

E ma-tom-ba, 116

E-ma-tom-bee, 138

*E matubbee, *120

E ma umba, 196

E maum bee, 235, 316

E m a um ber, 167

E maunte ah hoka, 395

Emayash tubbee, 925

E m bo tah, 527

R.C. E-me-cam-bee, 665

E meen tah honah, 520

E me ha, 525

E mei a hok ta, 194

R.C. E me la, 276, [R. c. 670,] 1054

E me la chubbe, 500

E me lah, 446, 875, 876, 1053

E-me-lah-ho-nah, 442

E me la hona, 229

E me la to nah, 550

E mele, 554

E mele honah, 542

E me le hubbe, 523

E me sha, 544

E mes hehona, 265

E meyah, or Amiyah, 543

E mi a cha tubbe, 167

E-mi-ah, 579, 621, 797

E mi ah tubbe, 501

*E mihinah, *182

*E miline, *128

E milla, 243

*Emilli, *182

R.C. E mily, 50, [R. c. 629,] 840

E min ta ham bee, 218

E min te honah, 522

R.C. E min te hoyo, 228, [R. c. 665⁻

E mis ah hoka, 551

R.C. E misha, 142, 254, 319, [R. c. 669,] 1049

E mish ah honah, 504

E mish te ubbe, 562

E mish te ubbee, 492

E mish too nah, 377, 501

*E mish toubbee, *84

*E mish tubbee, *100

E mis sah, 522

E mistaia, 190, 194

E mistona, or Istona, 204

E mis tubbe, 529, 542

E-mis-tubbee, 387, 478, 814, 827

E mita, 1034

E mith ta hubbee, 1041

E mith tubbe, 503

E mi-yah, 387

E mi ya tubbe, 520

E m lubbee, 184

E mmacamba, 191

Em-mah-le-ho ka, 377, 503

*Em mullah, *38

E mock-ah-ho-nah, 801

E-mock-ah-ho-nah, alias R. c. Mol-la-hoo-nah, 617

E mock he tubbe, 548

E mock mahn tubbee, 392

R.c. E mog lush a homa, 266, 319, [R. c. 629,]

E mok la hona, *300

E mok lam be, 569, 690

E mok onah, 267

E mol ah tubbe, 511

E mol-ah-tubbee, 375

E mol le tubbe, 1088

*E monabi, *162

*E monahe, *124

E mo nah ho ca, 789

E mo nah hoka, 186, 394, 520

R.c. E mo naho kah, 616

E-mo-nah-tub-bee, 817, 825

E mo-nan-tub-be, 90

E mo-nan-tub-bee, 137, 211, 213

E mona tubbe, 255

R.c. E monatubbee, 271, 319 [R.c. 641]

E monche hubbee, 277, 320, 942

E mo nola cho nah, 567, 689

E mon tubbee, 185

E mo nubbe, 508, 563

E mo nubbe, alias Im mo nubbe, 499

E-mo-nubbee, 386, 469, 492, 817, 827

E-mo-og-loosh-ah-homa, 88, 112

E-moog-lush-ah-homa, 817, 825, 847

E-moo-nah-to-ka, 579

E moon tubbee, 421

E moon ubbee, 421

E-morg-loo-shah-ho na, 137

E mothah tubbe, 536

*Empakna, *116

Em-pi-ah, 85, 140, 149

Em shille tubbe, 255

Em ton la hona, 252

E mubbee, 186, 198, 216

E muck a tona, 263, 316

E-mu-li-hah, 146

E-mul-lah-tub-bee, 146

E-mul-la-tubbee, 100

R.c. E-mul-te-bah, 615

E mul tu bah, 791

R.c. E-muth-pa-sa-hona, 251, [R. c. 667,] 922

E muth pa sa hubbe, 264

R.c. E-muth-ta-ha, 267, [R. c. 629,] 847

E-muth-tah-hah, 388

E-muth-tah-ho-nah, 389

E muth tah onah, 593

E muth ta hubbee, 250

E ne cune ubbe, 564

E-ne-cun-e-ubbee, 389, 493

*Englisha, *112

*E nilla, *176

*E nilli, *178

E n lah tubbee, 960, 961, 962

E no, or Enos Wade, 26

R.C. E noa hona, 226, [R. c. 661,] 1009

E no ha, 190

E-noon-tah, 579

E no wa, 184, 194, 201, 205, 216, 217

E nowah, 139, 141, 190, 198, 224, 316, 405,
    417, 418, 419, 422, 423

*E nowaid, *88

E no-yh, 103

E ntle Toner, 727, 728

Eo-ba-tub-bee, 145

Eo catubbe, or Tocubbee, 589

-Eo-co-to-nah, 442

Eo cutcha, 463

E-o-cutch-ah, 389, 497

Eo-gad-abbee, 102, 144

Eo-gad-tub-bee, 144

Eo-gad-ub-bee, 146

Eo-gad-un-nah, 95

E oka, 225, 406

E-o-kah-to-nah, 389

E o kah tubbe, 498, 528

R.C. E-ok-i-tubbee, [R. c. 636], 884, 885, 886

E-ok-tam-bee, 381, 504

E-ok-tum-be, 579

E ona, 279

*E-o-nah, 377, 387, 442, 497, *46

E o ta, 250, 384

E o tah, 404, 492, 559, *72

E o tim ah, 501

E o tubbee, 396

*Erastus, *202

E-Ro-us, 141

Er-ti-ah, 803

R.C.*Es-co-la-cha, R. c. 619, 717, *178

Es-co-lee-cha, 780, 806

E sha-ho-ka, 99, 139, 530

E shal etubbe, 550

E sha too nah, 511

R.C. E-she-a-ho-na, 665

E-she-ho-ka, 385, 471, 826

E she hona, 239

Esh-to-no-ho-yo, 148

E shul le tubbee, 906, 907

*E sicky, *128

Es-main-ha, or Spamba, 26

Es-pa-na-ha-joe, 138

Es-pa-nu-ha-joe, 106

Estah-ha-batche, 806

R.C. Es-tah-ho-bah-che, R. c. 619, 717

E-stah-ho-batche, 780

Es-ta-ho-yo, 383, 459, 531, 813, 826

Estamba, 114

Estamba, Charles, 191

R.C. Es-te-ah-ho-ka, alias Ah-pat-tah, 616

Estear-moo-ner, 798

Esteen pun a hoka, 233

Es-te-ma-la-cha, 140

Es te nulle, 523

Este-te-ma-ho-nah, 148

R.C. Es-ti-ah, 617, 799

*Estubotiah, *138

R.C. *E-tah-mi-ah, [R. c. 674], 1077, 1078, *300

E tamba, Charles, 194

E ta pam ba, 190

E te pok a nah, 514

Eth-la-po-ah, 735, 736

R.C. Eth-la-po-ah-mah, 623

E til ah me, 446

E-til-ah-wah, 390, 892

R.C. E-til-ah-we, 492, 563, [R. c. 637], 892, 893

*Etoheka, *296

E took la ha nah, 406

Et-til-a-wa, 92, 141

E*ttillawe, *290

*Everidge, Joel W., *206

*Everidge, Thomas, *206

Evi hovo (by Eli Tobah), 457

Evua tubbee, 158

E whah tonah, 587

*E yab an otubbe, or J. K. Palk, *2

E ya-chub-bee, 141

E yah ah to nah, 560

E-yah-che-chub-bee, 142

*E yahema, *322

E yah hah tubbee, 515

E yah ham ba, 542, 570

E yah ham bee, 512

E yah he tubbee, 530

E yah hi yah, 521

E yah hokah tubbe, 528

E yah hubbe, 564

E yah hubbee, 493

E-yah-ish-to-nah, 383, 531, *104

E ya-his-ti-ya, 137

E-ya-his-ti-yah, 817

E-yah-is-to-mah, 813

E-yah-is-to-nah, 459, 826

E-yah-is-to-ya, 111

E-ya-his-to-yea, 825

R.C. E-yah-kah-tubbee, [R. c. 683,] 1029, 1030

*E yah makin tubi, *148

E-yah-moon-tub-bee, 146

E ya-hoy-ar, 90

E ya-ho-yuo, 137

E-yah-tah-ho-nah, 579

E-yah-tal-ah-ho-mah, 381

E-yah-tu-nah, 388, 483, 520, 828

E ya-hu, 107

E ya ka tubbe, 562

E ya ka tubbee, 492

E-ya-ki-ah, 384

E-yak ki ah, 461

E yak tubbe, 529

E yal a hoka, 535

E yala honah, 547

E ya le, 517

E yan-ish-lock-ana, 138

E-yan-tah-ho-da, 385, 826

E-yan to hoka, 522

E-ya-pil-lah, 146

*Eyarsha, Wm., *292

*E yatambe, *30

E-ya-to-nah, 817

*E ya tubbee, 18, 137, *90

E ya-tu-nah, 137, 138

E yau-ish-lock a-na, 106

E ye-ho-na, 145

R.C. E-yel-la, [R. c. 665], 1033

E yem e tubbe, 506

E-yi-ho-yo, 382, 515, 816, 827

E

R.C. E yim mah hoka, 598, [R. C. 649,] 960, 961, 962

E yimmer, 190

E yi-tu-nah, 110

E yock a ma tubbee, 392

E yok a che, 531

E yok ah ho nah, 895

E yok-ah-hub-bee, 814

E yok a honah, 531

E yo kah tubbe, 449

E yo kah tubbee, 379, 442

E yok a hubbee, 474

E yok a toonah, 746

E yok a tubbe, 268, 515

E-yok-au-tubbe, 579

E-yok-kah-hub-bee, 826

E-yok-ki-ah, 537, 824

R.C. E yok-o-nubbee, R. c. 669, 1052

E yok o tubbe, 506

E yon tah, 522

E yosh moon tubbee, 497

*E yotambe, *248

E zam tah ho ka, 471

Fa-bo-ga, 143

Facha, 192, 193

*Fachabbe, Mary, *322

Fae a min to na, 917

Fa ha mah ho nah, 547

Fah cha, 436

R.C. Fah-lah-ho-nah, R. c. 676

Fah lah mah, 397

Fah lah mah hoka, 987, 988

Fah lah mah honah, 1123

R.C. Fah lam ah hoka, 597, [R. c. 658,]

Fah lam bee, 401

Fah lam bu, 451

Fahla min cha, 420

R.C. Fah o cha, 280, [R. c. 662,]

Fa he gee, 1013

Fa-hub-bee, 143

Faja, 243

*Fajo, *180

Fal ah mah honah, 1091, 1092

Fal ah moon tubbe, 505

Fal-ah-mo-tubbee, or Ah-fah-moon-tubbee, 378

Fal ah mo tubbee, 567, 689, 829

Fa-la-koo-ma, 26

*Fala humma, *256

Falame, 192

Fal-am-ah-ho-ka, 384, 542

Fa lam ah hon ah, 751

Fa-lam-a-tub-be, 574

*Fa-lam-a-tub-bee, 814, *102

Falam-e-tubbe, 518

Fa lam e tubbee, 384, 462, 478, 824

R.C. Fal-a-min-che, R. c. 628

Fa la min chi, 159, 163, 222, 838

Falaminchubbee, 274

*Falamintobi, Smith, *146

R.C. Fal-a-min-to-na, R. c. 642

R.C. Fal-am-in-tub-bee, 144, [R. c. 663], 1016

*Falamintubi, *130

Fal-a-mo-lin-tub-bee, 145

Fal a mon tubbee, 478

Fala moon tubbe, 532

Fa-lam-o-tubbee, 387, 827

*Falaun moon tubbi, Capt., *26

Fal-e-mon-tub-bee, 814

*Falemoontubbee, *66

Falicheto, 211, 213

Fal-ish, 143

Fallah moontubbee, 557

Fal-lah mo tubbe, 552

Fal-la-ho-la, 149

Fallam in cha, 419

Fal-lam-me, 146

Fal-la-mon-tubbee, 387, 827

*Fallamotubbi, *154

*Fallatubbee, *42

Falle che to, 269, 317, 817

Fallicheto, 110, 138, 825

Fal-li-ho-ma, 137

Falli-moon-tubbee, 114, 137

R.C. Fal-lo-ho-wah, R. c. 651

Fa-lo-mah, 386, 474, 520, 813, 826

Fa lo main tona, 256

*Falomoontubbee, *70

*Faluma, *176

Fal-um-in tubbee, 384

Fal-wat-to-nah, 141

Fa-mon-tubbee, 377

Fan-ab-bee, 145

Fa-nan-chee, 388

Fane-abbee, 97

Fane-ubbe, 535

*Fankah, *224

Fannubbee, 196

Fanubbe, 267

Fa nubbee, 190, 393, 422

Fa nublee, 423

Far-lar-mah, 141

Farver, Alexey, or Lixley Favre, 692, 693

Farver, Alexr., or Lixley Favre, 692

Farver, Bateas, 765

Farver, Bates, 765

R.C. Farver, Batteas, [R. C. 626,] 780, 783

Farver, Battees, 764, 765

R.C. Farver, Beteas, R. C. 626

Farver, Brattus, 785

Farver, Lexey, 749, 785

Farver, Lickesey, 694, 744

Farver, Licksey, 694, 744

R.C. Farver, Lixey, [R. C. 625,] 698, 781, 785

Farver, Lixy, 748, 807

*Farvor, Battiest, *180

Farvour, Alex, alias Lixy Farvour, 808

R.C. Farvour, Alexes, alias Lixey Favre, R. C. 614

Farvour, Lixy, alias Alex Farvour, 808

Farvr, Marey, 692

Farvr, Marrey, 692

*Favor, Battiest, *128

*Favor, Lexy, *144

Favour, Lixey, 760, 762

R.C. Farve, Lixey, R. C. 614

R.C. Favre, Lixey, alias Alexes Farvour, R. C. 614

Favre, Lixley, or Alexy Farver, 692, 693

Favre, Lixley, or Alexr Farver, 692

Favre, Lixey, 693

Farver, Licksey, 379

Faya, 316

Feby—should be Phoebe, 929

*Fechik homa, *198

Fee chub lee, 540

Fela, 889

*Felacatche, *104

Fe lah moon tubbe, 514

*Felamatubbee, *64

*Feleh kache, *216

Feleka chubbe, 547

Fe le kah, 503

Fele-mah-hon-ah, 388

Felemetubbe, 541

Fele moontubbe, 541

Fe le nubbe, 505

*Feleta, *126

Fe le tah, 508

*Feletah, Mrs., *228

Feletahhon, 1091

*Feleyeta, *158

Felik a chubbee, 446, 479

Feli kah chubbee, 445

Felik e chubbee, 444

Felik-ka-chubbee, 375

*Feliteah, *104

Fel-la-mat-ca, 146

*Fellimechubbe, *50

Fe look a che, 515

Fe-low-a-cha, 143

R.C. Fe-lub-le-chubbee, R. C. 637

Fem'-mah, 85

Fe te mah timah, 498

Fe tick ah chubbee, 497

*Fia hocha, *32

*Fielamowa, *200

Fi ho cha, 1013

Fik a bo nah, alias Tek a bottah, 746

Fil ah moontubbee, 689

Fi-la-ka-chubbe, 87

Fi-la-ma, 141

File-mar, 80

R.C. Fil-a-moon-tubbee, [R. c. 663,] 1018, 1019

Fil-a-tub-bee, 147

Fil e ah timah, 509

Fil e ah tubbee, 497

Fil-e-at-tah, 388, 484

Fil-e-cut-che, 386, 475, 573

Fil-e-mah, 382, 421, 571

File mah ho nah, 570, 690

Fil-e-mah-te-kah, 813, 826

Filemah tubbe, 562

Fil e mah tubbee, 382, 445, 492

*Filemah tubbee, *68

File mam be, 554

Fil e ma stubbee, 1061

Fil-e-moon-te-kah, 459, 813, 826

Fil-e-moon-tubbee, 375

File tan ho nah, 566

Fil e te mah, 1061

Fil-e-ti-yah, 387, 478, 519, 814

Filetonah, 570, 690

Fil e tubbe, 514

*Filikachi, *148

*Filih ka tohi, *164

R.C. Fil-la-ma-tubbee, R. c. 671

Filla mon tubbee, 1027

Filla moon tubbe, 244

Filla moon tubbee, 406

Fil la tah, 991

*Fillatah, *52

Filla toya, 192

Filla tubbee, alias Anok filla tubbee, 272

Fillatubbee, alias Anokfiillatubbee, 317

Fil-le-cah-ga, 139

Fille-congee, 115

Fille, or Noak filla, 517

Fillee taia, 197

*Filleharche, *28

Fille mon tubbee, 229, 270

Fille moon tubbee, 568

Fil-le-mo-wah, 146

Fil-le-tah, 376, 586

Filletah honah, 689

Fil-le-ti-yah, 827

*Fillihkotobi, *168

*Filli kottubi, 168

Fillubbee, 224

Fim-mah, 140

*Fimmentubbee, *82

*Fink ta homa, *156

Finmintubbe, 585

Fin-min-tubbe, 376

Finn, 756, 757

R.C. Finn, Louiza, [R. c. 626]

*Fisher, Charles, 312, 408, 433, *76

*Fisher, Joseph, *258

*Fisher, Silas, D., *248

*Fisher, Susan, *36

*Fisk, *308

Fit-chee-nu-wa, 137

Fit-chie-nu-wa, 113

Fitch ik noma, 457

Fitch-ik-no-wa, 817, 828

Fitch-ik-no-wah, 383, 514

Fith-le-at-am-bee, 143

Fith lio tubbee, 497

Flack, Eliza Ann, 376

*Flender, *320

*Fletcher, Mrs. Harris, *228

*Fletcher, Isom, *240, 246

*Fletcher, Capt. Jas., *240

*Fletcher, Moses, *200, 306

*Fletcher, Nancy, *128

*Fletcher, Wm., *240

Fo-am-bubbee, 145

Focatubbee, 276

Fo kah lin tubbee, 497

Foko lin tubbe, 536

Fola min to na, 918

Folivah, 87

Follama, 221

Fol-mo-tubbee, 442

Folo-mo-tubbee, 375

Fo look ache, 523

R.C. Fol-o-tah, R. c. 651, 966

*Folsom, Adam, *294

*Folsom, Alix, *294

*Folsom, Amanda, *20

*Folsom, Bradford, *16

*Folsom, Coffe, *30

Folsom, Colonel, 30

Folsom, D., 10, 12

*Folsom, David, 444, *20

*Folsom, Edmund, *2

*Folsom, Edmund B., *16

Folsom, Elias, 24

*Folsom, George, *260

*Folsom, I. N., *2

*Folsom, Isaac, *218

*Folsom, Israel, *306

*Folsom, Joel, *20

*Folsom, John, *262

*Folsom, McKee, *6

*Folsom, Nat., *16

*Folsom, Peter, *2, *30

*Folsom, Phoebe, *20

*Folsom, Polly, *128

*Folsom, Capt. Robert, *206

*Folsom, Robert, *234

*Folsom, Sampson, *218

*Folsom, Samuel, *236

*Folsom, Solomon, *10, *20

*Folsom, Ward, *8, *18

*Folsom, William, *236

*Folsom, Willis, *6

Fo-lubbee-chubbee, 389

Folub le chubbee, 493, 565

Fo-na-cha, 140

Fone, 144

Fo-ne-ab-bee, 145

Fo-ney, 143

Fo-ni-ah, 143

*Forb, Joe, *144

R.C. Forbes, R. c. 665

*Forbis, 250, *300

Forester, 409

Forester, John B., 408, 495

Forrester, 202, 412

Forrester, Col., 200, 410, 411

Forrester, J. B., 433

Forver, Licksey, 747

*Foster, 51, *32

Foster, Elijah G., 406

Foster, George W., 406

Foster, Hugh, 18, 77

Foster, James, 18

*Foster, Lucy, *212, *240

*Foster, Luke P., *208

Foster, Thomas W., 406

Foster, William, 18

*Fowler, Henry, *116

*Fowler, John, *224

*Fox, Peter, *46

*Frances, 451, 977, *130

R.C. Francis, 607, 654

Francois, 422, 425

*Frank, Benjamin, *106

*Frank, Tobias, *68

*Frank, William, *50, *58

*Franklin, Benj., *286

*Franklin, Betcey, *290

Fraser, Swany, 390

Frazer, Swany, 512

*Frazier, Alex., *242

*Frazier, Amos, *162

Frazier, Andrew, 840

*Frazier, Benjamin, *228

*Frazier, Betsy, *228

Frazier, Billy, 176, 177

R.C.*Frazier, Charles, 46, 48, 49, 50, 140, 170, 171, 176, 177, 179, 247, 319, [R. c. 629,] 839, 840, *320

*Frazier, D., *312

*Frazier, Daniel, *28

*Frazier, Davis, *224, *250

*Frazier, Elam, *130, *162

*Frazier, Ellen, *28

*Frazier, Fisher, *244

Frazier, Harry, 140, 142, 179

*Frazier, Heliche hona, *310

*Frazier, Jackson, *314

*Frazier, James, *224

Frazier, Jane, 839

*Frazier, John, *28, *138

*Frazier, J. R., *244

*Frazier, Lewis, *228

*Frazier, Lucy, *138

*Frazier, Mary, 840, *152, 154

Frazier, Maxwell, 840

Frazier, Molly, 46, 50, 78, 140, 142, 170, 172, 173, 174, *318, 319

*Frazier, Moses, *132

*Frazier, Nancy, 48, 50, 77, 140, 142, 179, 253, 319, *312, 318

Frazier, Nelly, or Nelly Dyer, 178, 179

Frazier, Polly, 50, 77, 79

*Frazier, Sameter, *226

*Frazier, Silas, *314

*Frazier, Simon, *152

*Frazier, Stephen, *152

*Frazier, Suky, *28

*Frazier, Swany, *152

*Frazier, Tobias, *310

*Frenay, Sally, *226

*Fry, Betsy, *212

*Fry, Billy, *294

*Fry, Edmund, *130

R.C. Fry, Elcey, 607, [R. c. 654]

*Fry, Lismore, *166

*Fry, Lucy, *224

*Fry, Thomas, *294

*Fry, Wm., *212

Fu-ches-ho-mah, 142

Fu-ches-two-mah, 92

*Fulamotubbee, *48

F

Fullamatona, 50

Ful-le-ha-mah, 816

Ful-le-ho-ma, 113, 114, 457, 499, 827

*Fulle homah, *100

Ful-le-ho-me, 382

*Fullemountubbee, *50

Fullo motubbe, 551

Fulsom, David, 26, 29, (?)

Fulsom, Isaac, 189

Fulsom, Israel, 29

Fulsom, John, 26, 189

Fulsom, Robt., 26

Fun-ne-ho-ma, 113, 384, 461, 824

Fun ne homah, 530

Fun-ne-ho-na, 138

*Funne howah, *102

*Funnka, *168

Fut-cha, 602, 610

Fut-choos-ho-mah, 478, 814, 827

Futch-us-ho-mah, 387

R.C. *Gaines, 238, [R. c. 662,] 1012, *134

*Gardner, Edmund, 20

*Gardner, Green, 238

*Gardner, Isaac, 238

*Gardner, Jackson, 204

*Gardner, James, 20

*Gardner, Jeremiah, 240

*Gardner, Josiah, 98

*Gardner, Salina, 16

*Gardner, William, 204, 240

*Gardner, Zacheriah, 238

*Garland, Febis, 256

*Garland, James, 20

Garland J., 12

*Garland, John, 156

*Garland, Peggy, 20

*Garland, Rhoda, 158

Garland, Samuel, 26

*Garland, Sarah, 148

*Garland, Silas, Jr., 146

*Garland, Silas, Sr., 146

Garland, Thomas, alias Wall Thomas, 27

*Garvin, Henry, 18, *164

*Garvin, I. L., 164

*Garvin, Lewis, 218

*Garvin, Sokey, 198

*Gary, Lucy, 304

*Gears, Billy, 192

R.C. George, alias Hopia shubbee, 50, 190, 197, 253, 399, [R. c. 670]

*George, Dixon, *244

*Gibson, 510, 551, *302

*Gibson, Anna, 242

*Gibson, Calvin, 242

*Gibson, David, 198

*Gibson, James, 266

*Gibson, John, 322

*Gibson, Mary, 288

*Gibson, Tom, 863

*Gillet, Nancy, 22

Gipson, James, and Goen, James, 27

Glenna, 483

Glertubby, 707

Goc ha ta, 169

Goch tie, 144

Goen, James, and Gipson, James, 27

*Goforth Loiza, 196

Goin, Jim, 451, 980

R.C. Gon a chubbee, 930, 931, [R. c. 668], 253, 222

Gosheworkaw, 440

Gowin, Betsy, 392

*Graves, Henry, 160

*Grayham, George, 152, 154

Grayham, Suhanna, 18

*Grayson, John, 8

Greggs, Leroy P., 425

*Griffith, Martha, 54

*Griffy, Charles, 56

*Griffy, Mark, 29, *56

Griggs, Leroy P., 981

*Guess, Billy, 64

Gun na bo nubbe, 107

Gwin & Co., 409

Gwin, Doct., 192

Gwin, Dr., 240, 410

Gwin, Edward, 192, 206, 207

Gwin, Fisher & Co., 408

Gwin & Forester, 413

Gwin, Wm. M., 408

H

Habanah, 542

Hab-beinta, 167

r.c. Ha-be-na-chubbee, 281, [r. c. 671], 1063

*Hablintubby, *222

Hacatcher, 714

Hacha, 141, 142, 376, 395, *46

Hachach, 418

Hachah, 417, 419, 448

Ha-chonah, 397

Hachoneo, 225

Hacubba, 316

Hacubbe, 539

r.c.*Hacubbee, 118, 191, 197, 222, 251, 375, 377,
379, 442, 497, [r.c. 619, 627, 667], 771,
785, 807, 808, 921, [*48, 59]

Hacubbey, 770, 780, 783, 785

Haccubby, 770, 771

Ha-gah, 146

Hagopionabbi, 50

Hah be nah, 553

Hah-cha, 501

Hah-gah, 105

Hah-la-chah, 422

Hah lah le, 532

Hah-lak-lama, 97

Hah-le-cha, 1083

r.c. Hah-lin-cha, 616

Hahmook la honah, 518

Hahnubbe, 571

r.c.*Hah nubbee, 386, 464, 476, [r. c. 616, 627,]
789, 789, *104

r.c. Hah-ta-chubbee, 615

Hah-tak-bil-ah, 580

Hah-tak-lam-ah, 502

Hah tak ubbe, 509

r.c. Hah-te-mah, [r. c. 625,] 746

Hah-tock-bil-ah, 387

Hah-tock-bill-ah, 509

Hah-yah, 103

*Haiakanubby, *244

*Haietima, *8

*Haiopahnobe, *300

Ha ka, 252

Ha kaahona, 507

Ha kah toonah, 912

Ha-kainlatubbey, 742

r.c. Ha kanlintubbee, r. c. 627, 743

Ha katona, 50

Ha keta, 1027

*Haklohima, *162

*Haklohona, *137

*Haklohonah, *258

Hala, 46, 50, 75, 172, 173, 178, 179, 198, 377,
442, 513

r.c. Ha-la-be-ho-nah, 616

*Hall a chu bbe, *20

Ha-la-gah, 104, 145

r.c.*Halah, 250, 407, 465, 910, 911, [r. c. 666,
673,] *232

Halak, 319

*Halalechobi, *160

*Halatubbi, *24, 40

*Hale, John, *208

r.c.*Ha-le-cha, 675, *152

Haletubbe, 504

Ha-le-tub-bee, 144

Haley, 399

Halison, 225

*Hall, Jone, *292

*Hall, Louis, *196

*Hall, William, 18

Halla, 401

Hallache, 557

*Hallahtubbe, 18

Hallatahhoma, 1042

Hal-le, 143, 507

*Halloway, Thomas, 104

Hallubbee, 275

Hal-lun-tubbee, 26

Halotahoma, 250

Halotahona, 319

*Halston, Charles, 86

*Halston, Henry, 6

*Halston, Stephen, 4

*Halston, William, et al, 6

*Halth-tenubbe, 100

Halubbe, 481

Halubbee, 379, 442, 555

Ha-ma-co-lee-cha, 148

R.C.*Ha-mah, [R. c. 679], 1106, *48

Ha-ma-lah, 825

Hamayotubbee, 235

Ham ba, 462, 463, 475

*Ham be, Mrs. Lauris, 204

*Ham be, Lauris, 278

Ham bee, 378, 568, 689

*Ham bi, 200

*Hamilton, Wellington, 222

Hammond, John T., 45, 47, 48, 49, 50, 75, 245, 249, 319

Ha-moog-ib-le-tub-bee, 103, 138

Ha-mook-lah-tubbe, 517

*Hampton, 280

*Hampton, Jas., 220

*Hampton, Melissa, 228

*Hampton, Nicholas, 314

*Hampton, Phebe, 188

*Hampton, Willis, 214

*Hampton, W. W., 314

Hanachito, 264

Han-ah-che-to, 817, 825

Han ah to nah, 542

*Han cha (widow,) 272

*Hancock, Albert, et al., 14

*Hancock, Benj., 32

*Hancock, Betsy, 26

*Hancock, Bob, 118

*Hancock, John, 26, 108

Hancock, Robert, 18

Hancock, Robert, jr., 75

*Hancock, Robt., 108, 188

*Hancock, Siny, 188

Haniss, 279

Hannah, 407

Han-nan-chi-to, 137

Han nan-ho-mo, 140, 149

Han-nan-hoom-ah, 142

Han-nan-hoona, 89

*Han-no-chito, 308

Han-nubbe, 269, 542

Hannubbee, 317

Hannubbey, 703

Han lubbe, 530

Han-on-cheta, 111

Han-tub-bee, 108, 137, 385, 471, 826

Han-ub-bee, 767, 814, 825

Haoletimah, or Ah-ho-latimah, 508

*Hapakintubbee, 322

*Haparkintubbe, 26, 36

Hapiahishtalubbee, 1005

Hapo tubbee, 1028

Happ a lab hona, 1072

Hardaway, Hartwell, 18

*Harkin, D. F., 312

*Harkins, George, 312

Harkins, G. W., 432

*Harkins, George W., 222

*Harkins, Stephen, 44

Harland, Jno. T., 77

*Harle, 272

R.C. Harlin, 254, [R. C. 639]

*Harlo, 58

*Harly, Thomas, 132

Harmbey, Piser, 711

Harmbey, Tear, 711

Harris, 50, 403, 905, 906

Harris, Ailsy, 234

*Harris, Daniel, 234, 236

*Harris, Elcy, 234

*Harris, Mrs. Elcy, 234

*Harris, Mrs. Elsie, 236

*Harris, H. C., 130

*Harris, John, 172, 234

*Harris, Joseph, 82, 84

*Harris, Robinson, 36

*Harris, Solomon, 36

*Harrison, Mrs. Betsy, 216

*Harrison, Daniel, 236, 238

*Harrison, Hickman, 298

*Harrison, J., 296

*Harrison, J. D., 302

*Harrison, Peter, 40

*Harrison, Zadoo, 216

R.C. Harriss, [R. C. 640]

Harry, 273

*Hart, Susan, 262

H

*Hartemer, 302

*Harney, Joseph, 196

*Hashe homma, 242

*Hashemingo, 100

Hash-e-no-wa, 826

Hatah honah, 690

*Hatahtoch billah, 114

Hatak-lam-bee, 145

Ha-tak-lam-ma, 145

Hata mah honah, 559

*Hateahonah, 46

*Hatei-labbee, 284

Hatemah, 50

Hatemah, 1043

*Hatimahah, *272

Hathahonah, 530

Hathla, 548

Hathtenubbee, 474

*Hatona, 204, 229, 406, *90

Ha-to-nah, 141

Hatook-lubbe, 524

Haltubbe, 266

Hatty, 50

Hatubbee, 27, 147

*Haxagie, 206

Hayes, Betsy, 1057

*Hayes, Charles, *206

Hayes, Phil., 239

Hay-ky-o, 107

*Hayliss, 168

Hay-mah, 148

Hayopa, 269

*Hayopatubbe, 18

*Hayoper, George, 204

R.C. Hays, Betsy, 239, [R. C. 670]

Hays, Charles, 27

*Hays, Cornelius, 214, 218

*Hays, Jane, 214

*Hays, Nickman, 190

*Hays, Rachel, 218

*Hays, Stephen, 290

*Hays, Capt. Thomas, 190

Hay ubbee, 188, 881

Hea-ca-te-nah, or Widow Radford, 26

He-ah-kah, (dead) 377, 442

He-ah-ka-ishtonah, 523

He-ah-ke-lub-bee, 146

He-ah-ke-tub-bee, 104, 145

He-ca-amba, 218

R.C. Hecatona, 255, [R. C. 641,] 912, 913

Hechalle, 561

Hechatte, 384

Hecubbe, 510

He-e-ho-nah, 145

Hegah, 105, 145

Hein timah, 508

Hein-tuner, 722, 723

Hei on tanah, alias Ah-hatonah, 723

He-ion-to-nah, 380

R.C. He-i-on-to-nah, alias Ah-ha-to-nah, [R. c. 623,] 724, 783

Heith-lah-tho-nah, 522

Hekan, 382, 556, 584

He-kah-che-honah, 533

He-kah-tim-ah, 505, 508

He-kah-tubbe, 504, 530

He-kah-tubbee, 500

He-ke-ab-honah, 506

R.C. He-ke-ah, or Ho-ke-tah, 717, [R. c. 620]

*He-k-tona, 160

He-ki-yubbe, 517

He-la-tom-bee, 111

He-lubbe, 537, 337

*Helubbee, 102

He-mah-ho-mah, 376

He-ma-ki-ah, 146

Hemanche, 540

Hem-ock-a-to-na, 140

He-mok-o-nubbe, 522

Hemonahtubbe, 545

Hemonatubbi, 50

Hem-te-a-ka, 146

He-nah-homah, 448, 548

*Henderson, John, 172

He-neah-honah, 403

*Henry, Amos, 32

*Henry, Matthew, 96, 102

Hent-lar-to-nah, 729

He-ock-co-nubbee, 392

He-oh-com-oh, 423

Heo-po-ho-mah, 147

Heotemah, 566, 689

He-o-to-nah, 379

Heo-tubbee, or Utubbee, alias Mr. Shoat, 271

Heoun-ubbee, 504

Her-lin-cha, 791

Her-lin-epa, 702

He-teah-ho-nah, 500

He-tock-looah, or Ah-noon-pisah-cha, 401

*Hetty, 253, 590, *294

He-tu-capa-homa, 112

Henah-le-tubbe, 535

*Heyakabe, 272

*Hey as honubbee, 108

*Heyo, 4

He-yope-hajo, 469

Hi-a-can-tu-na, 65

Hi-a-ca-tub-bee, 799

*Hiacutcha, 102

Hiacut-chee, alias, Hiyocache, 275

Hiacutchee, or Hyocache, 317

Hi-ah-ca-tubbee, 619

Hiah-comah, 422

Hiah conubbe, 544

Hi-ah-cubbee, 109

Hi-ah-kah, 437, 467

Hiah kamahtubbee, 588

Hiah-ka-tubbe, 537, 547

Hiah-katubbee, 379, 552

Hi-ah-ke-che, 813, 826

Hi-ah-ke-chee, 459

Hiah-ki-mah-tubbe, 588

Hiah konubbe, 585

Hiah-la-ho-nah, 395

R.C. Hi-ah-too-nah, 797, [R. C. 619,]

R.C. Hiaka, 158, 159, 163, 166, 197, 225, 232, 318, [R. C. 661]

Hi-a-kah, 512, 1002, 1004

Hi-ak-ah-ton-ah, 384

Hi-ak-a-tema, 264

Hiaketubbe, 571

*Hiakitubbee, 266

Hiala, 393

R.C. Hi-a-la-lah, 808, [R. C. 614]

Hi-a-lee, 516, 517

Hi-ank-ah, 108, 109

Hi-ar-cha, 140

R.C. Hi-a-temah, [R. C. 625,] 747

R.C.*Hi-a-to-nah, 396, 760, [R. C. 621,] 717, 781, 788, *74

Hiatubbee, 18, 270, 799

Hichon-na, 105

Hic-am-tub-bee, 139

Hic-an-to-nah, 756

Hic-a-tea-cha, 85

Hic-a-tee-cha, 149

Hic-a-tes-cha, 140

Hick-a-te-mah, 397

Hick-a-tom-bee, 393

Hick-a-tubbe, 269, 594

R.C.*Hick-a-tub-bee, 117, 138, 140, 376, [R. C. 619,] 788, *72

R.C. Hick-a-yo-tubbee, alias Ka-yo-cubtee, 678, 994, 995, 996

Hick-a-yo-tubbee, 1102

R.C. Hick-in-to-nah, 585, [R. C. 659,] 994, 995, 996

*Hickman, A., 50

Hic on-to-nah, 780

Hicon-tunah, 737

*Hieantona, 144

R.C. Hi-e-an-to-nah, 626

Hi-een-ah-tubbe, 525

Hi-e-le-honah, 553

Hi-emstemah, 516

Hi-ene-chubbe, 459, 518

Hi-en-e-chub-bee, 383, 813, 826

Hie-on-to-nah, 783

Highabey, 694

High-a-ger-sto-ner, 780

R.C. High-ah-gah-sto-nah, 624

High-i-no-na, 234

Highorga-stoner, 739

Hig-horger-stoner, 379, 739, 740, 783, 785

High Tim, 741

Hi-ille-ho-nah, 109

Hi-il-le-na-ho-nah, 137

Hik-ah-che, 527

*Hi-keah, 32

Hiketenah, 514

Hikeyah, 537

*Hikin, 310

Hikintubbee, 234

*Hikitambi, 136, 138, 180

Hikiteah-ho-nah, 561

Hi-le, 144

*Hilitobi, 132

*Hill, James, 20

*Hill, McAlester, 20

Hill-a-tubbe, 529

Him-a-bar-to-nah, 141

Himah-kiah, or Himmockah-yuh, 690

*Himakattona, 266

Him-ak-ubbe, 533

Him-an-am-bee, 143

Him-is-a-hoga, 145

Him-man-ne-tubbee,

Himmo-catana, 157, 192, 199

Him-móck-abbee, 394

Him-mock-am-bee, 394

Him-mock-ah-to-nah, 446

Him-mock-ah-tunah, 437

Him-mock-ah-yah, 375, 569

Him-mock-ah-yah, or Him ah kiah, 690

Him mock a-tona, 194

Him-mok-am-bee, 147

Himmokatona, 321, 316

Him-moon-nah-tubbe, 597

Himmucatona, 198

Himmuccatona, 162

Himmuk-ubbe, 523

Him-ok-a-toona, 1064

Him-o-nah-tubbee, 497

*Him-on-obi, 156

Him-o-nubbe, 502

Him-o-nubbee, 567, 689

Hin-a-ho-mah, 148

*Hin-a-hooma, 184

Hi-ne-ubbe, 509

Hin-che, 386, 475, 523, 825

Hinola, 544

Hintimah, 561

Hi-och-tubbee, 1018, 1019

Hi-o-ga-be, 139

Hi-o-gale, 529

Hi-o-galee, 110

Hi-o-ga-lu, 137

Hi-ok-a-tema, 274

R.C. Hio-ka-tona, 250, [R. C. 666]

R.C. Hi-o-pah-nubbee, [R. C. 674,] 1077, 1078

Hiotah, 398

Hi-o-temah, 445, 497, 637, 746

*Hi-o-tonah, 499, *64

Hi-o-tubbe, 244, 516, 548

Hi-o-tubbe, or Ah-hi-o-tubbe, 580

R.C. Hio-tubbee, 380, [R. C. 618, 663,] 761

Hio Tubby, 712

His-ka-tub-bee, 148

Histeia, 267, 317

His-tubbee, 780

Hi-tak-e-pa-ho-ma, 386

Hitcha, 184

Hith-ah, 394

Hith-la-ho-ka, 579

R.C. Hi-to-wat-cha, alias Eliza Edmond, 670

Hito-watchir, alias Eliza Edmon, 281

Hit-tuch-ho-mir, 137

Hit tuck a pa ho ma, 138, 475

Hit-tuck-kome, 113

Hittukhoma, 211, 213, 817, 825

Hituk, 144

Hituk-e-pa-homa, or Yo-ki-ah, 516

Hi-tuk-e-pa-homa, 825

*Hix, Pilot, 258

Hi-ya-kubbe, 529

Hi-yo-cacha, 212

Hi-yo-cache, alias Hiacutchee, 275

Hi-yo-catonah, 1037—1037

Hi-yok-a-che, 814, 825

Hi-yok-a-chi, 138

Hi-yok-ah, 520

Hi-yok-hubbee, 387

Hiy ok kubbe, 542

Hiy ok kubbee, 478, 814, 827

Hi yola, 524

Hi yope ah hah cho, 383

Hi-yop-e-ah-hajo, 542

Hi-yo-pe-e-ah-ha-jo, 813

Hi-yope-e-ha-jo, 385, 817, 826, 827

Hi-yope-hajo, 521

Hi-yo-tubbee, 98, 139, 825

Hi-you, 885, 886

Hizopeah-hah-cho, 459

Ho-au-tubbee, 101

Hobacha, 191

*Hoba-cha-hon-ah, 56

Hobah, 375, 468, 567, 1087

Hobah cha, 905

Ho-bah-cha-ho-nah, 378, 500

Ho-bah-chee, 379, 454, 619, 788

Ho-bah-tam-be, 492, 563, 690

Hobahtambee, 569

Ho-bah-tishubbee, 406

Ho-bah-tamah, 525

*Hobahtubbe, 536, *40

Hobahtubbee, 407, 452

Hobalot, 515

Hobataka, 270

Ho-ba-tambee, 111, 146

Ho-ba-ta-sha, 141, 192, 198

Hobateia, 266

Hobateia, alias Abasiya, 275

Hobateia, alias Abatuja, 320

Hobatisha, 204, 224

*Hobatishubbe, 90

Hobatishubbee, 229, 331, 408

Hobatiyah, 516, 816, 827

Ho-ba-tubbee, 393

*Hobbintobi, 170

R.C. Hobelah, 683, 1130

*Hobert, Jerry, 296

Hobeteyah, 457

Hobetiyah, 523, 525, 382

Hoblee, 524

Hob-nubbee, 1073

Hoca, 392

Hocha, 103, 192, 193, 199, 240, 242, 319, 551

Hochafa, 191

Hochah, 435, 580, 390

Hochefo, 193, 228, 402, 417, 418, 421, 439, 580, 600

Ho-che-fo-tubbe, 545, 147

Ho-che-mah, 392, 521, 547, 983

Hochepo, 1051

*Ho-chia-homa, 320

Ho-chon-chubbe, 518

Ho-chubbe, 502, 517, 529, 148

Ho-chub-bee, 219, 442

Hoc-ka, 139

Hock-a-fa-tubbee, 451

*Hock-a-la-tubbee, 148

R.C. Hock-a-loo-tubbee, 615, 780, 806

Hock-a-loo-tubbey, 699

Hock-a-lo-tubbee, 379, 398, 406, 761

Hoc-ka-to-hub-bee, 147

Hock-ba-to-nah, 140

Hock-co-o-to-nah, 148

Hock-e-lan-Tubbee, alias Tucke-lantubbee, 721, 720

Hock-e-lan-tubbe, or Nuck-er-lan-tubbe, 783

Hock-e-lantubbee, 762, 780

Hock-e-lo-tubbee, or James Alley, 382, 493

Hock-il-lo-tub-bee, 138

R.C. Hock-kah-la-ho-nah, 596, [s. c. 659,] 997, 999

Hock-la-honah, 502

R.C. Hock-lah-to-nah, 403, 465, [s. c. 631,] 859

R.C.*Hock-lan-tubbee, alias Tuck-ah-lan-tubbee, 623, *286

*Hock-loo-a-tubbee, 116

*Hock-loon-tubbee, 144

Hock-o-lo-tubbee, 1027

*Hock-sachi, 308

*Hock sage, 202

*Hoc-loon-tubbee, Capt., 24

Hococha, 198

Ho-cc-lo-tubbee, 1032, 1033

Hocombe, 767

*Hocowatubbee, 110

Hocubbee, 395

Ho-cut-tubbi, 80

Ho-de-gah,

Ho-de-kah, alias Hotick-oh, 141

Ho-dik-ah, 144

Ho-e-ho-nah, 501

Hoe-to-ney, 379, 691

Ho-fah-cubbee, 916, 917

Hoga, 978, 145

Hogay, 96, 145

Hogee, 145

Hogla, 397, 465

Ho-ho-na, 50

Hoh-ta-nah, 380

Hoh-te-mah, 747

Hoh timah, 937, 938

Ho-ish-ah-ho-nah, 144

Ho-it-ish-ti-ah, 144

Ho-ka, 138, 178, 242, 277, 386, 475, 518, 528, 551, 631, 825, 857, 901

Hokah, 622, 678, 717, 813, 826, 945, 947, 1097, 1098

Ho-kah-tubbe, 580, 388

Ho-ka-la-jah, 26

Ho-ka-la-pissa, 169

Ho-ka-loche, 264

Ho-ka-lo-chubbee, 377

Hoka-lohona, 218

Ho-ka-lo-tubbee, 229

Hokan-ta-lubbey, 741

Ho-ka-to-nah, 147

Ho-ka-tubbee, 224

Ho-kee, 106, 145

Ho-ke-lo-tubbee, 446

Ho-ke-lo-tubbe, or James Alley, 564

Hoketa, 274, 406, 585, 630, 659, 994, 995, 996

Hoketah, 379

Ho-ke-tah, alias, Hekeah, 620, 717, 761, 781, 801

Ho-ki-a, 380, 625, 752, 753, 762, 780, 783

Hok-honah, 220, 508

Hokla, 147

Hok-la-chub-bee, 144

Hok-la-hattah, 509

*Ho-kla-jah, 34

Hok lo hattah, 509

Hok lo tubbe, 525

*Hok-obe, 290

Hok-ob-eont-ab-bee, 143

*Hok olo chi, Wilson, 68

Hokolo-chubbe, 538

Hok sa gee, 520

Hok sa jah, 28

*Hokti, Kam, L., 242

Hok ubbe, 540

Hola ba tubbee, 84

*Holabbee, 228

Holah, or Stem-a-hal-ubbee, 1073

Holah bah honah, 505

Holah cha, 566, 689

Holah temah, 569, 690

Holaiya, 32

*Hola ta, 208

Hola tah homa, 1042

Hola ta homa, 1288

R.C. Hola to homa, 178, R. c. 666

Hola tom bee, 137

R.C. Hola to pah, 149, [R. c. 682,] 1126

Holbach, 316

Holbache e, 219

Hol ba chubbee, 234

Hol bah, 264

Hol bah chubbee, 399

Hol bah tub bee, 379

Hol ba ti yah, 525

Hol bu honah, 545

*Hol dufield, Richard, 196

Hole bi cha, 437

Holemioka, 587

Hole-tah-ho-nah, 421

Hole-tah-mah-cubbe, 580

Hole-tham-a-gub-bee, 143

*Hole to pah, 389, 589, *72

Holet tah ho mah, 392

Holet tah honah, 421

Holey by ho nor, 789

Holicka, 199

*Holimalah, *272

Holina, 502

*Holin labi, 196

*Holipubbee, 158

Holisah tubbe, 559

Holis ah tubbee, 492

Holis-so-honah, 529

Holis subbe, 512

R.C. Holis subbee, 107, 138, 386, 470, [F. c. 635,] 817, 827, 875, 876

Ho-lit-ab-bee, 143

Holla, 190, 399, 437

Hollah-hun-nah, 147

Hall-ba-cha, 163, 197

Hall-ba-che, 156, 193

*Hollis subbee, 258,

*Hollotahoma, 316

Hollotubbee, 55

*Holloway, Billy, or Ahpah hah, *36

*Holloway, Thomas, 114

*Holloway, William, 86

*Holmes, Abner, 266

*Holmes, Wiless, 110

*Holmes, Wiley, 114

Ho-lo-ba-lubbee, 85

*Holson, Malinda, 24

Holson, Charles, 26

Holth-te-nubbe, 522, 523

Hol-ubbee, or Ho-tub bee, 26

*Holubbee, 42

*Homa, Anna, 310

*Homa, Jincy, 126

*Homa, Selina, 264

*Homa, Thomas, 260

Homa a che, 242

Ho-ma-ca-la-tub-bee, 137

*Homah, 99, *172

Homah, Chuffah, 715

Homa-ka-tona, 84, 85

*Homar, Mrs. Anna, 202

*Homar, Nancy, 222

Home ho tubbe, 569

Home hotubbee, 690

Homi-a-cha, 141

*Homma, Allen, 296

*Homma, Cornelius, 226

*Homma, Estona, 298

*Homma, J., 226

*Homma, Nokon, 206

*Homnoh, 168

*Homuli, 190

Hon-a-che, 146

*Honah, 147, 378, 387, 478, 501, 537, 542,
566, 689, 814, 827, *40

Honah, or Ma-ho-nah, 698

Honah, Malla, 702

Honah, alias Nah ho nah, 791

R.C. Hon nah, alias Na-ho-nah, 615

R.C. Ho-nah-hah-tubbee, 400, [R. c. 632,] 860

Ho-nah-te-mah, [R. c. 617,] 806

Hon-a-tona, 912

Hone mah, 536

Hone qurah, 595

Honer, 698

Honer, or Ma-ho-nah, 698

Honer, Atchey, 717, 718

Honer, By, 784

Honer, Ma-La, 704

Honer, Moley, 710

Honer, Staga, 704

Honer, Tonley, 702

Honelambe, 535

Hong-kio, 158, 191, 194, 197, 316

Hong-ky-o, 162

*Honia, 216

Honk-ley, 145

Honl-bah, 26

Hon nub bee, 212, 213

Hon tah etub bee, 916

Hon tona, 482

Hon tonah, 569, 690

*Hook ela, 448, *50

Hooker chupper, Stimer, 697

Hook-la, 377

*Hook-la-che, 268

Hook-la-chubbee, 104

Hook-le-la, 548

Hook-lin-tubbe, 580

Hook-te, 853

Hoola to-pah, 84, 140

Hool-bah-ho-nah, 537

Hool-bah-tubbe, 446, 532, 542

Hool-bah-tubbee, 388, 446, 472

*Hool-ba-tubbee, 826, *70

Hool-lo, 376, 448, 551

Hoon-ah, 569, 690

Hooner, 698, 718

Hoo sah tubbe, 520

Hoo taner, 712

Hoo tener, 709

Hoo too nah, 386, 470, 521

Hoo tubbee, 547

R.C. Ho-pa-co-nubbee, [R. C. 668,] 1047

R.C. Ho-pa-cubbee, [R. C. 642,] 917

Ho-pah-cubbe, 592

Hopah-cubbee, 405

Hopah-ha tubbe, 566

Hopah kah, 517

Hopah ka-tubbee, 375, 468, 689

Hopah ken tubbe, 380, 783

R.C. Hopah ken tubbee, [R. C. 624, 627,] 737, 761

Hopah ken tubby, 737

Hopah ken tubbey, 738

*Hopah kiah, *14

Hopah kin tubbe, 780

Hopah kin tubbee, 491, 827

Ho-pah-ko-nubbe, 597, [R. C. 660,] 999, 1000, 1001

*Hopai hemitta, *306

*Hopais, 304

Hopa-ka-che, 267, 317, 825

Hopa-ka-ge, 138

Hopa-ka-nubbee, 1047

Hopa-kea-ge, 99

*Hopakinhona, alias Nancy Durant, 2

*Hopakintobi, 170

*Hopakintubbee, 387, 478, 572, 814, *62

Hopa kon ubbee, 252

Hopa nah, 395

Hopa pa nubbi, 79

Hopar kanubbi, 50, 77

*Hoparke, 276

Hopar rintubbe, 767

Hopar ubbi, 50

R.C. Hopa-ya-Shubbee, 671

*Hopenah, 296

Ho-pe-nah-ho-yo, 445

Hope-nahoyo, 390

*Hopia, 258, 1060, *194

R.C. Hopiah, 141, 497, R. c. 645

Hopiah, or Abbetook chiah, 600

Hopiah homah, 415, 416, 417, 418 419, 601

Hopiah-Iske-tina, 389

Ho pi ah shubbee, 1059, 1060

Ho piah ska tena, 979

R.C. Ho-pi-ah-ska-te-na, or Ab-be-took-chi-ah, R. c. 655

Ho pi ah tubbe, 521

*Hopia ish tonake, *248

*Hopiamatube, *320

*Hopian che hubbee, Capt., *250

Hopia Shubbee, 281, 320

R.C. Ho-pi-a-shubbee, alias George, R. c. 670

Hopia ska tena, or Abbi took cheah, 465

Ho pi a sto lubbee, 1005

Ho pi es ka te ne, 62

Ho pi es ka te ne, or Little Leader, 61·

Ho-pi-im-che-ab-bee, 139

Hopiishtalubbee, 225

Ho pi oh, 939

Ho pi yah, 521

*Hopiye, *296

Ho pok onah, 560

Ho-polth-lah, 142

Hop pah lah tubbee, 404

Horoma, 249

Ho-se-to-mah, 146

Ho sheen she homa, 174

*Hoshe homa, *296

Ho she no mah, 459

Ho-she-no-wah, 383, 813

*Hoshe she humma, *250

*Hoshe she mahaha, *252

*Hoshesh mataha, *194

*Hoshe huma, *126

Hosh in she homa, 249, 319

*Hoshin she hona, *230

Hos-ka, 104

Hos to noche, 529

Hota, 403

Ho ta che ho nah, 502

Ho-ta-chub-bee, 140

Hota cubbe, 593

*Hota cubbee, 271, 317, 376, *52

Hotah, 18, 389, 465, 587, 689, 992, 993

Hotah at tubbe, 504

Ho tah ho nah, 403, 405

Ho tah lah ha mah, 398

Ho tah na, 194

Hota honah, 569

Ho-tah-tah, 143, 510

Hotah timah, 558

Hotalah, 242

Hotaina, 191

*Hotaiye, *8

Hotaka, 1005

R.C. Ho-ta-kah, 376, [R. C. 676,] 1089, 1090

Ho-ta-kub-bee, 825

*Hotala hooma, *254

Hotamah, 552, 908, 910

Hotamba, 737

Hotambe, 767

R.C. Ho tam bee, 397, 403, R. C. 624

Hotambee, or Ick bush ko, 417, 418

*Ho ta na, 28, 158, 197, *138

R.C. Ho-ta-nah, 163, 437, [R. C. 618, 661,] 760, 781, 788, 1004, 1005

Hotanah, or Hoth tena, 225

Ho tan te mah, 397

Ho tan tu nah, 525

Ho-tan-yah, 382, 506, 580

Ho tan yah, or Oth-te-yea, 388

*Hotatah, *164

Ho ta ta homa, 1046

Ho ta tim ah, 492

Ho ta tubbe, 267

*Hotawah che, *276

Ho-tay-ah, 145

*Hote, Wina, *256

Ho te ah, 498, 560

*Hoteah honah, *46, 48

Hoteah ke, 510

Ho-te-an-ah, 384, 492, 558

*Hote che hona, *314

Hote cubbee, 88

Hote hoka, 264

*Hotekabbe, *322

Ho te kah, 580

Ho te kubbe, 523

*Hotelabbee, Capt., *246

Ho te lubbe, 524

R.C. Ho-te-ma, 50, 91, 116, 138, 255, [R. C. 641]

Ho-te-mah, 138, 148, 242, 378, 396, 529, 531, 569, 575, 594, 600, [R. C. 649, 655,] 690, 829, 955, 956, 957, 979

Hote mahlah, 546

Ho te ma la, 267

*Ho-te-ma-lah, 142, *272, 274

*Hotemey, *144

Hotemiah, 401, 415, 551

Ho te min chi, 1058

Ho te mi ya, 418, 594

Ho-te-mo-nah, 442

Ho te mon okoka, 269

Hotena chubbee, 198, 216, 217

Ho-te-na-chub-bi, 141

R.C. Ho te nah, 517, 530, 532, R. C. 649

Ho te nah chubbe, 539

Ho-te-nah-chub-bee, 142, 392, 395, 418, 419

Ho te nah honah, 517

R.C. Ho te nah tubbee, [R. c. 619,] 803

Ho te nan cha, 403

Ho tenan chubbee, 417

*Hoten labbee, *284

Ho te nubbee, 400

Ho te o a, 391

Ho te ocka, 193, 402, 435

Ho te ock ka, 463

R.C. Hote oka, 192, 199, 243, 569, R. c. 663

Hote o kah, 1014, 1015

Ho-te-ok-kah, 375

Hoteyah, 573

*Hoteyaki, *4

Hoth ta na, 163, 205, 221, 316

Hoth te na, 201

Hoth tena, or Hot an ah, 225

Hoth te na ho, 218

Hoth-te-nubbee, 386

Hoth tim na, 158

Hoth ton ah, 419

*Hotia, *322

Ho-tia-chub-bee, 138

Ho-ti-a-ka, 103

Hoti cha, 205

*Hoti chi hona, *132

Ho ticka, 193

Ho tickah, 331,

Ho-tick-ah, alias Ho-cle-kah, 141

Hotick kah, 435, 436

Ho ti ka, 201, 243

*Hotik abbee, *194

Ho-tik-i-a, 380, 512, 584

Ho ti koh, 408

Ho tim ah, 503

Ho-tim-ah-che, 388, 580, 557

Ho tim e ah, 508

Hoti mi ya, 417

Ho-ti-na-chubbee, 184

*Hotinah, *12, 14

Ho tin lubbe, 505

Ho-tin-lubbue, 143

Ho-ti-o-ka, 103

Ho tish le ah, 472, 573

Ho tish tam be, 505

Ho-tish-te-ah, 385

Ho-tish-tim-ah, 380, 506

Ho-tish-tin-ah, 584

Ho-tis-ka, 142

Hotiya, 571

*Hotobi, Johnson, *142

Ho-to-chub-bee, 148

Ho to mah, 404

Hoto manka, 570

Ho Tomba, 737

Ho tom bee, 738

Hotona, 192, 255, 330, 408, 1027

*Hotcnah, 404, 464, 515, 535, 541, 569, 592, 690, *224

Ho to nan cha, 451

Ho to ney, 781, 785, 807

R.C. Ho-to-ney, alias Ho-tun-nee, [R. c. 613,] 808

Ho-ton-ho-yo, 147

Ho to nub-bee, 903

Ho to pahle, 522

*Hotmah, *10

Hotroka, 690

Ho tubbe, 514, 522, 527, 580

R.C.*Ho tub bee, 144, 147, 176, 278, 381, 384, 388, 461, [R. c. 647,] 824, 947, 948, *116, 200, 312

Ho-tub-bee, or Hol-ubbee, 26

R.C. Ho-tun-nee, alias Ho-to-ney, [R. c. 613,] 808

Hougkio, 221

Houm-tubbee, 100, 146

How a chubbee, 173

How ah to nah, 789

*How anotema, *122

R.C. How-a-to-nah, alias Te ah hoo kah, R. c. 619

*How atubbee, Capt., *114

Howell, Calvan, 18

Howell, Calvan H., 151

Howih, Oklih, 786

Howta, Chubby, 697, 803

Howyar, 706

Hoxaga, Capt., 433

Hoxager, Capt., 427

Hoxager, 428, 432, 604

Hoxagu, 451

Hox-e-cha, 442

Hoya, 1126

Hoya, or Ahoya, 222, 316

*Hoyabbee, *270

Hoy-no, To-ke, 139

*Hoyo, 242, 268, 399, 437, 561, 1028, *126

Hoyo an tubbe, 569

Hoyo an tubbee, 690, 832

Ho-yo-at-i-ga, 146

*Hoyobi, Willis, *142

Ho-yo-ga, 106, 145

Ho yo hi ah, 514

*Hoy oh oka, *166

R.C. Ho-yo-ho-nah, 376, 549, 574, 593, [R. c. 648,] 953, 954, 955

Hoy ohonubbee, 236

Hoy oka, 590

Hoy opa, 224

Hoyo pah, 399

Hoyo pah tubbee, 500

R.C. Ho-yo-po- nubbe, [R. c. 641,] 908, 910

*Hoy op otobi, *170

*Hoy o pu, Geo., *278

Ho yo ta ma, 229

Ho yo te mah, 383, 461, 824

R.C. Hoy o tubbee, 234, [R. c. 675,] 1083

Ho-you-hun-na, 92

Ho yo ubbe, 560

Ho yo ubbee, 388

*Ho yubbe, 512, 516, 531, 541, 544, 563, *204

R.C.*Ho yubbee, 99, 117, 138, 141, 145, 198, 204, 207, 375, 382, 398, 465, 492, [R. c. 636,] 834, 879, 880, *86, 90

Hu ba tubbee, 185

Hubbe, or Tick bone tah yubbe, 549

*Hudson, Elsey, *190

*Hudson, George, or George Hutson, 26 *152

*Hudson, James, *164

*Hudson, Joel, *152

H

*Hulbah, Capt., *90

Hul-ba-tub-bee, 145

*Humak vtona, *188

*Humma, Ace, *210

*Humma, John, *240

*Humma, Saini, *210

Humphius, 280

R.C. Humphreys, R. C. 670

Hunahoka, 319

Hun oon pah, 603

*Hunter, Sylas, *218

Hup-ah-ka-tub-bee, 146

Huse, Mingo, 117

Hush ah e tunah, 517

Hush cumma, 204

Hush e homah, 524

Hush e lah tam be, 506

Hush e mingo, 268, 317, 825

Hush e no wah, 516

Hush e te mah, 519

Hush hook homah, 515

Hush-ke-ah-hook-te. 826

Hush ok homah, 459

Hush-o-me, 105, 145

Hush-oom-ah, 144

Hush oon ah mustubbee, 113

Hush-shok-ho-wah, 813

Hush-shook-ho-ma, 139, 383, 457, 317, 828

*Hush shook homah, 530, *68

Hush-shoon-ah-mus-tubbee, 138

Hush sok ho ma, 826

Hush-spoon-ah-mis-tubbee, 137

Hush ta sho nah, alias Ah tah sho nah, 574

Hush to mubbee, alias Tishu mustubbee, alias Ak wat o cubbee, alias Og leis teia, 275

Hus ke ah hooc ta, 459, [R. c. 638], 896, 897

Hus ke ah hooc te, 813

Hus ke ah hooe ta, 531

Hus ke ah hook tah, 383

Hus se min go, 138

Hus shook ho mah, 383

Hustep, or Io gle tubbee, 394

Hutson, George, or George Hudson, 26

Huttuk homa, 276, 317

Hyo cache, or Hia cutchee, 317

Iache, 103, 137

Ia che ho na, 138

Ia che ho nah, 386, 476, 517, 825

Ia con ubbee, 1047

Ia gle, 1126

Ia ha, or Ayaha, 220, 316

Iah che honah, 509

Iah ka, 191

R.c. Iah ho nah, [R. c. 681,] 1117, 1119

Iah ho to nah, 535

*Iah ish to na bee, 194

*I ahish to nubbe, 210

I ah ka hoche, 517

I ah lepan, 689

I ah min tubbee, 401

*I ah oko tahi, 190

I a hubbee, 403

I ah wa cha, 437

I aith le pah, 375, 862

*I ak an tobi, 186

I ake be to lah, 448

*I akin to bi, 188

I alba, 542

R.c. I a mah, 391, 394, 397, 407, [R. c. 650,] 964

Ia main tubbee, 938

Ia mata, 178

Ia min tah hoka, 592

Ia nah, 382, 457, 525, 590, 600, 816, 827

Ia nean tubbee, 173

Ia nim tubbee, 18

Ia nin tah, 420

Ian ta tubbee, 540

*Ian ta tubbee, 319, 388, 483, 484, *230

R.c. I an ta tubbee, alias Antatubbee, 928, R. c. 643

I ape ah tubbe, 520

I ash ka mah, 516

I ash ta, 142

Iata, or Hiata, 190

Iata, 199

*Iatah, 401, 440, *244

Iath lah, or Ia tubbee, 690

Iath le pah, 382, 509, 566, 568

Iath le pah, or Ah se ta ho nah, 580

Iath le pah, or Iskatenah, 690

Iath le pah ish ke te na, 468

Ia to lubbe, 267

Ia tone lah, 442

Ia tubbee, 392, 421

Ia tubbee, or I ath lah, 690

Ia wa che, 239

Ia wa gee, 1008

I bah ash tah, 384

I bah ho yo, 382

I bah no wah, 529

I bah osh ta, 538

I bah osh tay, 824

*I bah o tubbee, 158

I bah wa che, 518

*I baka habbe, Capt., 254

I bak ah hubbe, 530

I bak ash tah, 462

Ib bah e lubbee, 925

*Ib banoah, 34

Ic ah cubbee, 452

Icha, 225

Ichin tubbee, 146

Ich la nat chee, 190

Ic ho nah, 142

Icho wa, 580

Ickana, 270

Ick bush co, 419

Ick glen ahn cha, 397, 464

R.C. Ick ki o nubbe, [R. C. 652]

Ick ki o nubbee, 604, 971

Ick ko nah ho nah, 399

Ick neth lo, 404

Ick nith co, 464

Ick sa nam pulli, or O nah cha tubbee, 398

Ic misha, 1048

Ico nah, 141, 396

Icon nah, 398, 417, 418, 419, 451

I eah cubbee, 378

I e ah honah, 536

I een la hubbe, 519

I e lah ho tubbe, 518

I e ma, 252

I e mah, 922, 923

Ie mah to kah, 540

Iem na, 522

Ie my, 146

Ie ne timah, 497

*Ie nin tubbee, 42

Ie ton lah, 569, 690

I et tu lah, 385, 470, 472

I e tu lah, 471

Ig oh ohubbee, 228

I ha gah tubbee, 532

I ha gah tubhee, 387, 478, 814, 827

*I haithea, 132

R.C. I haith la, 603, [R. c. 651]

I haith lah, 450, 968

I ha kah tubbe, 520

I ha kah tubbee, 386, 475

I ha kom bee, 531, 895

I ha me ubbee, 386

I ha neah, 390

I ha ne ubbe, 574

I ha ne ubbee, 475, 825

I heeth la tonah, 875

R.C. I heeth la too nah, [R. c. 635], 876

*I he ka tobbe, 198

I hik e tubbe, 521, 542

I hik e tubbee, 387, 478, 814, 827

I hio tubbe, 518

R.C. I ho lo tubbe, 651

I ho na ee, 115

I hove bah tubbe, 517

*I ho wa, 154

I huth la toona, 512

Iik len ah, 521

Iilla, 789

Ii nean tubbee, 174

I in toa nubboy, 1037

R.C. I ish e tubbee, [R. c. 683,] 1131, 1132

I ish tin ag we ah, 96

I ish to no ho yo, 101

I is ka ti oak te, 99

I is toke cha, 191

I it ah nubbe, 513

I ith la pa, 468

I it ta lah, 826

I it toon lubbee, 829

I it tu lah, 514

*I it u lah, 104

I kah po lubbe, 537

*Ik be honah, 531, *304

Ik be tubbe, 515

Ik ea him na, 145

Ik e be honah, 580

Ik e be tul lah, 97

Ike bit ulla, 145

Ik ha nah, 568, 689, 830

Ik ho pom ko yo, 143

Ik ione mah, 552

Ik lan abbe, 18

*Ik lan abi, 176

Ik lan ah tah, 516

Ik lan ubbe, 541

Ik le nah, 441

Ik o nah te mah, 497

R.C. Ik o man tubbee, [R. C. 680,] 1110

*Ik o no Ward, 212

*Ik san opola, 206

Iks a num pulla, 451

Ik sa num pulli, 970

Ik so num pulli, 142

Ik tan nalth la cha, 442

Ik tan nath la cha, 376

Il ah e mah, 516

I lah ha be tonah, 518

Il ah he kah, or E lah ha cubbee, 381

Il ah he kah, 580

Il ah hoyo, 457

Il ah ish te mak, 548

Il ah ish to noh, 515

Il ah no la, 387, 826

I lah o kubbee, 894

I la bo nah, or I ye le he mah, 497

I lah ta shubbee, 377

*Ila hullo, 212

I lah yo kubbee, 895

I lap im hah, 532

*I la pish taya, 212

*I la pish taya, Moses, 212

I lap o nah, 522

*I lap o tube, 38

*I latoh noche, 196

I la tubbe, 529

I la tubbee, 386

*I la wi tubi, 130

I la yo kubbe, 531

I-le-hoh-poh-nubbee, 905

I le ho yubbe, 580

I le ho yubbee, 388

Il i ah ho nah, 580

Il ie o tubbe, 501

Ili ho ka, 140

**Ili kau chi tobi, 126

Ili yo kah tubbe, 580

Ilk co tubbe, 90

Ilk co tubbee, 91

Illa aho chubbee, 420

*Illa banna, 264

Illa bo tonah, 928

Illa cha, 376

Illache, 595

Illa con ah tubbee, 393

Illa con a tubbee, 401

Illah chaf fubbee, 525

Illah e ka, or Elah ha cubbe, 509

Illah ho ka, 396

*Illah hona, 134

Illah honah, 983

Illa hiah, 401, 464

Illa hin ubbee, 147

Illah ish te mah, 526

Illah no la, 532

R.C. Illa ho chubbe, 606, R. c. 653

Illa ho chubbee, 392, 464, 973

Illahoka, 5J6

*Illaholo, 136

*Illahona, 188

Illahonah, 395

Illa hoyo cubbee, 985

Illah payn to nah, 404

Illa mo to nah, 399

Il la na la, 814

*Illanola, 478, *66

Illa no lah, 827

Illano wa hubbee, 196

Illanowatchee, 172, 179

Illa piah, 147

*Illa po nubbee, 108

*Illa po nuby, 102

*Illar ho tubbee, 276

Il la tah lo ah, 932

Il la tonah, 440

Il le cun ne chubbee, 142

Il le hi ah, 142, 452

*Ille hin yah, 304

Ille ho chubbee, 142, 983

Ille ho chubbi, 108

Ille hona, 192, 198, 220

Ille honah, 571

Ille ho yubbe, 505

Ille nawa, 212

*Illenowa, 213, 266, 319, *186

R.c. Ille no wa che, 645

Ille no wah cha, 940

Ille no watchee, 179, 258

Ille no watchie, 319

Ille nu wa, 139

Ille nu wah, 114

Iller fa lubbi, 82

Ille tubbe, 509

Ille wo wa che, 941

Illi che tah, 472

*Illi ho vo bi, 142

*Illil rochobi, 176

Illook chah, 446

Illug lah to nak, 396

I lok cha ya, 28

Ilth co tubbee, 451

*Ilth koli, 162

R.c. Im ag hah, alias Im mah o glagh, [R. c. 622,] 717, 791

Im ah ag hah, 786

*Im a hanta, William, 216

Im ah chiah, 509

Im ah han ah, 144

Im ah hath lah, 580

Im ah ho ka, 505

Im ah ho tonah, 384, 560, 922

Im ah ho yo, 382, 449, 505, 556, 570, 584, 690

Im ah illa, 497

Im ah isha, 517

Im ah kan che, 525

Im ah lahho nah, 555

Im ah le honah, 498, 509

Im ah no ah timah, 561

Im ah no le hambe, 533

Im ah no wabbe, 542

*Im aho glah, 385, *148

Im ah o glah, alias Im ag hah, 79I

*Im a hona, 130

Im ah o nah, 504

*Im ah o tona, 134, 260

Im ah pis ah tim ah, 498

*Im ah sah che, 72

Im ah ta be, 384

Im ah tah, 498

Im ah tale, 462

Im ah talle, 521

Im ah tha ka, 471

Im ah tha kah, 385, 516

Im ah tickah, 952, 953

Im ah tish e honah, 506

Im ah to ka, 377

Im ah tonah, 514

Im ah yah, 521

*Im ai chitobi, 166

*Im aishe homa, 282

Im aka, 173, 319

Im ak ka, alias Onaka, 932, 934

Im ak po lo tubbe, 548

*Imala habby, 222

*Im aiahokta, 204

Im ai tah honah, 492, 536

Im ai to bah, 503

Im ai tova, 501

Im am be, 584

Im am bee, 382, 506

Im an o tika, 503

*Im an o tobi, 172

Im asacha, 193

Im as he, 143

Imath pisa tambe, 569, 690

*Im a tona, 294

Im e lubbe, 502

Im enah ho ka, 478

*Imeullube, 34

Imi a chubbe, or Soc ka, 580

Im i a chubbee, alias Miah chubbee, 1116

R.C. Im i ah hubbee, alias Mi ah chubbee, 681

Im ie ah ha tubbe, 535

*Imi le, 106

Im illa hona, 273

Im ille, 384, 491, 517, 558, 581, 582, 583

*Im in la hona, 134

Im in tubbe, 588

*Im i oh aklah, 88

Im io nah, 891, 892

*Im ishi hona, 176

Im ish leah, 516

Im ish tam be, 562

Im ish tam bee, 492

*Im ish taya, 314

Im isht eah, 146

Im ish to nah, 442

Im ish too nah, 516

Im ish tuma, 95

Im isht un nah, 146

Im ma, 95, 146

Im ma cam ba, 199

Im ma chubbee, 143

Immah, 535

Im ma ha tubbee, 140

Im ma ha yo, 50

Im mah ho bah chubbee, 417, 418

Im mah honah, 405

R.C. Im mah ho to nah, 389, 597, [R. c. 658, 660,] 951, 967, 987, 988, 999, 1000

Im mah la chubbee, 399

Im mah lah hubbee, 401, 463

Im mah lah te mah, 400

Immah la hubbee, 973

R.C. Im mahn chah tubbe, 596, [R. c. 659]

Im mah nola, 597

R.C. Im mah no wah honah, 397, [R. c. 652]

Im mah no wa honah, 971

Im ma hoba chubbee, or Ma ho ba chubbee, 204

Im ma ho ba chubbee, 207

Im ma ho bah chubbee, 417, 418

R.C. Immah o glah, alias Imagnah [622, R. c.] 717

Im ma hoka, 190

R.C. Im ma hoka chubbee, 228, R. c., 665

Im ma hola chubbee, 140, 1031

Im ma honah, 146

R.C. Im ma ho to nah, 439, 597, [R. c. 648]

Im ma ho ya chubbee, 1031

Im mah sah cha, 403

Im mah sha hoka, 593

Im mah sho mah, 594

Im mah ta le, 824

Im mah thah kah, 826

Im mah ti yah, 587

R.C. Im mah to nah, 591, [R. c. 659,] 950, 993

Im mahu cha tubbee, 997, 999

R.C. Im ma ka, alias Onaka, 668

Im ma la tah, 141

R.C. Im ma lubbe, 601, [R. c. 655]

Im ma lubbee, 465, 978

*Im ma luchah, 28

Im man e lo hoyo, 265

Imma noahoka, 553

Im marthla chubbee, 405

Im matebohona, or Atoba, 229

Immatha chubbi, 598

Im math la chubbee, 451, 464

Im math la tubbee, 916

R.C. Im math pa sa hona, 661

Im me cha, 389

Im me ho ba tubbee, 400

Im me hoka, 537

Im me ho nah, 526

Im me ho nubbee, 982

R.C. Imme lah tubbee, [R. c. 682,] 1120, 1121

Im mella, 973

Im me ne lah, 591

Im me sha, 596, 597, 610

Im mey ahhonah, 589

Im mia cha honah, 966

Im miash tubbe, 256

R.C. Im miash tubbee, 643

Im mi cha homah, 602

R.C. Im mi cha honah, 651

Im mi cha tubbee, 442

Immi choketa, 466

Immi eah ho to nah, 401

Immilahona, 273

Immil la hona, 273

R.C. Immil la hoyo, 604, [R. c. 652,] 969

Im min tah, 422

Immin ta hubbee, 396

Immin to hoyo, 1031

Immish ti yah, 399, 465

Immish tonah, 384, 391, 462, 824

Immis te wah, 243

Immith to mah, 859

Immi yash tubbee, 925

Immiyowa, 979

Immoc cayo, 203

Immock ah honah, 397

Immock fo quah tubbee, 403

Immogla chubbe, or Ogleah chubbe, 586

Immohakachubbee, 318

Immo ho to nah, 601

Immɔ kai yo, 252

Immɔkayo, 319

Immɔlla tubbee, 1013

Immɔnah, 588

Immɔ nah hoka, 591, 814

*Immɔ nah hoke, 74

R.C. Immɔ nah ho kah, 627

R.C. Immɔnahoka, 141, 587, [R. c. 649,] 827

Immɔnahoka, or Nah wa, 376, 591, 962, 963

Immɔ na hoyo, 243

Immɔ nah tonah, 595

Immɔ na tubbe, 601

Immɔ nubba, 865

Immɔ nubbe, alias Emo nubbee, 499

Immɔ nubbe, 525, 866, 875

Immɔ nubbee, 874

Immɔon ah hoka, 767

Im moon ah hora, 767

Im moon tubbee, 417, 418, 419, 399

Im moon tubbi, 141

Im mubbee, 394

Im muk ah ta tubbee, 142

Im mul ta hubbi, 50

Im mum be, 141

Im mus ha tub bee, 142

Im mus tah hobbee, 1041

Immuth baah honah, 921

Im muth pas a hona, 225

Im mut teah, 461, 521, 824

Im mut ti ah, 384

Im my, 497

*Im m oa, Stewik, 154

Im oc cum ba, 1031

Im og hah, 781

Im ok la tubbee, 140

*Im ok tish tiyah, 202

Im o nah ho ka, 387

*Im o nah hoke, 62

Im o na hoka, 514

R.C. Im o nubbee, [R. c. 634], 866

Im oon ubbee, 504

Im pi ah, 376, 594

*Im po nah, 75, 376, 434, 535, *48

*Impson, Caleb, 260

Impson, Dennis, 977

*Impson, Harot, 322

*Impson, Harris, 232

*Impson, Isaac, 260

*Impson, Lewis, 318

*Impson, Sally Ann, 18

*Impson, Wm., 150

Im punah, or Is tim pon ah, 378

*Im punah, 503, 507, *58

Im pun nah, 424

Im ti ca, 142

Im ubbee, 397, 417, 418, 451, 975

Im uk tah nubbe, 509

Im ulth ta ha tonah, 525

Im un no ubbee, 570, 690

Im ust ubbee, 146

*Im uth pisabi, 168

*In a char hoke, 8

In ah lubbee, 561

In ah tah honah, 508

R.C. I na in tubbee, 667

In che le tubbi, 50

*In chok ma ho yo, 290

In chuk mah hoyo, 529

In co ne ya, 92, 142

In cun eah, 455

In cun e yah, 390, 446

In e tubbee, 107

In hoah to nah, 535

R.C. In how che tubbee, [R. C. 675,] 1085, 1086

I nin tubbee, 1043

Ink kun nis la to nar, 80

In lah cubbe, 584, 380

In lah cubbee, 380, 555

In lah honah, 509

In lah o nah, 580

In lah tim ah, 500

In lah to nah, 507

In lah tubbe, 504

*In leowah etubi, 180

In mok in too nah, 143, 580, 827

In na tubbi, 141

In no tubbe, 517

In no tubbee, 139, 386, 469, 817, 827

R.C. Inock che to, [616, R. c.] 789

I nok che to, 704

In pak nah ho nah, 497

*In shah tona, 300

In sha la tubbe, 515

In tah hubbe, 542

In tah hubbee, 384

In tah tubbe, 542

In ta la honah, 922, 924

R.C. In to la ho na, 668

In tone la hona, 923

R.C. In to nubbee, [666 R. c.], 1037, 1038

*In toolah, 387, 478, 532, 814, 827, *118

In tubbee, 190

In tu la hoka, 522

*In ul le cha be, 296

In ulth paesahonah, 1003, 1004

In water, 81

Ioa hona, 272

I oath ah, 516

Io bon ubbe, 527

Io chaffubbee, 690

Io co ma, 190

R.C. Io ga be, [634, R. c.] 869, 870

Io ga lee, 519

Io ga lu, 871

R.C. Iogla, 378, 394, 452, 594, 598, [R. c. 657,] 983, 985

Ioglah tubbee, or Hustep, 394

I og la tema, alias Oe la tema, 273

I og le tema, 575

I oh lo tubbe, 603

I oka, 386, 476, 537, 825

I o ka chubbee, 391

I o kah tona, 503

*I o ka tonah, 398, *50

I ok che me hoka, 522

*I ok gla, 144

I o kla, 492, 564, 895

*I ok la shubbee, 262

I oklo hubbe, 564

I ok lo hubbee, 492, 497

I oko nubbe, 525

I o koom ah, 530

Io kubbee, 491, 572

Io ma, 269

Io mah, 389, 594

R.C. Io mah te kah, [R. c. 635,] 873, 874

*Io mah ti ka, 228

Io na he ma, 270, 317

Io nain ta, 197

R.C. I o nubbee, 405, R. c. 631

Ioosta, 395

Iopa chee, 523

Io pa nubbe, 559

Io pinna, 468

Io pon na, 375, 544

Io pun a chubbee, 398

Io punne hoyo, 203, 256

Iose, 393

Iotah, 463

Iota niah, 911, 912

*I oth la, 395, 464, *94

I oth lah, alias Iotubbee, 375

I oth lah, 569

Io to ma ho yo, 191

Iotonah, 442

R.C. Iotonaha, 255, [R. C. 641]

Io tubbee, alias I oth lah, 375

R.C. Iowache, 272, 319, R. c. 670

Iowatchie, 201

*I pak na, 24

*R.C.Isaac, 50, 255, 279, 280, 497, 553, [R. C. 641,]
    908, *34, 278

*Isaac James, 70

*Isaac, William, 96

*Isabell, 204, 220

R.C. Isabella, 614

Isabelle, 808

Is cha fubbe, 570

*Is cum mah, 405, 424, *76

Ish an hok ta, 387, 557

Ish an honah, 422

Ish an hook ta, 584

Ish a honah, 393

*Ish ah to na, 304

Isham, 491, 572

Ish am ah, 144

Ish a tubbee, 393

Ish cola, 198

Ish e ha to nah, 388

Ish e hi nah, or Ish e ho to nah, 580

Ish e hona, 209

Ish e ho to nah, or Ish e hi nah, 580

R.C. Ish e tak e u nah, [R. c. 674,] 1080

R.C. Ish e tubbee, 281, 320, [R. c. 670,] 1058

Ish e tuk im mah, 144

Ish hish hal lo, 145

Ish hish hullo, 104

Ish ho mata, 111

Ish ho ni ye, 377, 503

Ish ho te mah, 389, 445

Ish ho ya, 377, 570, 690

Ish hoyo, 397, 419, 549

Ish i hona, 200

Ish im ah ho ge, 144

Ish im ma ho yo, 95

Ish in tubbee, 147

Ish ka chubbe, 523

Ish ka te oak te, 139

Ish kumma, 223, 316

Ish lah, 448

*Ish lah hoka, 58

Ish lah, or Ish lah ho ka, 378

Ish lah hoka, or Ish lah, 378

Ish la hoka, 138, 384, 462, 500, 523, 825

Ish le bah ne, 382

Ish li yah 525

*Ish lo hoke, 102

Ish ma am ba, 203

R.C. Ish ma am bee, 668

Ish ma ham ba, 319, 922

Ish mah ho nah, 580

r.c. Ish mah la le ho nah, [r. c. 678,] 1102, 1103

Ish ma ho nah, 144

Ish ma kia ba, 912

Ish mam bah, 922, 923, 924

*Ish mam bi, 174

Ish man tubbe, 544

Ish ma ubbee, 141

Ish me ah, 529

Ishmia, 192

Ish miah, 436, 546

Ish mi ah ho ka, 388, 507, 580

Ish miah honah, 509

Ish mie ha, 146

Ish mi ke oh, 28

Ish mi yah, 435

*Ish niaiy ubbee, 222

Ish no akke, 538

Ish no wa, 265

*Ish no wah, 377, 554 *76

Isho mata, 117, 139

Is hoka, or Ath le ho ka, 505

Isho kambee, 436

Isho nah, 146

Isho na hoka, 117, 163, 191

Ish pah lah te, 382, 507, 584

Ish pah na, 391, 414, 415

Ish pah nee, 417, 418

Ish pa hona, 190

Ish pa la, 140

*Ish pam be, 252

*Ish pane, 298

Ish pa we, 141

Ish sham ba, 395

Ish she hona, 169

Ish she hora, 196

Ish shish pool la, 442

Ish sho na hoka, 955, 956, 957

r.c. Ish sho no hoka, 594, 595, [r. c. 649]

Ish stanthly, 602

Ish sto nah tubbee, 378

Ish taah ha cubbe, 593

Ish taah hona, 503

Ish ta ba wala, 899

*Ish tabola, 112

Ish ta bo lah, 385

Ish ta bo la tubbee, 551

Ish ta cha hoyo, 580

*Ish tache, 74

*Ish ta cubbe, 202

r.c. Ish tah cubbee, [675, r. c.], 1082

Ish tah ah homah, 570

Ish tah ah honah, 790

Ish ta ha mah, 569

Ish tah bola, 471, 514, 826

Ish tah bo le, 539

Ish tah buk ti ya, 580

Ish ta he mah, 567, 569, 690

Ish tah ha kah, 377

Ish tah ham me, 384, 492, 559

Ish tah he mah, 570, 689, 690

*Ish tah ho bache, 78

Ish tah ho bah, 580

Ish tah ho cubbe, 512

Ish tah ho ho tubbe, 575

Ish tah hona, 542

Ish tah hook tah, 493, 565

Ish tah ho vah honah, 380, 498

Ish tah ho we cha, 389, 596, 610

Ish tah ka, 395

Ish tah ke le homah, or Ish tah ukla, 580

Ish tah ko pah, 376

Ish tah lah, 400

R.c. Ish tah lah him ah, 1089, 1090, [R. c. 676]

Ish tah la ho nah, 584

Ish tah lubbe, 504, 595

Ish tah lubbee, 376, 834

Ish tah nah, 1027, 1028

Ish tah nosa, 580

Ish tahn tah, 592

R.c. Ish tah nubbbee, 400, [R. c. 632] 860

Ish ta ho bah, 144

Ish ta ho ge, 144

*Ish ta ho ka, 56

Ish ta hola, 825

Ish ta ho lubbe, 521

Ish ta ho nah, 503, 570

Ish ta ho pah, 595

Ish ta ho ta ma, 170

Ish ta ho te ma, 167

Ish tah pa sah, 422

Ish tah pok mah, 515

Ish tah shubbee, 399

Ish tah te mah, 523

Ish tah tubbe, 524

Ish tah tubbe, or Big Jacob, 563

Ish tah tubbee, 139, 375, 386, 445, 476, 689, 825

Ish tah tubbee, or Big Jacob, 942

Ish tah uk la, 505, 584

Ish tah uk la, or Ish tah ke le homah, 580

Ish ta huna, 147

Ish tah yo co mah, 505

*Ish taimaheta, 8

Ishtaka, 81

Ish ta kubbee, 483

Ish tal ah honah, 388

Ish tal ah hoonah, 388

Ish tal ath i ah, 504

Ish tallah, 542

Ish tal lah honah, 505

Ish ta lubbe, 509

Ish tam ah, 144

Ish ta ma ha, 167, 198

Ish tam ahah, 417, 418

Ish ta mah honah, 376, 448, 500

Ish tamalhoga, 50

Ish tam ba, 207, 316

*Ish tam be, 90

Ish tam bee, 223

Ishtam eha, 1011

Ish ta min cha, tubbee, or Mincha, 400

Ish tam ma ha ubbee, 143

Ish tam mi hah, 419, 420

Ish tam mo, 380, 508

Ish tamo, 580

*Ish ta moon chubby, 270

R.c. Ish tana, 227, R. c. 664

*Ish tan hoke, 224

Ish tan ho nah, 378

Ish tan ho pah, 89, 140, 149

*Ish tan oah, 116

*Ish tan te ma, 280

Ish tan te mah, 522

Ish tan to nah, 567, 689

Ish tan tubbe, 542

Ish tan tubbee, 817, 825

Ish tan we che, 381, 504, 584

Ish tape mah tubbe, 568

Ish ta pe mah tubbee, 690

*Ish ta tema, 278

Ish ta tubbee, 94, 141, 569

Ish ta tubbee, or Big Jacob, 382

Ish te abbee, 105, 145

Ish te ah hoka, 492, 563

Ish te ah honah, 388, 498

Ish te ah ho nubbee, 601, 950, 951

Ish te ah hoyo, 388, 483

Ish te a hoyo, 146

Ish te bah ne, 498

Ish te ga hoyo, 143

Ish te ha hubbee, 386

Ish te he mah, 378, 454

Ish te ho lubbee, 817, 469

Ish te ho mah, 143

R.C. Ish te ho mia, 642

Isht e ho miya, 917, 918

Ish te ho tubbee, 827

Ish te hoyo, 814, 827

Ish te hubbee, 387

Ish te ja hona, 142

*Ish teke lubbe, 40

Ish te kubbee, 474, 814, 827

Ish te la mah, 539

Ish te ma, 137, 502, 515, 594

R.C. Ish te mah, 387, 389, 390, 474, 515, [R. c. 683,] 814, 826, 1131

*Ish te mah e labbe, 214

Ish te mah ka, 397, 419

Ish te mah kah, 385, 471, 826

Ish te mahn ta, 585

Ish te mah onah, 500, 532, 569, 690

*Ish te mala, 266

Ish te ma le chubbe, 512

Ish te mau te, 140

*Ish te mayah, 250

Ish tem bola, 389, 509

Ish tem e hah tubbe, 584

Ish tem eia, 275

Ish tem ei anubbee, 237

Ish te me le hoka, 508

Ish te me lubbee, 536

Ish tem hu kubbee, 81

R.C.*Ish te miah, 378, 603, [R. c. 651,] 967, *60

Ish te miahe, 501

Ish te miah hoka, 509

Ish te mi onah, 507

Ish te miyah, 523

Ish te mok ah, 515

*Ish te mona, 266

Ish te monah, 144

Isht e mona hoka, 179

Ish te moth lah, 508

Ish tem po tubbee, 550

Ish te ne ah u a chubbee, 402

Ish te oh to nubbee, 1003

Ish te onah, 547

*Ish tewa, 142

Ish tiah, 422, 507, 508

Ish tiah, or Okish tiyah, 524

Ish tiah honah, 540

*Ish tia homubbe, 278

*Ish tia honubi, 130

Ish ti hok ta, 570

Ish tik ah tubbe, 515

Ish til ak feya, 158

Ish tilla bolatubbee, 169

Ish tilla mah, 397

Ish tillonah, 395

*Ish timah, 581, *130

Ish tim ahae, 1003

*Ish timah futche, 52

*Ish tim ah honah, 56

R.C. *Ish tim ah la, [649, R. c.,] *162

R.C. Ish tim ah las, [R. c. 649,]

Ish tim a soya, 404

*Ish tim a yoke, 152

Ish tim bola, 580

Ish tim ea, 144

Ish tim ele chubbee, 553

*Ish tim ia hoke, 174

Ish tim la he mah, 568

Ish tim ma chubbee, 985

Ish tim mah la, 594

R.C. Ish tim mah lah, 594, [649, R. c.,] 955, 956,
     957

Ish tim mah oka, 604

Ish tim ma hoya, 393

R.C. Ish timme chubbe, 598, R. c. 657

Ish tim me hayo, 422

Ish tim me hoya, 417

Ish tim me hoyo, 452

Ish tim mi hoyo, 418

Ish tim mo na chubbee, 393

Ish tim monah, 590

*Ish timona, 302

Ish tin ho me yah, 916

Ish tioh, 423

Ish ti ok lee, 540

Ish tionah, 517

Ish tiopa, 492, 563

Ish tish tam be, 566

R.C. Ish to ah ho nubbee, 648

Ish to hoyo, 98, 534

Ish to i timma, 145

Ish to ka ho timah, 536

Ish to kubbee, 388

Ish tollah, 1031

Ish to mah bone chubbee, 400

Ish to mah honah, 402

Ish to man to, 149

Ish tom bee, 141

Ish tome, 146, 502

Ish to me hah tubbe, 509

Ish to me hah tubbee, 380

Ish to miah, 538

*Ish tonache, Billy, 268

*Ish to na chi, B., 308

*Ishtonachi, Mary S., 308

Ish ton ack fu lah, 89

Ish to nah, 568, 689

Ish to naha, 788

Ish to nah che honah, 504

Ish to nah kueah, or Ish ton ok we ah, or
     Nokweah, 535

*Ish to nak homa, 20

*Ish to nak i hijo, Capt., 182

Ish to nan che, 391

Ish to nan chi, 415

*Ish to neah meah, 60

Ish ton eah tonah, 533

Ish toniye, 382, 509, 584

Ish ton ock fa la, 140

Ish ton ock falah, 149

Ish ton ok we ah, or Ish ton ah kue ah, or
     Nok weah, 535

*Ish tonsi, 12

Ish tontemah, 403

Ish ton timah, 571

*Ish tonuke, 122

Ish to pah nubbe, or Okalache. 522

Ish to pah nubbee, or Ok a lache, 826

*Ish to pa ney, 246

*Ish to panny, 270

Ish to pa nubbee, or Ok a la cha, 385

*Ish torpa kna,

Ish to tam bee, 101

Isht tubbee hoka, 382

Ish tubbe, 549, 580

Ish tubbee, 143

R.C. Ish tubbee hah tah, 378, 422, [R. c. 675]

Ish tubbee hat lah, 1083

Ish tubbeehat tah, 139

Ish tubbe hoka, 504

Ish tu ha mah, 148

*Ish tu ho bakka, 140

Ish tuh tam bee, 689

Ish tum a ka, 141

Ish tu nah, 146

Ish tu nah tubbe, 502

*Ish tun ah tubbee, 78

Ish tun a tubbee, 145

Ish tun lah he mah, 689

Ish tunna, 146

Ish un ah hoka, 535

Ish wa caba, 173, 179, 1049

Ish wah ki yah, 397

*Ish wa ke ya, 212

Ish wa kia, 932

*Ish wak iabe, 312

R.C. Ish wak kiaba, 255, 319, R. c. 641

*Ish wa tobi, 126

Ish yoya, 449

Isim, 393

Iska tena, or Little Leader, or Iath le h, 591, 690

*Isk lo shabbee, 298

Isk te kubbe, 574

*Isk te kubbee, 98

Is ma ham ba, 252

Is ma la honah, 378

Ismya, 199

Is o polla, 89

Is paahona, 194

Is pa hona, 197

Is pia, 18

*Israel, 78

Is shabbo tabbee, 156

Is shan ke hoyo, 503

Is shon ke hoyo, 377

Is spalla, 149

Is spolla, 140

Issusa, 424

Is sta cha, 448

Is stilla bo la tubbee, 196

Iss tubbe, 466

R.C. Is ta a hoka, 255, R. c. 641

Is ta boke tiah, 144

Is ta ca pona, 177

Is ta cha, 142, 377

Is ta cha hoyo, 580

Ista che, 535

Is ta haga, 209

Is tah hotemah, 1024, 1025

Is tah oke leahamah, 388

Is ta ho la, 814

Is tia ho lo, 265, 316

R.C. Is ta ho ta ma, 664

Is tah o tema, 227

Is ta homei, 256

Is ta ho tima, 192

Is tah pa sa, 139

Ist ta ia, or Emistaya, 198

Istaka, 191

Istalubbee, 192

R.C. Is ta ma ha, 170, 192, 196, 201, 205. 238, 319, [R. c. 662], 1011

Is ta man cha, 213

Ista ma no la tubbee, 941

Istam ba, 137, 183, 203

Is tam bal a lee, 237

Ista me ha, 184, 216, 224, 316

Is tan tona, 264

Istam tubbe, 264

Is ta pa sa, 191, 194, 199

Ista po ca nubbee, 235

Is tap o cona, 176

Is tau tubbee, 316

Is ta we ge, 144

Is te abbee, 442

Is te ah ho ca, alias Ar patter, 789

Isteam or Yeahn, 401

Is te che, 509

Is te chubbee, 236

Is te ho bak ka, 783

Is te ma he jo, 140

Is te ma hoyo, 85, 198

Is te man cha hona, 275

Is te ma ya, 199

Is te mei, 243

Istemeia, 316

Is te me lio, 982

Is te mi chubbe, 560

Is te mionah, 566

*Is temmaha, 138

Is tem ona chubbee, 176, 177

Is tem ona hoka, 251, 319

Is tem ona tubbee, 190, 199

Istemoncha, 212

Is te neg weah, 145

Is te ubbee, 375, 553

Is ti a to nubbe, 225

R.C. Is ti a to nubbee, [R. c. 661] 1004

Is tib a bola, 167

R.C. Is ti ho bah ka, 380 [R. c. 623,] 725, 726

Is ti ho baka, 780

Is ti hoka, 768, 769

R.C. Is ti ho kah, 627

R.C. Is ti ho ke ta, [R. c. 622,] 717, 807

Is ti hok ta, 879, 785

Is ti ho tah ka, 761

Is ti ho tiahka, 725

Is tik a tubbee, 1005

Is til iah hoka, 492, 562

Is til la bola, tubbee, 236, 316

Is tilla bo tubbee, 194

Is tilloc faya, 197, 1020

Is tilloc fayah, 163, 164

Is tilloc foya, 191

Is tillok faya, 221, 227

Is tillok fayha, 194

Is tim ah hambe, 559

Is ti ma kiya, 250

Is ti ma la hona, 235

Is tim aya, 192

Is tim cah, 141

Is tim haya, 225

R.C. Is tim i ah honah, 392, [R. c. 631]

Is tim i hoyea, 1037

Is tim min cha tubbee, or Mincha, 463

R.C. Is ti mo haya, [R. C. 661,] 1003, 1003, 1004

Is tim pon ah, or Im punah, 378

Is tin a hoyo, 142

Is to ma hoyo, 149

Is to ma la hokta, 147

Is tomba, 1032

Is to mionah, 689

Is to naka, 264

Is to nan chi, 414

Is ton e hook tah, 442

Is to no ka, 219

R.C. Is to pan ah, [R. C. 626,] 754, 755

Is tubbe, 551

Is tubbe hattah, 502

Isum, 392, 393

Isum na he, 146

Is wa lubbee, 255

I tah ha, 454

It ah hoba, 529

It a hom ba, 199

It an ubbe, 560

It an ubbee, 384

It a pesah, 500

R.C. It ath le ah, [R. C. 621,] 797

*Iteak chokka, 100

It e lok na, 515

It e lok nah, 461

It e miya, or Manya, 536

It e ok chokko, 575

It e pisah, 97

It hanah, 147

Ith co tubbee, 389, 417, 418, 419

*Ith ko tubbe, 34

*Ith ko tubbe, Joseph, 34

Ith ko tubbee, 184, 216

R.C. Ith leo hah, 227, [R. C. 664]

Itim i ah honah, 857

Itin lah himah, 569, 690

Itoba, 271, 317

Ito chubbee, 402

Itoko, 190

Ito lah, 580

*Iton la homa, 22

It tah hu kah, 81

It tah lowe chah, 595

It tah nuth ubbee, 499

It ta lok ra, 824

It ta tam be, 201

It techea, 902

It te ho mis tubbee, 386, 469, 499, 817, 827

It te lok nah, 383

It te oak chocco, 139

Itte oak choe co, 99

It te ok chocka, 459

It te ok chok ko, 383, 813, 826

Ittobah, 141

Ittoobah, 147

*Itto ta cha hubbi, 322

*It to te mas tobi, 204

Itubbee, 146

Itulah, 138

Itum la tubbe, 561

Itunah, 461, 529, 824

Itunahe, 383

I-tune-lub-bee, 148

Itunla, 146

*Itunona, 172

*I uk pan tubbee, 8

I um pah, 390

I um pah, or Chumpah, 565

I ush kam ah, 388, 505, 580

I yah, 515

Iyaha, 198

Iyah ha, 162

I yah hubbe, 515

*I yak a tobi, 198

*I yak a yabi, 224

R.C. I yat ah nubbee, 679

I ya tubbee, 197

I ye le he mah, or Ila honah, 497

I yem an te mah, 566

I yemetubbee, 388, 483, 484

I yit ha nubbee, 1107, 1108

I yo arch cha, 141

I yock ubbee, 983

I yo coma, 198

I yo co nubbee, 492, 562

I yo co tonah, 148

*I yo honah, 535, *82

I yok abbee, 109

I yok a honah, 895

I yo ke mubbe, 520

I yo ke pee e ta, 179

I yok e tubbe, 535

I yo komah, 569, 690

I yok ubbu, 142

I yola, 570, 690

I yomah, 763, 764

I yo ma hoka, 85, 149

I yo mah hoka, 574

I yo nah, 380, 506, 580

I yo nah te mah, 512

*I yon na, 220

I yo pa tubbee, 275

I yo thea, 147

I yoth lah, 144

I you ah, 179

I you car ta nah, 1037

I yo wa, 248, 319

I yo wa cha, 1056, 1057

*I yo watcha, 258

I ze me honah, 867

*Jacaya, *138

Jack, alias Onatubbe, 235

R.C. Jackson, 144, 158, 159, 163, 220, 227, 229, 279, 395, 400, 406, [R. c. 617, 664,] 796, 1024,

Jackson, Billy or Moomintamba, 445

Jackson, Billy or Momintambe, 493, 564

*Jackson, Billy, *108

*Jackson, Davis, *240

*Jackson, Jacob, *70

*Jackson, Joe, *118

*Jackson, Lymon, *282, *284

*Jackson, Mingo, *54

Jackson, Saly, 709

*Jackson, Suckey, *240

*Jackson, William, *2

*Jacob, 546, *28

*Jacobs, A. M., *114

*Jacobs, Betsey, *94, *100

*Jacob, Big, *94

Jacob, Big or Ishtahtubbee, 492

*Jacob, N. M., *98

*Jacob, Morris, *94

Jafferson, 442

Jaha, 194

Jakcheto, 704

Jake, 567, 689

Jama, 234

James, 50, 117, 139, 540

James, Doctor, 147

*James, Abel, 94, 100

James, Adam, 10, 28, 181, 261

*James, Benjamin, Capt., 160

*James Bob, 140

*James, George, 10

*James, Isaac, 27, *10

*James, John, 126, 160

*James, Lora, 166

*James, Lucy, 126

*James, Martin, 232

*James, Mrs. McKee, 18

*James, Sally, 126

*James, Silis, 18

*James, S. W., 94

Jamintubbi, 141

Jamy, 279

*Jancy, *200

R.C. Jane, 50, R. c. 629

Jantatubbe, 259

Jath-le-pah, 378

Jefferson, 95, 146, 501

*Jefferson, Adam, *152

*Jefferson, Celia, *40, *54

*Jefferson, Gaines, *198

*Jefferson, Sarah, *16

*Jefferson, Solomon, *240

*Jefferson, Thomas, *16, *314

Jefferson, Tom, 147

*Jefferson, Wallace, *256

R.C. Jema, 668

Jemer, 776

Jemmy, 191, 219, 316

Jenison, 280

Jenkins, Jack, 18

Jenny, 690

Jeremiah, 50

*Jerry, 282

*Jerry, Jim, 288

Jess, 401

R.C. Jesse, 500, [R. c. 631,] *319

Jessee, 400, 403, 859

Jetumlah, 147

Jim, 398

Jimabubee, or Jmbubbee, 422

R.C. Jimey, 380, [R. C. 616,] 705, 789, 781, 760

Jimmah, 144

R.C. Jimme, 672

*Jimmerson, *32

Jimmie, or James Carn, 425

*Jimmy, 158, 163, 194, 198, 405, 1071, 1072, *178, *192

Jimsey, 401

*Jimson, *80

R.C. Jimson, Vina, alias Malacha, 669

*Jincy, *56

*Jinks, Wm., *222

Jinny, 501, 568

Jno-pissa, 140

*Joe, Austin, *260

*Joel, 50, *244

Joel, Thomas, *290

R.C. John, 392, 393, 405, 544, [R. c. 626,] 757, 756, 764

John, Billy, or Kamshononchehubbee, 492

*John, Billy, *108

*John, Norris, *180

*Johnson, Dick, *272

Johnson, Mary, 389

Johnson, Nancy, 18

Johnson, Sally, alias Mahaona, 140

Johnson, Silas D., 388

*Johnson, William, *76, *276, *308

*Johnson, Wilsey, *76

Johnston, Col., 210, 212, 213, 214

Johny, 514, 574

Jonas, 403

Jones, Anna, 218

*Jones, Cornelius, *148

Jones, Delilah, 26

*Jones, Elijah, *19

*Jones, Fred, *118

Jones, Frederick, 28

*Jones, Gincy, *254

Jones, Holin, 218

*Jones, Isaac, *4, *22

*Jones, Jack, *298

*Jones, Jackson, *42

*Jones, James, *148

*Jones, Mrs. Jane, *204

*Jones, Jesse, 4, 22

*Jones, Jimmie, 114

Jones, Jimmy, 273

*Jones, Jimpson, *82

*Jones, John, 18, 139, 1055, *28, *122

*Jones, Joséph, 140, *28

*Jones, Levi, 117, 158, 162, 191, 194, 198, 415, 218, *126

*Jones, Logan, *144

*Jones, Mahale, *20

*Jones, Capt. N., *258

*Jones, Nat., 438, *206

*Jones, Norris, *18

*Jones, Phillis, *222

*Jones, S., *42

Jones, Sabala, 218

*Jones, Samuel, 29, *82

Jones, Sinah, 218

*Jones, Siney, *4, *22

*Jones, Solomon, 280, 320, *238

Jones, Tennessee, 378, 553

*Ka-anjah-tubbee, *88

Kacha (dead), 198

Kachah, 141

Ka che, 184, 186

Kachien, or Carson, 226

Kaha lehona, 519

R.C. Kah chee, R. C. 619

Kah chu, 788

Kah chubbe, 557

Kah lambee, 515

Kah la tubbee, 491

Kah lo tubbee, 572

Kah no mahonah, 530

Kah roon tah be, 480

Kah rote ubbe, 520

Kah po tubbe, 523, 542

Kah se tah, 518

Kah sone ta, or Tush-ho-nah-tah, 580

*Kaihona, *16

Kaka, 382

Kak ne tah, 529

Kal ah it im ma, 95

Kalehona, 264

Kalistah, 446

Kam pa lubbe, 524

Kam pe tubbee, 515

Kampilla, 540

Kampillah, 537

Kam sho non che hubbee, or Billy John, 492

*Kanabbe, *4

*Kanah hotubbe, 376, *48

Kanahoyo, 163

Kanah tonah, 575

Kanaia tubbe, alias James Patterson, 255

Kanalle, 378, 555

Kanaur entin tubbee, 558

*Kanan to-coyer, *306

Kan-an-un-tin tub bee, 491

Kanatubbee, 825, 935, 936

Kan cha, 90, 137, 273, 317, 825

Kanchatomba, 517

Kancha tubbee, 167, 499

Kanche, 517, 531, 538

Kanche hoge, 143

Kan che hoka, 521

Kan che honah, 522

Kan che le, 524

Kan che maha, 471, 530, 826

Kan che mehah, 382

*Kan che moliah, *10

Kan che tambe, 530

*Kan che teah, *72

Kan che tiah, 535

*Kan che tonah, *50

*Kan chi, *188

*Kan chubbe, *22, *110

*Kan chu na, *24

*Kan clubbe, *14

Kan e ah toonah, 541

*Kane moon tobi, *182

Kane tom be, 525

Ka ne yo he ka he, 817

*Ka ni a cha be, *198

*Kania tubbee, *272

*Kani man tubbee, *270

*Kani ma tobi, *158, 186

*Kani yah ekabe, *200

Kani yohi kaba, 457, 828

Kani yohi-kabbee, 383

R.C. Kan neah toonah, [R. c. 636], 881

Kan nomehemah, 515

Ka nohotema, 243

Kanone tabbee, 163

Ka nonta shubbe, 256

Ka no onta tubbee, 535

Kan oon timah, 525

*Kanoontobi, *174

Kan oon tubbe, 502, 504

R.C. Kanoon tubbee, 221, 277, 316, 320 [R. c. 645,] 936, 937

Kanoon ubbe, 510

*Kan ot abe, *300

Kan ot onah, 538

Kan ountubbee, or Ka on oon ta ubbee, 377

Kano yo he kubbe, 515

Kan sha hok a, 276

Kanshononchehebbe, or Billy John, 564

Kanshononchehubbee, 389

Kan tun tubbee, 143

Kanun ta chubbi, 50

Ka ocubbee, 567, 689

Ko on oon ta abbee, 442

Ka on oon ta ubbee, or Kan oun tubbee, 377

Ka otubbe, 585

R.C. Ka po tubbee, R. c. 664

Karl ahohar, 81

Kar neo tubbee, *250

Ka sa, 502

Kasa hook tah, 146

Kash a hok ta, 97

Ka she hoh tee, 146

*Kash e nah la, *276

*Kashonata, *196

*Kashoonamostobi, *188

Ka tah bee, 143

R.C. Katharine, R. c. 625, 626, 765, 766, 748, 749

*Kathrine, *76

Ka tonah, 462, 515, 824

Ka tubbe, 521

Katy, 279

R.C. Ka yo-cubbee, alias Hick a yo-tubbee, R. c. 678

Ka yocubbee, 1102

Ka yo he mah, 511

Kayu hubbe, 516

Ke ah na chubbee, 405

Kearney, Charles, 398

Kecher, 81

Keille, 523

Keka, 505, 580

Ke lah it im mah, 146

Ke-lis ta, 472, 575

Kellehona, 190

*Kelley, Betsey, *6

*Kelly, Sopha, *120

Kemp, Tim, 140

Ken tuc kay, 107

Ken tuckey, 145

Kentuckey, John, or Emah shah chubbee, 480

Key o cubbe, 498

Keyohonah, 575

Ke yok ubbee, 143

*Ke-yu, *294

*Ki ah ar, *196

Kil estah, 385

Kimahochubbee, 186

Kim e an che hubbee, 385

Kim ne monubbi, 930

Kincade, Capt. James or Joseph, 26

*Kincaid, Andrew, 28, *322

*Kincaid, George, *130

*Kincaid, Jenny, *26

*Kincaid, Joseph, *14, 322

*Kincaid, Lyman, et al, *14

*Kincaid, Vicey, *24

*Kinchis, William, *96

*King, Anne, *106

*King, Harris, *72

*King, Capt., James M., *14

*King, Levi, *102,

*King, Margarett, *238

*King, Mary, *116

*King, Matilda, *110

*King, McKee, *10, 108, 116

*King Milevit, *126

Kirksey, E. B. W., 495

Kisahnah, 552

Kish a mus tubbee, 98, 139

Kish er amba, 139

Kish u mus tubbee, 825

Kis tubbe, 531

Kis t mus tubbee, 814

*Kitini Hopaies, *182

Kitty, 50

*Ki Ya Ish wa, *226

*Kiz zie, *89

K neck a ma shubbee, 100

Knok ho ma bache, 137

R.C. Ko a ne wa, R. C. 630

Ko a nu wa, 854

Kobah tombee, 518

Kochabbee, 157

Koch a tubbee, 236

Koc hubbee, 162

K o ck amashubbee, 148

K o ck ene tubbee, 441

Koheia, 265

Ko he lu, 186

*Koh n ohi, *282

Koh po tubbee, 1027

*Kaihoma, *8

*Kaitube, Capt., *28

Kok e na tubbee, 455

*Komah, *60

Kom pil lah, 382, 507

Kompil lah, or Compil lah, 579

Komp il ubbe, 580

Ko mubbe, 524

Kona chubbee, 236

Kona chubbi, 930

Konah ho tubbee, 553

Kon am chubbee, 529

Kon che a tubbee, 194

Kon che at unah, 144

Konchehoka, 377, 503, 580

Konche hona, 378, 502

Konche tambe, 505

Kon che toah, 536

Kon che to nubbe, 504

Kon che ti ah, 377, 535

Kon che ti yah, 378, 442

Kon che tubbe, 501

Kon che tubbee, 378, 454, 455, 556

Kon che tu nah, 580

Kon chi tim ma, 145

Kon e maon tah, 442

*Kon e mier, *312

Kon e moon tah, 378, 498

*Koner, *146

K

Kon e toon tubbe, 381, 507, 580

Kong ki yo, 420

Konhooha mustubbee, 1st, 457

Konkahnooskabo, 827

Kon kah nooskabo, 386, 470, 541

Kon ka noos kabo, 817

Konnemahtubbee, 535

Konolahona, 263

Konoo tubbe, 528

Konowa, 274

Kon sha tubbee, 169

Kon she ho tema, 223

Konshe tia, 243

Kon ubbee, 1009

Koocha, 382, 527, 580

Koochabbe, 525

Kooch ati yah, 525, 817, 828

Koochi ti ya, 383

Koochubbe, 542

Koostaha, 531

*Koostinche, *62

Kootah, 386, 470, 520, 817, 827

Kootonah, 817

Koo too nah, 827

Kopot ubbee, 227

Koshon ahhona, 381

Kosh oon nan cha hubbe, 445

Kov chi ti ya, 457

Kot a, 190, 194, 198

Ka tah, 379, 399, 440, 550

*Kotubbee, *252

Kouoon bamba, 551

Ko we lomah, 143

Kon oon tah tubbe, 536

*Krebs, Exther, *66

*Kuchan tubbee, *22

*Kullish ubbee, Capt., *250

Kunah ho tubbee, 525

Kunahochubbee, 184

Kunahoka, 252

Kun ah tubbee, 814, 825

Kun a monetubbee, 212

Kun a moon tubbee, 209, 227

Kun an tubbee, 947

Kun a tubbee, 139

Kun e ah, 137

Kune ah hon ah, 385, 471

Kun eah tonah, 514

Kun e at honahe, 514

Kun eah tubbee, 385, 826

Kun eau che habee, 469, 525, 817

Kun e auche hubbee, 827

Kun e a tam ba, 1058

Kunemahonah, 575

Kun e moon tubbe, 505

Kuneotubbee, 471

Kun e pah honah, 826

Kune tah honah, 522

*Kunillubbee, Semus, *276

Kunish tonah, 524

*Kun mell ubbee, *276

Kunnahoyo, 196

Kunnal le tubbee, 499

Kun nam one tubbee, 213

Kun na moon-tubbee, 318

*Kun na tic ker, *194

R.C. Kunnat ubbee, 278, 320, R. c. 647

Kunnea, 224, 265

Kunneah, 113

Kun ne ah honah, 518, 531

Kunne ah tonah, 525, 880

Kunn eah toonah, 879

Kun ne atubbe, 515

Kun ne ma, 512, 870, 871, R. c. 634

Kun ne me, 869

*Kun ne mon ubbe, *230

Kun ne mo nubbe, alias Monubbe, 253

Kun ne mon ubbee, alias Monubbee, 319

*Kun neo tubbe, *26

Kun nubbi, 80

Kunnullenoyo, 445

Kun otema, 268

Kun otom bee, 537

*Kuppon chajo, *28

Kush ah hooc ea, 388, 484, 540

Kush ah nambee, 518

Kush ooah chehubbee, 817

Kush ooma mustubbee 2d, 457

Kush oon ack chi ah, 138

Kush oon ah che hubbe, 518

Kush oon ah che ubbee, 469

Kush oon ah chi ah, 827

Kush oon ah chi hubbee, 827

Kush oon ah mus tubbee, 482

Kush oo na mues tubbee, 382

Kush oon a mus tubbee, 483, 512, 1st and 2d, 816, 817, 827, 828, 863, 864, R. c. 633

Kush oon an cha haba, 541

Kush oon an cha ha bee, 383

Kush oon an che habee, 457, 817, 828

Kush oon an che hubbee, 384, 462, 824

Kush oon an che ubbee, 386

Kush oon mustubbee, 456

R.C. *Kush oon ok chiah, 386, 470, 499, [R. c. 635,] 817, 877, *288

Kusk oo nuck chiah, 112

Kus oo na mus tubbee, 383

Kut cha, 144

Kuth lee lee, 514

Kut-tah hah, 519

L

Laam ba, 274

R.C. Laam bee, 630

Lab ah tubbee, 442

Labasa, 191

Lach chist ab bee, 146

Lack it un ma, 145

*La fah mah, 270

*La fa mar, 246

Lah at ub bee, 143

Lah bah tubbee, 548

Lah fa tah, 392

Lah ha nubbe, 529

R.C. Lah he cubbe, 528, R. c. 637

Lah he cubbee, 390, 445, 891

R.C. Lah ho tea, 621

Lah la, 607

Lah lis, 903

Lah ma, 403

Lah meah ho nah, 1082

La ho la, 167

Lahouse, Marthew, 15

Lah pa chubbe, or Pa chubbe, 528

Lah pah ho nah, 405

Lah pah la tubbee, 889

La pahm ba, 455, 533

Lah pahm bee, 379

Lah pah na tumah, 497

Lah pakah, 1075

Lah pa nubbee, 406

Lah pa sa honah, 531

Lah pa te mah, 401

Lah pe te mah, 501

Lah pim e ho ka, 512

Lah pish tiah, 580

Lah po chubbee, 604

Lah po ho nah, 598

Lah po ho yo, 589

Lah po ka, 399, 451

Lah poon te mah, 947

Lah sa, 398, 405

Lah sho ma, 883

Lah ta kah, or Tom Billy, 492, 562

Lah tubbe, 569

Lah tubbee, 690

Lah wah honah, 549

Lah yok ah tubbe, 580

Laie, mahona, 271

*Laise, 296

*Laise, Lohmi, 296

*Laisma, 8

*Laiwa, 202

*Lake, Betsey, 262

*Lake, John, 262

*Lakna, Ette, 244

*Lakna, Robert, 244

*La ko toon ubbee, 284

*Lalase, 235

R.C. Laliss, 231, [R. c. 640,] 903

*Lalona, 300

Lam a che, 864

Lam ah hona, or Ele mah hona, 508

La march, 699

Lam ba, 138, 853

Lambee, 91

Lanache, 864

*Lan a po chubbee, 290

*Lan e tubbee, Mrs., 200

Lanige, 756

*Lan win cha, 149

Lapa chubbee, 566, 689

La pah hooc ta, 516

La pah la, 530

R.C. La pa nubbee, [R. c. 640,] 905, 906

La pa sa, 264

R.C. La pa te ubbee, 274, [R. c. 630,] 853

R.C. La pe ma, 256, [R. c. 645,] 940

*La pe na huma, 280

La pe ne tee nap, 148

R.C. La pi ma, [R. c. 643,] 919, 920

La pin tubbee, 170, 223

*La pis ha ha cho, 190

La pish a ha jo, 147

La pish tam bee, 143

*La pitta, 196

R.C. La pon e tema, [R. c. 630, 647,] 947, 948

La pon te ma, 274, 278

La pon ubbee, 234, 275

La poon ah hah, 516

Lap oon te mah, 854

Lappatemah, 544

*Larles, 194

*Lar pat imma, 238

*Lasaha, 166

La sham e hona, 253

R.C. La she ma, 630

Lashoma, 949

La sho mah, 394

Lasin, 220

Latah, 146

R.C. Latalla wa hona, [R. c. 668,] 932, 933

*La tam as tubbee, 284

La te ma, 1031

La tim a sha, 243

La te cha, 142

La te ka, or Tom Billy, 382

*Lattie, 222

*Latty, 288

La tubbee, 105, 145

Lau ha, 145

Lau pin tubbee, 147

Lavina, 280

R.C. Lavina, Anna, 670

*Lawa, 222

Lawa chubbee, 274

Law at am ba, 235

Law ba tubbee, 148

Law stah, 1030

*Law wa chubbe, 274

Law wa tubbee, 882

Law wincha, 140

*Lawyer, 308

Leah hoka, 497

Leah honah, 501

*Leana, 60

Lec tam bee, 143

Leflore, 289

*Leflore, Anna, 248

*Leflore, Annie, 238

*Leflore, Basil L., 226

Leflore, Forbis, 29

Leflore, Greenwood, 27, 429, 430, 431

*Leflore, Isaac, 27, *278

*Leflore, Joel, 27, *222

*Leflore, Judy, 90

Leflore, Michael, 29

*Leflore, Michel, 256

*Leflore, Millie, 66

*Leflore, Narcissa, 258

*Leflore, Robert, 96

*Leflore, Thomas, 27, *256

L

*Leflore, Capt., Thomas, 27, 432, *148

Leflore, Tom, 468

*Leflore, Wallace, 66

Leflore, William, 26, 155, 430

*Lehona, 162

*Lekema, 300

Le mah honah, 522

Le noah tubbe, 580

Le no wat ubbee, 143

Leomah kap, 196

*Le sho he mitta, 238

*Le sho hi mitta, 320

*Les ho latta, 228

*Les ho pia, 232

*Lettie, 122

Leuki mahona, 930

Levi, 50

*Levi, Silan, 304

*Levi, Simeon, 246, 250

*Levi, Susan, 208

Levis, 223

Lewellen, Annie, V., 18

Lewis, 279, 405, 764, 971

*Lewis, Benj., 258

R.C. Lewis, Dixon W., 592, R. C. 649

Lewis, Dixon W., alias Mintubbee, 957, 958, 959

*Lewis, Isom, 100, 112

*Lewis, James, 158

*Lewis, Jesse, 252

*Lewis, Joe, 182

*Lewis, John, 60

*Lewis, Malwell, 132

*Lewis, Sampson, 198

*Lewis, Seria, 108

*Lewis, Simon, 288, 290

*Lewis, Widow E., 288

Lewisa, Timmeece, 709

Lewiss, 219

*Lialy, 132

Lie gad abbee, 144

Lies unna, 101, 145

Lightfoot, William, 18

Lila, 401, 403, 404, 407

Lile, 553

*Lilie, *190

*Lily, 92

*Lina, 228

Lincome, John, 83

Lismah, 402

Lismon, 141

*Lis tubbe, 20

Little Leader, 18, 61, 150, 154

Little Leader, or Iskatena, 591

Little Leaders, 856

*Liza, 395, 1127, 1128, *174, 206, 270

Lizaam, 607

*Lizer, 54, 78

Lizma, 197

Lizy, or Elizabeth, 109

*Lizzibeth, 264

Loamah, 147

Lockna, 1054

*Logan, Davis, 34, 90

Loh mah ta ker, 141

Lohomete mah, 448

Lo ho me tubbee, 192

Loka, 237

Loka tam bee, 551

*Loma, 220, 228, 283, 394, 457, 541, 817, 942, 993, *302

*Lo ma chabi, 164

R.C.*Lo mah, 192, 193, 199, 242, 316, 435, 436, 437, 451, 465, 517, 531, 548, 580, 608, [R. c. 655,] 980, 1031, 1032, *162

Lomah, or Lomahtah, or Lomahtah cubbe, 602

R.C. Lomah, or Lomahta, or Lomatah cubbee, 650

Lomah ho shubbee, 388, 527

Lomah ka, 391, 393

Loma hona, 264

R.C. Lo mahta, or Lomah, or Loma tah cubbee, 650

R.C.*Lo mah ta che, R. c. 680, *54

Lo mah ta cubbe, or Lomah, or Lomahtah, 602

Lomahtah, or Lomah, or Lomah ta cubbee, 602

Lo mah ta ka, 400

Lo mah ta kah, 417, 418, 419

Lo mah to nah, 530

Lo mah tubbee, 395, 417, 418

Lo mah utah, 965

Lomaka, 190, 608

Lomakah, 212

Lo man to nah, 504

Lo ma ta cha, 1111, 1112

R.C. Lo ma tah cubbee, or Lomah, or Lo mah ta, 650

Lo ma ta ka, 185, 186

Lo ma te ka, 198

Lo ma tubbe, alias Elalomatubbe, 548

*Lo ma tubbee, 186, 198, 419, *10

Lomee, 828

Lomiah, 143

Lomoka, 269, 317

Lo mokka, 825

Lo mut ege, 105, 145

Lon ah ho yo, 580

Lon a hoyo, 251, 319, 918

Lon ah tubbee, 690

*Lone, 784, *180

Lonie, 596, 749

Lonubbee, 588

Loo ak ish tubbe, 525

Look a la tubbee, 454

Look fan cha, 316

*Look fan chah, 180

Look fan cha ha, 221

Look fan cha pa, 163

Look fan che ha, 201, 205

Look fan che hah, 419

Look fon ge aha, 158

Look a la tubbe, 502

Look a la tubbee, 379

*Look ta, 324

Looma, 114, 137

Loom abbee, 137, 139

Loom a ho ma, 87

Loom a ho na, 138

Loom a honah, 116

Loomaka, 169

Loom a to cha, 148

Loom a to cubbee, 1016

Loo ma to nah, 148

Loom a tubbi, 141

Looma tulha, 142

Loom it te abbee, 137

Loom ma tonah, 422

Loonaia, 178

Loon ul lubbi, 82

L

Loo sho ma, 854

Lo pish nowah, 551

Lo po te ma, 219

*Loring, Jackson, 18

*Loring, James, 18

*Lose, 306

Loshoma, 223, 274, 944, 507

Loshomah, 507, 521

*Loshomma, 262

Losho na, 553

Losimah, 192

Losy, 859

Lotahoma, 926

Louaka, 142

R.C.*Louis, [R. c. 625,] 748, 749, *222

R.C. Louisa, [R. c. 617,] 908

Louise, 757

Louize, 797

*Lou na chubbey, 288

*Lou sanna, 288

*Lousia, 156

*Louwa, 134

R.C. Lowa, 191, 197, 227, 318, 594, R. c. 663

Lowac he, 114, 137, 523

Lo wa chubbe, 517

Low ah chubbee, 378

Low a hoka, 553

Lowahoka, 235

Low ah te mah, 394

Low ah tubbe, 580

R.C. Low ah tubbee, 442, 554, 569, R. c. 616

Lowatona, 234

Lowa tubbee, 148

Loway, 435

Low in cha, 376, 595

Low in tubbee, 397

R.C. Low is oo nah, [R. c. 679,] 1108

Low wa che, 137

Low wa che ho yuo, 138

Low wa tubbe, 515

R.C. Low wa tubbee, 553, [R. c. 636,] 883

Low way, 1020

Low win che, 436, 517

R.C. Lay sin, Logan, 208

Lubbee, 590

*Lubbin, 292

Lucas, Adam, 26

*Lucas, Capt. James, 24

*Lucas, James, 116

*Lucas, Jinny, 4

*Lucas, Sam, 116, 122

*Lucas, Samuel, 116

*Lucas, Sophia, 30

Luce, 140

*Luce, John, 68

Lucey, 407

Luchu na hona, 930

Lucinda, 50

Luck homa, 190

*Lucly, 170

R.C.*Lucy, 252, 405, 424, 497, 507, 567, [R. c. 668, 672,] 689, 1047, 1071, 1072, *28, 254

*Louis, Jefferson, 200

Lumah, 465

*Lunah, 396, *132

Lunatubbee, 142

Lu ock ho mah, 397, 464

R.C. Lushomahona, [R. c. 668,] 690

Lusho min tubbe, 544

Lush pah, 387, 474, 532, 814, 826

Lush pam be, 497

Lush pan tubbee, 142

Lush pee, 75, 76

Lush ta, 223

*Lusick, 248

Luspa am ba, 138

Lu un abbee, 143

*Lyda, 254

Lyha, 927

Ma a cham ba, 916, 917

Ma-ah-ho-nah, 380, 709, 761, 781, 788

Maa lehema, 237

Maan to nah, 574

R.C. Ma-a-sham ba, 642

Maa she mahoka, 270

Macambee, 228

Macatona, 1032

Machaia, 218

R.C. Ma-cha-to-na, 665

Ma che a hona, 269

Ma che tubbe, 501

Ma-che-tubbee, 378

Ma chubbe, 542

Ma chubbee, 173, 78, 378

Ma chubbi, 50

*Mackey, David, 262, *210

Mackey, Billey, 385

R.C. Mackey, Billy, alias Ah-sti-lubbee, R. c. 620, 717

Mackey, Billy, 780, 786

Mackey, Billy, alias Ahsticubbee, 796

Mackey, the Interpreter, 577

Mack hah le tubbee, 789

Mack kin, 399

Mac o lona, 1033

Ma com ba, 1031

*Magie, Lousan, 308

*Maggie, Cherlis, 306

Ma haamba, 275

R.C. Mahacha, 399, R. c. 633, 862

Ma-ha-chah-tubbe, 580

Ma-had-isht-ea, 144

R.C. Ma-hah-che-ho-nah, R. c. 677, 1093, 1094

*Ma hah honah, 234

Ma hah neyo, 591

Mah ah tah honah, 507

Mah-ah-to-hon-ah, 388

Ma hah tubbee, 1027, 1028

Ma hain teah, 218

Ma hala, 266

Ma-ha-la-hona, 99

R.C. Ma-ha-le, 616

Ma-ha-lee, 781, 788

Mah-al-it-mu-ah, 143

Ma ha lo ma tubbee, 394

Ma-ha-lu-an, 788

Ma-ham-ba, 138

Ma-ham-bee, 144, 385, 515, 826

Ma-ha-o-na, alias Sally Johnson, 140

R.C. Ma-ha-o-tubbee, 615

Ma Ha O Tubby, 698, 803

Ma ha tai o nubbee, 219

Ma ha te lubbe, 517

Mahatona, 163, 167, 169, 196, 235, 318

Mahatona, alias Wahatona, 220, 316

R.C. Ma-ha-Tubbee, 26, 227, 318, R. c. 664

Ma he o tubbee, 950

Ma he tubbe, 522

Mah-ha-cubbee, 376, 554

Mah-hah, 148

Mah-hah-lee, 761

Mah-hah-la-hoonah, 728

Mah-ham-be, 580

Mah-ham-tonah, 589

Mah-han-tubbe, 502

Mah-han-tubbee, 442

Mah-he-ah-tah, 379, 454

Mah he cubbe, 504

Mah-hil-le-tu-na, 580

M

Mah ho kah tubbe, 509

R.C. *Mah honah, 377, 399, 463, 536, 580, 969, R. c. 617, *74

Mah-ho-nah-tubbe, 580

Mah ho tonah, 689, 987

Mah ho tubbe, 516

Mah hubbee, 475

Ma-him-tibbee, 104, 105

Ma-hin-to-nah, 405

R.C. Ma-hin-tubbee, R. c. 643, 919, 920

Ma hi ye, 552

Mah ka tubbe, 515

Mah ke, 504

Mah kin tubbee, 905, 906

Mah ko chah, 516

Mah la, 399, 454, 569, 690

Mahla, or Suckey, 591

*Mahlah, 384, 462, 523, 824, *104

Mah lah ho nah, 397

Mah la hoka, 512

Mah la honah, 540

Mah la hoyoche, 445

Mah la ta cubbe, 598

R.C. Mah-la-ta-cubbee, R. c. 649, 960, 961, 962

Mah la tubbe, 597

Mah-le, 382, 542

Mah le ah, 492, 559

Mah le ah tah, 501

Mah le hoka, 528

Mah-le-le, 381, 556, 580

Mah le le honah, 509

Mah li, 457, 521, 816

*Mah lia pesa tubbe, 320

R.C. Mah-li-ha, R. c. 676, 1087

*Mah lon tikubbe, 12

Mah ma tubbee, 198

Mah no te mah, 498

Mahn to nah, 605

Mahn tubbee, 760, 762

Ma hoba chubbee, or Imma hoba chubbee, 204

Ma hobatubbe, 272

Mahobatubbee, 273

Mahobbee, 138, 883, 825

Ma-ho-been-tub-bee, 148

Mahoka, 517

Ma hom bee, 471

Ma hona, 191

*Ma-ho-nah, 103, 137, 379, 420, 760, 781, *62, *66, *146

Mahonah, or Honah, 698

Ma ho nah, or Honer, 698

Ma-ho-ne-ab-bee, 144

Ma-hoo-too-nah, 139

Ma-ho-rat-ab-bee, 143

Ma-ho-wa-tub-bee, 138

Ma-ho-yah, 104, 144

Mah-sho-la-cah, 789

Mah sho bah homah, 689

R.C. Mah-sho-la-kah, 616

R.C. Mah-thah-tah, alias Me-shah-tah, R. c. 621, 717

Mah that a tah, alias Me-shahtah, 797

Mah-ti-ya, 580

Mah-to-ho-nah, 580

R.C. *Mah-ton-ah, 381, 504, 531, 580, R. c. 652, *114

Mah tub bee, 883

R.C. Ma-hubbee, 93, 98, 139, 260, 270, 317, 386, R. c. 636, 825, 882, 883

Mahubbe, 515

Ma-hun-tub-bee, 145

Mah yah, 515

Mah-ye, 380

Mah ye, alias Ok lah mi ah, 505

Ma-hy-chub-by, 803

Maia chubbee, 1005

Ma-it-ah-ho-na, 143

*Maize, Salina, 222

*Maize, Selina, 238

*Mak ah a yah, Liza, 276

R.C. Mak-ah-ha-tubbee, R. c. 676, 1091, 1092

Mak ah hi ah, 503

Makatona, 242

Makay, 10

Mak-e-chub-bee, 143

Mak e ubbe, 507

*Mak he tubby, Fallis, 322

Mak in tubbe, 560

*Mak in tubbee, 471, *220

*Mak kar har tona, 220

Mak ke hatona, 237

Ma ko ka, 523

*Mako chabbee, 268

Mala, 401

Malacha, or Vina, 280

R.C. Ma-la-cha, alias, Vina Jimson, 669

Malacha, 1050

Malachubee, 260

*Mala heyock, 84

R. c. Ma-la-ho-nah, 616

Ma la honer, 789

Ma la ho yo che, or Math le hi o ja, 492, 563

Ma la la ho nah, 501

Ma-la-ley-chubbee, 380, 761

R.C. Ma-la-le-chubbee, 616

Malaley chubbey, 704

Mala-tomba, 750

R.C. Malatubbee, 280, R. c. 662

Malehona, 264

R.C. Mal-e-te-ma, 629

Ma ley chubbey, 781

R.C. Malinda, 250, R. c. 665

Ma-lin-ga-liah, 140

Malissa, 279

*Malitaya, 150

R.C.*Malla honah, 791, R. c. 616, *80

Malla ta ha ka, 728

Malle tubbee, 505

*Mallobbe, 318

*Malthally, Seily, *30

*Malteah, 142

*Maly, Mary, 248

Mam-ba, 387, 474

Mambah, 531, 814, 826

*Mampoli, 188

Man-ah-a-gee, 143

Manc che, 316

*Manche honah, *48

Manchubbe, 558, 581, 582, 583

Manchubbee, 223, 384, 491

Manchubbe, Captain, 581

Maneche, 217, 224

Manin tuluy, 712

*Manotubbee, 58

Man sha tubbee, 272, 275

*Mantama, 218

*Mantehubbee, 108

*Man tonah, 310

Man tubbe, 523

Man Tubbey, 712, 725, 760

Man Tubby, 712

Mantubby, Con on Timer, 712

Manu stoo nah ha, 772

Manya, or Itemiya, 536

Ma-pa-la-ho-na, 137

Ma-pa-tu-na, 138,

Mar car ley, 707

Mar-har-le, 379, 701

*Mar kin tubbee, 76

Marsalla, 201

Marsh-ho-ner, alias Me-ah-sho-nah, 780

Mars Honer, 706, 714, 715

Mars Hoone, or Neah shonah, 714

Mars Hooner, 705

Marssauther, or Me ah shuts ah, 711

Martha, 403, 406

Martin, Henry L., 495

*Martin, Henry, 264

*Martyan, Henry, 322

R.c.*Mary, 50, 224, 748, 749, 756, 757, 764, 1127, 1128, R. c. 626, R. c. 629, R. c. 683, *202, *222, *254, *294

R.c.*Mary Ann, 398, 808, R. c. 614, *160

Masala, 158, 163, 205

Ma-sha, 147

Mashambe, 50

Mash-he-ab-bee, 144

Mashia, 277

Mash-o-ba-ho-mah, 100

Ma-sho-la, 385, 471, 542, 826

Ma sho letubbe, 559

Mash on timer, 700, 701

Mashpa nubbe, 580

Ma-shun-ta-tub-bee, 147

Mason, 405

Massala, 225

Massahla, 419

Ma tha tubbee, 917, 918

Mathe chubbee, 218

Mathla, 500

Math-la-chub-bee, 146

Math la tubbe, 256

R.c. Math la tubbee, 569, R. c. 642, 690

Math-le-hi-o-jah, 382

Math le hi o ja, or Ma la ho yo cha, 492

Math le hi oja, or Mala hoyo che, 563

Mat-la-chubbee, 96

Matona, 242

Matona, alias Onatona, 276

Mat-tubbee, 442

Ma-tubbe, 778

R.c. Ma-tubbee, R. c. 619, 717, 781, 799

Maun thla tubbe, 50

*Maxwell, 50, *629

May hue, 42

Maytubbee, 393

McCan, Cornelious, 29

*McCann, Cornelius, 24

*McCann, Allen, 24

*McCann, Wall, 24

*McCann, William, 24

*McCann, Thos., 252

*McClish, George, *6, *114

*McClure, James, 26, *184

*McClure, Liley, 16

*McClure, Liza, 16

*McClure, Wallace, *154, *156

*McClure, Walter, 154

*McClure, William, 16

R.c. McCown, Lucy, 141, 192, 198, 1030, 229, 318, R. c., 665

McCoun, Lucy, 1030

McCoy, James E., 142

*McCoy, James, 234

*McCoy, Nelson, 128

*McCoy, Oliver, S., *242, *252

*McCoy, William, 26, *252

*McCurtain, A., 298

*McCurtain, Allen, 44

*McCurtain, Daniel, 176, 177, *44

*McCurtain, Delilah, 14

*McCurtain, E., 52

*McCurtain, H., 52

*McCurtain, Huston, 80

*McCurtain, Thomas, *14, *44, *52

*McCurtain, William, *14, *44

*McDonald, Sophia, 80

McDonold, Hugh, 408

*McFarren, Jenny, 28

McGee, Ann, 1055

*McGee, Amy, 238

*McGee, Eliza, 270

McGee, Humphreys, 1055

McGee, Lavinia, 1055

*McGee, Louis, 308

*McGee, Malina, 230

McGee, Polley, 1055

R.C. McGee, Samuel, 60, 82, 140, 280, 320, 1055, R. c. 670, *238

McGee, Umphries, 1055

*McGelbeny, Mickle, 34

McGelvroy, Jno., 75

McGelvroy, Lucy, 75

*McGibbeny, Wallace, 30

McGilbey, Lucy, 83

McGilbey, Jno., 83

McGilbey, Lucy, 142, 390

McGilbey, Robert, 142

McGilvery, Gordon, 18

McGilvery, John, 18

McGilvery, Robert, 18

McGilvery, Turner, 18

*McIntosh, John, 29, *126

McKee, 443

McKee, Alexander, 29

McKee, Davy, 447

McKee, Middleton, 444, 447

*McKenny, Capt. John, 66

*McKey, Billy, 54

*McKey, E., 54

*McKey, Ellis, *62, *64, *88

McKinney, Billy, (Tun-al-up-kah,) 147

McKinney, Catharine, 26

*McKinney, Catherine, 260

*McKinney, Mossa, 138

*McKinney, Silas, 28, *156

*McKinzie, Coleman, 138

McLaughlin, Matthew, 23

*McNael, Elwood, 36

Me ab sho nah, 456

Me a chia, 942

Me-ah-che, 381, 508, 580

Me ah chubbee, 534

R.C. Me ah hoka, 603, R. c. 651, 968

R.C. Me ah honah, 528, 793, R. c. 619, R. c. 622

R.C. Meah ho tubbe, 596, R.c. 659

Meah ho tubbee, 997, 999

Meahiahchunah, 535

Meah ish tam be, 500

R.C. Me-ah-shah-tah, Capt., 617

Me-ah-shambee, 85, 140

Vol. XIII—6.

M

Me ah shan tah, 480, 481, 547

Meah shane tubbee, 400, 465

Meah shatta, Capt., 804

Me-ah-shattah, 696

Me ah shattah, Capt., 781

Meah she cubbe, 527, 580

Me-ah-she-cubbee, 381

Me-ah she mah, 542, 561, 569

Me ah she mah, 690

Me-ah-shim-tah, 580

Meah shin tubbe, or Meashin tubbe, 509

Me-ah shin tubbe, 584

Meh sho ka, 512

R.C. Me-ah-sho-nah, 378, 380, 399, 456, 547, 568, 584, R. c. 620, 690, 760, 801, 803

Me-ah-sho-nah, alias Marsh-ho-ner, 780

Meah shootubbee, 568

Meah sho tubbe, 503

Meah sho tubbee, 400, 689

Me-ah-shul-ah, 380

Meah shu nah, 505, 528

Me ah shut ah, 761

Meah shutsah, or Marssauther, 711

Me-ah-tah-tah, 580

Meah tambe, 557

Me ah te ubbee, 391

Meah tim ah, 405

Meah tim mah, 598

Meah to chubbe, 690

Meah-to-chubbee, 375, 568

Meah to co nah, 492, 562

Meahtonah, 436, 788

Me-ah-too-chubbee, 100

Me-ah-tubbe, 586, 690, 780, 783

R.C. Me-ah-tuebee, 376, 379, 404, 570, R. c. 623, 731, 761, 731

Me ah tubbey, 730

Me-al-ishl-eah, 380

R.C. Me-an-tubbee, R. c. 614, 695, 696

*Me antubbe, 300

Me an Tubbey, 695

Measen tubby, 785

Me-ash-ah, 382

Me asham ba, 256

Me asham bee, or Mesh shambe, 589

Meashatta, Capt., 719, 722

Me ash e mah, 503

Me ash en tubbee, 770

Meashen tubbey, 770

Me ash fane ubbe, 508

R.C. Meashia, 265, R. c. 646, 943

Me-ash-ik-ab-bee, 143

*Me ash in ta, 84

Me ash in tubbe, 540

R.C. Me ash-in-tubbee, 380, R. c. 619, R. c. 627 780, 807, 808

Me ash i yah, 942

Me-ash-on-cha-hub-bee, 143

*Meas hon ubbe, 24

Meas hoonah, 731

Meashoontemah, 540

Mea showtah, 489

Me-ash-pul-la, 98, 139, 461, 824

*Me-ash-pullah, 383, 520, *106

Measin, Tubbe, 774, 775, 780

Me-as-in-tubbe, 783

Me asin tubbee, 785

Measin Tubbey, 774

Meas-in-tubby, 379

Me-at-at-ah, 143

Meatubbe, 586

R.C. Meatubbee, 658, R.C. 991, 992, 591

Me cam bee, 525

Me-chubbe, 87, 510, 580

Me-chub-bee, 138, 148, 381

Me-chi, 95. 146

Meck a howier, 733

Meein loketubbee, 274

Meek A. B., 495

Me-e-shan-tah, 375, 377, 442

Me-ka-che, 385, 471, 522, 524, 826

Me ka che honah, 515

Me-ka-che-lub-bee, 826

Me ka che to nah, 573

Me ka che tubbee, 385, 471

Me ka che tubbe, 517

Me-kad-isht-ea, 144

Me-ka-ga-tub-bee, 143

Me-ka-gee-tub-bee, 138

Me-ka-ge-ho-na, 143

Me-ha-ge-tubbee, 144

Me-kah, 95, 147, 528, 566

Me-hah-che-hu-nah, 580

Me-hah-che-tubbe, 580

*Me hah cubbe, *248

Me-hah E-lappish nowah, 442

Me-hah Kah timah, 557

Me-hah-tah-tah, 382, 508, 584

Me-hah-tish-teah, 509

Me hah tonah, 405, 442, 569, 690

Me hah to nubbee, 396

Me hah took honah, 544

Me-hah-tubbee, or Tim-ah-ha-tubbee, 377

Me hah tubbee, 448, 498

Me hair tubbe, 256

Me-ha-la, 139

Me ha la ho nah, 540

*Me hambe, 290

R.C. Me-ham-lah-ho-nah, 651

Me hane lah ho nah, 603, 967

Me han to tubbee, 566, 689

Me ha nubbe, 531

R.C. Me-ha-nubbee, R. c. 638, 897

Mehashia, 199

Me-ha-ta-cubbee, 109, 110, 137

Me ha ta ka, 270, 317

Me-hat-at-tah, 144

Me-ha-te-ah, 826

Me ha te cubbe, 525

*Me-ha-te-ka, 138, *164

Me-ha-te-kah, 110, 813

Me-ha-te-kubbee, 382, 457, 816, 821

Me hat e she, 515

Me ha tim ah, 561

*Me ha tisk teah, 106

*Me hatona, 192, 266, *38, *92

Me ha tonah, 540

Me ha to nam bee, 491, 572

Me ha tubbe, 521

Me ha tubbee, 190, 197

Me haw, 491, 572

Me he ah chubbe, 563

Me he ah chubbee, 492

Me hea tema, 271

Me heah te mah, 528

Me he be cubbe, 1076, 1077

R.C. Me-he-be-cubbee, 674

Me-he-be-kah, 580

Me he le hona, 505

Me he looth tubbe, 508

Me he loth temah, 547

M

Me he mah, 542

Me he o timah, 507

Me heo tubbe, 603

R.C. Me he o tubbee, R. C. 651, 690, 967

Meh e tambe, 535

Me he ubbe, 504

Me he yo ka tubbe, 505

Meh ho to nah, 987

*Me hia chubbee, Joe, 262

Me hi a tonah, 402

Me hi a tubbee, 392

*Me hin loh mubbe, 34

Mehi-o-tubbee, 391

Me-hi-to-nah, 141

*Meh mah tona, 274

*Meh mar tona, 220

Mehn Tubbee, 707

Me-hoh, 145

Me ho nub bee, 896

Me ho shia, 190

Me-ho-te-ah, 386, 474, 518

Me ho te mah, 567

Me ho timah, 539

Me ho to mah, 689

*Meh teah, 70

Me-ish-attah, 95

Mela, 502, 932

Melah, 689

Me la ho nah, 497

*Melarma, 58

Melah tonah, 419

Me lingaliah, 228

Me linge liah, 330, 406, 408

*Melissa, *204, *304

Me-lot-ab-bee, 143

Me lo tubbe, 525

R.C. Me mah tam be, 567, R. C. 675, 1083

Me mah tam bee, 689

*Me mah tubbe, 136

R.C. Me mah tubbee, 436, R. C. 682, 1124, 1125

Me ma tubbee, 190

Me mock almah, 436

Me mock a mah, 395

M enta, 191

Me o chubbe, 507

Me oho he kubbe, 522

Me o sham bee, 916

Me o tubbe, 389

Meotubbe, 562

*Merryman, James M., 12

*Merryman, Lucy, 12

R.C. Me shah tah, alias Mah-thah-tah, R. C. 621
717

Me shah tah, 761, 780

Me shah tah, alias Mah that a tah, 797

Me sha lakah, 767,

Me sha mah honah, 554

Me sham ba, 459

Me sham be, 569, 530, 28

Me-sham-bee, 138, 383, 385

Me sha tah, 797

Me sha tubbe, 542

Me she mah, 544

Me she mah honah, 518

Me she mah tubbe, 509, 580

Me-she-mah-tubbee, 381

Me she ma tubbe, 533

Meshem ta tubbe, 558

R.C. Me-sho-la-kah, 627

Me sho la rah, 767

Me-shone-tah-tubbee, 375, 567, 689, 834

Me shoon kubbe, 516

Me shoon tah tah, 528

Me shoon ti yah, 472, 573

Me shoontiyah, alias Glennah, 473

Me shune tubbee, 570, 690

Me shune tah tubbee, 491

Mesh shambe, or Meash am bee, 589

Mestia, 139

Metah, 508

Me tah ba, 523

Me yah tubbe, 517

*Mey ashin tobi, 172

*Mey osh pollo, Lewis, 272

*Mey otema, *112, *118

*Meyotimah, 96

Me yotonah, 535

Me-you-yoh-cubbee, 90

Mia, 781, 803

R.C. Mi-ah-chubbee, alias Im-i-ah-hubbee, 681

Mah chubbee, alias, Im i a chubbee, 1116

Mi ah tim ah, 510

Mi-ah-to-chubbee, 146

Mi ah tubbe, 507

Mi-ah-tubbee, 387, 388, 557

*Miashaya, Forbis, 284

*Miash in tubbee, 212

*Miatikobi, 128

Mill hi tubbee, 194

*Mihahoke, 174

Mihah timah, 571

Mi-ha-tub-bee, 137

Mi ha ya tubbe, 264

*Mih motoli, Thomas, 136

*Miho tobi, 128

Mi-ho-to-nah, 141

Mi hotona, 192

Mi in to nah, 972

Mik-ko-ah-ho-mah, 384

R.C. Mi-la, R. c. 668, 932, 933

Mila tam ba, 799

R.C. Mil-a-tam-bee, 620

Mile, 253, 942

*Miller, Daniel, *268, *276

*Miller, Siney, *270, *278

*Miller, Vicey, 268

*Milley, 34

*Milly, *152, *276

Mima, 403

Mina, 393

Mincha, 417, 418, 419, 464

Minche, 201, 205

Minchubbee, 417, 418, 420

Min-chub-bi, 141

Min-ga-hoak-ta, 789

Mingo, 147

*Mingo Cocha, 276

Mingo faliah, 483

*Mingo falleeh, 304

R.C. Min-go-fal-li-ah, R. c. 678, 1100, 1101

Mingo ho mah, alias Captain Bob, 508, 576, 579

*Mingo homa, 126

Min-go-ho-nah, alias Captain Bob, 382, 581

Mingo-ho-pi-a, or Ne tah cubbee, 387

*Mingo-ho-pia, 162

Mingo ho piah, alias Ne tah cubbee, 499

Mingo, Mush-u-la-tubbee, 29

Mingo, Popia, 166

Min-ta-cha, 580

Minta chubbe, 536

M

Min tah chubbe, 517

Min tah hubbe, 502

*Min tah hubbee, 22

R.C. Min-ta-ho-ka, R. C. 642, 256, 394

Min ta ho koh, 916, 917

Minta hona, 275

R.C. Minta-ho-nubbee, 681

Minta hotona, 234

R.C. Min-ta-ho-yo, R. C. 621, R. C. 622, 718, 791

Minta hubbee, 234, 393, 378, 442

Min-ta-tubbee, 103, 138

Min te chubbe, 560, *270

*Min-te-chubbee, 384, *58, *60

Minte cubbe, 535

Mint-e-gee, 144

Min te hamah, 535

Min te ham bee, 399

Minte honah, 523, 983

R.C. Min-te-ho-yo, 381, 386, 469, 509, 522, 580, R. c. 620, 791, 796, 817, 827

Min te hubbe, 445, 505, 513, 570, 580

Min-te-hubbee, 381, 690

Minte nubbe, 535

Minte nubbee, 224

*Minti hambe, 324

Min to ho nah, 974

R.C. Min-to-ho-yo, 622

Min tor ho nubbee, 1117, 1119

*Minttubbee, 76

Min tubbe, 602

R.C. Mintubbee, 233, 400, R. c. 628, 834, 835

Min tubbee, alias Dixon, W. Lewis, 957, 958, 959

Mio, 761

Mio nubbe, 530

Mise mi yah, 512

Mish ah moon tubbee, 420

Mish ah oyo, 1048

*Mish amia, 164

Mish amom tubbee, 191

Mish amone tubbee, 197

Mish amon tubbee, 318, 230

*Mish amoon tobi, 132

R.C. Mish a moon tubbee, 158, 898, 899, R. c. 639

Mish-an-tu-tub-bee, 146

*Mish atta, Capt., 142

Mish a tubbee, 1010, 1011

Mish ean ah tubbe, 548

Mish e emah tonah, 492, 559

*Mish emah tubbee, 88

*Mish emah tubbee, Mary, 92

Mish-e-ma-tub-bee, 143

R.C. Mish-e-mi-yah, R. c. 635, 876

Mish-e-my-ah, 875

*Mish-imah tobe, 38

*Mish imah tubbee, 64

Mish-o-me-ah, 26

*Mish oon tubbee, 462, 540, 824, *102

Mis-horn-tubbee, 139

Mish-shambee, 376

Mish ta tubbe, 535

Mish tubbee, 1051

Mis ta bo yea, 459

Mis tai ahoka, 271

*Mis te boye, 68

Mis-te-bo-yea, 139, 517, 813, 826

Mis-ti-bo-yea, 383

Mis tubbe, 521

R.C. Mis tubbee, 228, R. c. 669

*Mitchell, Johnson, 20

*Mitchell, Joe, 20

*Mitchell, Stewart, 154

Mit-tub-bee, 147, 1052

R.C. Miya, 605, R. c. 653, 708, 973

Mi ya chubbee, 483, 817, 828

Mi ya chubbe, 517

R.C. Mi-yah, 380, 403, 514, R. c. 617

Mi-yah-chubbee, 388

Mi yah honah, 530

Mi yah tubbe, 514

Mi yah tubbee, or Ona hain be, 593

*Miyas hin tobi, 168

Mi ye obbee, 103

Mi-yub-bee, 137

Mo-bee, 144

Moc ah be, 505

Moc a howier, 732

Mocala, 158, 163

R.C. Mock-a-hah-wah, R. c. 623

Mock a hiah, 799

Mock ahhiyah, 589

Mock-ah-ho-yo, 389, 580

R.C. Mock-ah-la-mah, 623

Mock a hower, 733, 734, 735

Mock a howier, 732

R.C. Mock ah to nah, 400, R. c. 617

Mock ain tubbee, 404

Mock-a-lah, 147

R.C. Mock-a-li-ah, 619

Mock co nah, 967

Mock-e-na-e-la, 139

Mock en Toner, 710

Mock-en-tub-bee, 148

R.C. Mock-hah-la-tubbee, 616

R.C. Mock-in-tubbee, R. c. 623, 721, 722

Mockin Tubbey, 720

R.C. Mock ko nah, 630, R. c. 651

Mol-ah-to-nah, or Neal a hoo nak, 801

Mo heotubbee, 568

Mohola, 177

*Mohubbee, 190

Mok a cubbe, 498

Mok-ah-la, 735, 736

Mok-ah le hoka, 503

Mok ah le honah, 501

Mok a tubbe, 533

Mok in lubbee, 567, 689

Mo ko nubbe, 267, 534

Mo lah chubbee, 690

Mo la tubbee, 569

*Molcy, 180

Mo le ah, 392

Molla, 380, 538

Mollah le howah, 513

Mollahoka, 587

R.C. Mol-la-hoo-nah, alias E mock-ah-ho-nah, 617

R.C. Mol-la-ta-ha-ka, R. c. 623, 783

Mol-la-to-ha-kah, 379, 729, 762

Mol la to ha kat, 727

Mol-la-to-ha-kah, 382

Molle, 535

Molle tiah, 393

Molle-to-ho-kah, 780

Molli clah, 1050

R.C. Molly, 141, 219, 223, 250, B. c. 641, R. c. 665 908, 910, 1058, *308

Moma cha, alias Momintubbe, 504

Mo-ma-cha, 580

Mo-mah, 148

*Mo-ma-tubbee, 26, *214

Mo-me-cha, 144

Mo-men tubbee, 381

Mo-me-tam-bee, 94, 141, 390

Mo me tim ah, 497

Mo-min-che, 139, 383, 387, 457, 478, 524, 531, 814, 817, 827, 828

Mo-mint-ab-bee, 143

Mo-min tambe, or Billy Jackson, 493, 564

Mo min tomba, 537

*Mo min tubbe, 515, *32

*Mo-min-tubbee, 384, 403, 462, 824, *108, *214

*Momin tubby, 222

Mo-nah-ho-ka, 389, 580

Mo nah tubbe, 510

Mo-nam-be, 580

Moncrief, Sampson, 18

Mone tubbee, 191, 199, 227

Mo nim tubbe, alias Mo ma cha, 504

Monim tubbee, 224

Mo no ho key, 703

Monta, 190, 196, 199, 393, 399

Montah, 395, 465

Montah, or Montubbee, 401

Montona, 264

R.C. Mon tubbee, 117, 194, R. C. 618, 725, 799

Mon tubbey, 726

Monubbe, alias Kun ne monubbe, 253

R.C. Mo-nub-bee, 139, 227, 318, 421, R. C. 664, 930, 1025, 1026

R.C. Mo-nubbee, alias Cun na mo nubbee, 668

Monubbee, alias Kunnemonubbee, 319

Mook ka fa, 514

Mool a tubbee, 1013

Moo min tamba, or Billy Jackson, 445

Moon-tah, 113, 138, 383, 460, 461, 521

Moon tah, or Moontubbee, 589

Moon tubba, 76

Moon-tubbe, 179, 255

R.C. Moon-tubbee, 27, 81, 82, 142, 147, 170, 172, 177, 179, 181, 245, 319, 395, 399, 468, 569, R. C. 641, 689, 907, 908, 909, 910, 978, 1122, 1123, 375

Moon tubbee, or Moontah, 589

Moon-tubbee, 375

*Moon tubby, 232

Moon tubbi, 46, 47, 49, 50

Moon-ub-bee, 142

*Moore, John, 18, *316

*Moore, J. B., 316

*Moore, Nancy, 46, 47, 49, 50, 75, 170, 171, 172, 253, 319, *286

*Moore, Susan, 294

*Moore, Thomas, 294

*Morgan, 292

Moritah, 422

*Morrell, Louisiana, 286

*Morris, Rhodia, 198

*Morris, Sippie, 234

Moses, 909, 910

*Mo-sha-kah, 387, 478, 526, 814, 827, *72

Mo she la kah, 759

Moshen tubbey, 770

Moshola, 176, 178, 179

Mo-sho-la-ka, 383

R.C. Mo sho la kah, 459, R. c. 626, 813, 826

Mo-sho-le-tubbee, 384

Mo she le tubbee, 492

Mo shu la ca, 531

Mo shu la rah, 758

*Mosis, Henry, *204

*Mosley Lafayett, 226

*Mosley, Mrs. Mary, 204

*Mosley, Samuel, *226, *286

*Mosley, Yanis, 286

*Moss Gilford, 248

Mot Tubby, 776

Mo-wam-bee, 389

Muc-cam-bee, 111, 137

Muc-ha-mo, 140

Muchatona, 229

Muck an a tona, 914

Muck-a-to-nah, 825

*Muck en tubbee, 112

Muck intubbi, 50

Muk-a-an-ab-bee, 145

Mukah hotinah, 506

Muk-am-ba, 382, 457, 816, 827

Muk am bee, 517

Muk-in tubbee, 385

R.C. Muk in tubbee, 385, 491, 572, R. c. 640, 826

Muk oh to noh, 1032

Muk onubbe, alias Okla honubbe, 517

Mulae honah, 542

Mul-a-te-ma, 847

Mul a tubbe, 522

R.C. Mul-e-ti-ah, R. c. 620, 799

Mul e ti yah, 542

Mul labe chubbee, 470

Mul-lah-be-chub-bee, 827

Mul lah le honah, 519

*Mul-la-le-chubbee, 386, *106

Mulla lee chubbee, 499

Mul-la-lu-chubbee, 817

Mul la le honah, 573

Mulla-lu-chub-bee, 138

*Mulla luh hoke, 80

R.c. Mulla ti ah, 750, R. c. 625

Mulla Tiger, 751

Mulla-tubbe, 446, 516

Mul-la-tubbee, 92, 141

Mul-le-chub-bee, 138

Mullee-chubbee, 113

*Mullen, James, *68

*Mullen, John, 176

R.c. Mul-ti-ah, R. c. 614, 695

Multier, 694

Multiere, 785

Multior, 692

Multire, 379, 694, 695

Mul ti yah, 693, 780, 807

Multh toombah, 589

Multur, 717, 785

Mun-shon-tubbee, 107

Munt-ab-bee, 145

Mun-tubba, 105

Murcgey, or Paysubey, 1037, 1038

*Murphy, George, 18, *92

Muscle, 423

Muscoga, 176, 177, 203

R.c. Muscogee, or Pasubbee, 250, R. c. 666

Muscogy, alias Pasubbee, 1037

Mus cogy, 1039

Mus he leeker, 757

Mush-e-le-kah, 825

Musho aler, 703

Mush-oo-le-kah, 386

Mu-shoon-tub-bee, 137

Mush shu leekah, 690

Mush u la cah, 473, 474

Mush u lah kah, 523

Mush-u-la-tubbee, Mingo, 27

M

Mush-u-la-tub-bee, 139

Mush-u-le-a-kah, 376

Mush-ule-ca, 104

Mush-ule-e-ca, 144

Mushu leekah, 569

Mush u le kah, 475

Musko botokolo, 568

Muskogee, or Pashubbee, 319

Mutchey Allo, 757, 758

R.C. Muth-ta-hubbee, R. c. 666, 1041

Mutta, 179, 912

Muttahona, 269

Mutta lee chubbe, 113

Muttubbe, 268, 512

Muttubbee, 376, 452, 1126

*Muttubbee, Capt., 226

Mya, 142

My-atta, 143

My-yea, 145

Na ah ho tubbee, 404

Na ah tembee, 1125

Nac a tubbee, 85

Na chia stiah, 715

*Na chi ma, 308

*Na chi mer, 314

Na chubbee, 377, 448

Nacka chue a ma, 117

Nack a nam bee, 96, 97

Nack ne tubbee, 104

Na con sha, 479, 547

Naconsha, Billy, 492

*Nahamastabe, 192

*Nahayubbe, 26

R.C. Nah cee, 620, 796

Nah ho lubbe, 592

R.C. Nah ho lubbee, 140, 376, 957, 958, 959, 960,
    R. c. 649

Nah ho nah, 761, 781, 791

Nah ho sa, 387, 474

Nah ho sah, 814, 826

Nah ho te mah,

Nah ho to mus tubbe, 517

Nah ho to nah, 566

*Nah ho yabbee, 114

Nah ho yo, 379, 702, 761, 781, 792, R. c. 616

*Nah la hona, 284

Nah mi ah, 939

Nah na e mah, 392

Nah ne mah to nah, 393

Nah nim ah ho ka, 393

R.C. Nah nis teah, 791, R. c. 615

Nah no ma ho nah, 420

Na ho lah mustubbee, 115, 139

Na ho la mustubbee, 817, 827

Na ho lo mus tubbee, 386, 469, 877

*Nahoma, 324

Na ho mah, 104

R.C. Na ho nah, 615

Nahoosa, 99, 139

Nahosah, 518

Na ho te ma, 199

*Na ho yo, 140

Nah po lubbee, 149

Nah sah, 392

Nah she ba ho mah, 147

Nah sho bah, 580

Nah sho bah ho mah, 567

Nah sho bah ho nah, 375

Nah wa, 376, 591, 962

Nail Benjamin, 553

Nail, Daniel, 26, 27

Nail, Daniel W., 27

*Nail, E., 210

Nail, Greenwood, L., 553

*Nail, Jeny, 86

*Nail, J. H., 210

Nail, Joel H., 27, 380

Nail, John M., 390

Nail, Marcheline, 553

*Nail, Maurice, 86

*Nail, Sally, 20

*Nail, Wilson, 86

Naka cha, 8

Naka che, 87

Na ka chubbee, 827

*Na ka chuk ina, 134

*Na kah chuk mubbee, 306

*Nak an a tubbee, 886

*Nak chat tah, 158

Nak chu nubbee, 832

Nak e hattah, 817, 827

*Nak ei ma sha, 264

*Nak e na che, 80

Nak e na tubbee, 442

Nak e ne fe nah, 825

Nak fille, 143

*Nak hillabbee, 300

*Nakh labbe, Fallis, 300

Nak ho ah ho mah, 380

Nak ho mah, 828

Nak ho ma ha jo, 817

*Nak im pa ya, 170

*Nak in ho nubi, 170

*Nak in ta hubbe, 2

*Nakishi, 136, 138

*Nak ish taya, 318

*Nak ish tiah, 62

Nak ish ti yah, 455

*Nak ish to nubbe, 246

*Nak ish tubbee, 200

Nak ista shubbe, 263

*Nak neen tubbee, 74

Nak ne o ka tubbee, 826

*Nak ne tah, 1101, *296

Nak ne ubbee, 827

*Nak ni chi, 138

*Nak ni honobi, 170

*Nak ni taya, 178

Nak no ma hajo, 827

*Nak o a homa, 166

Na ko mah, 945

Na kon cha, 446

Na kon che, 445

Na kon sha, 382, 444

Na konsha, Billy, or Elashubbe, 563

Na kon sha, James, 382

*Nan a he ka, 318

Nan a ma ho na, 194

Nan a ubbee, 944

R.C.*Nan a yubbee, 277, 320, 817, R. C. 646, *270

Nan cha, 140, 580

Nan cha be, 89

R.C. Nan che ho ka, 801, R. C. 616

R.C. Nan che mah, 614

Nan cho mah, 808

R.C.*Nancy, 233, 256, 506, 925, R. C. 643, *106, 110, 116, 220

*Nanema, 50, 236, *140

R.C. Nanemah, [R. C. 621], 788

Nanena, 1039

*Nan e wa, 142

Nanna yhbbee, 943, 944, 945

Nanne ubbee, 598

Nanno ma honah, 388, 559

Nanomahona, 198

Nan ta ho yow, 1063

Nan ten ma, 26

Nan tinye, 381

*Nan to wah, 76

Nan to wah ya, 497

Nan tubbee, 925

Naoka, 499

*Na pis tona, 288

Nasakah, 417, 418, 421

Nase, 224

Nash in tubbee, 422

*Nashoba, 12

Nasho bah no mah, 1045, 1046

Nasho ba noah, 1043

*Nasho bonowa, 316

Nat, 159, 163, 222, 419, 201, 205, 316

*Natakeche, 92

Na to kun lubbee, 199

*Natubbee, 377, 442, 554, *46

Na wa tom bee, 385

*Naw yoke, 110

Ne an shah ho nah, 1125

Ne an shambee, 149

Neah sho nah, 714

Neal a hoo nak, 801

Neash o nubbe, 516

Ne cha che to, 386

Ne chubba, 102

Ne chubbee, 97, 145

*Ned, 298

Neeter, 764

Neetuck a chee, 692

Ne go ah ho mah, 143

R.C. Nela, 592, 952, 953, R.C. 648

Nele. 507

*Nelson, Betsey, 176, *240

*Nelson, Brown, 174

*Nelson, C. E., 244

Nelson, Chilocco, 176

Nelson, Dixon, 226

*Nelson, Eden, 170, 171, 172, 174, 176, 177, *152, 162

*Nelson, Ganet, E., 175, *200

Nelson, Garrett, 173

Nelson, Garrett E., 245

*Nelson, George, 172, 174, 176, *262

Nelson, Isaac, 172, 174

Nelson, Jenny, 176

R.C. *Nelson, Jesse, 146, 177, 190 198, 226, 318, 453, 1015, 1016, 1017, 1018, R.C. 663, *80

*Nelson Joe, 176, 255, 319, *260

*Nelson Joseph, 152

*Nelson Michell, 266

Nelson Mitchell, 176

*Nelson, Mrs. Molcie, 244

*Nelson Rhoda, 242, 264, 270

*Nelson Mrs. Rhoda, 242, 262

*Nelson Simon, 36, 240

*Nelson Simon F., 36

*Nelson Solomon, 176, *240

*Nelson Wm., 80

*Nenak am be, 220

Ne nak kam bee, 826

Ne nok kom ba, 385

Ne nok kom bee, 522

Nen tubbee, 142

Neohoyo, 1026

Ne tah che tah, 475

Ne tah che to, 103, 148, 537, 825

Ne tah cubbee, 307, 499

*Ne tan osh ko bo, 296

Neth yubbee, 571

Netoch oosh tah, 580

Ne tock ah ubbee, 382

Ne tock am be, 493, 565

Ne tock in ja, 425

Ne tock oosh tah, 381, 506

Ne tok un lubbee, 223

Ne tu can lu bee, 266

Ne tuck a chuch ma, 137

Ne tuck ah chik e mah, 817

*Ne tuck o ka, 138, *112

Ne tuk a chee, 29

Ne tuk ah che, 530

Ne tuk ah chik e ma, 383, 457, 828

N

Ne tuk ah chik e mah, 516

Ne tuk a ka, 472

Ne tuk e lubbe, 525

Ne tuk e mah, 537

Ne tuk la hubbee, or Ne tuk la tubbee, 27

Ne tuk o ka, 385, 499

R.C. *Nicholas, 280, 604, 970, R. c. 652, *230

Nigho, 319, 699, 761, 781, 791, R. c. 615, *138

Nighoe, 700

Nighor, 699

*Nigo, 74

Nik wah tubbee, 880

Nin nok ha cubbe, 503

Nin te hubbee, 389

Nish e om ah, 101

*Nitaannchubbe, 162

*Nitak, 188

*Nitakichi, 160

*Nitak tahubi, 130

Nit tuk ka chee, 695

Nit tuk kie chee, 696

Ni tuck a chick ma, 87

Ni tuck a sha, 911

Noachi, 144

*Noah, John, 172

Noahamba, 236

*Noahaya, Thompson, 250

Noah che, 382

Noahhonah, 491, 550, 558

Noah hon nah, 148

Noah ho yo, 89, 140, 149

Noah hubbe, 533

No a ho ka, 178

No a hona, 225, 406, 1008

R.C. No a no nubbee, 225, 1004, R. c. 661

Noah timah, 18

*Noah ton abbee, 246

Noah to nubbee, 406, 440

Noah tubbe, 527

*Noak falah, 52

*Noar a temer, 314

Noar tubbey, 705

No a tema, 235

No a te mah, 73

No a ti cha, 942

Noca chock ma, 197

Noca chuc ma, 163

Noc a ho la gee, 817, 825

Noc a maia, 169

Noc a maya, 167

Noc a na ho nubbee, 464

Noc any ho go tubbee, 1005

Noc a tubbee, 140, 149

Noch a chuk ona, 191

R.C. Noch e na chubbee, 632

Noch ish tia, 801

Noch is ti ah, 806

Noch steah, 763

No chubbe, 265

R.C. Nochubbee, 497, 799, R. c. 618

Noc is stut ah, 791

Nocka che tubbee, 403, 464

Nocka chook ma, 316

Nock a ho la go, 211, 213

Nock a howier, 732

Nock ah tubbe, 592

R.C. Nock ah tubbee, 376, R. c. 648

Nock ah tubbee, alias Billy Bob, 951, 952

Nock a la ho temah, 393

Nock a na chook mubbee, alias Noca na chook u, 156

Nock a na chubbee, 397, 400, 440

Nock a na eew lubbee, 1045

Nock a na hoka, 596, 997, 999

*Nock a na ho nubbee, 405, 463, *114

r.c. Nock a nee on tia, 629

Nock a ne lah, 396

Nock a nubbee, 398

r.c. Nock a sha, 603, 957, r. c. 651

Nock a stiah, 380

Nock a stiah to, 697

r.c. Nock a stu tah, 615

Nock a tuh na, 138

Nock a way chubbee, 393

Nock e ah chubbee, 398

Nock e chick e ma, 435

Nock e chook ma, 194

Nock e chuck e mah, 1020

r.c. Nock e chuck ma, 663

Nock e chuk ma, 1020

*Nock eh tubbee, 306

Nock e mah shubbee, 503

Nock e mam bee, 101

Nock e mia, 191

Nock e miah, 145

Nock e na chubbee, 860

r.c. Nock e na ho ka, 659

r.c. Nock e nan che, or Nock e na chubbee, 632

Nock e na tubbe, 547

Nock e ne tubbe, 448

Nock e ne tubbee, 148, 376, 570, 690

Nock en tubbee, 196

Nock en ucha kopah, 451

Nock e ny it tubbe, 106

Nock e ny it tubbee, 138

Nock eny tubbee, 117, 138

Nock eo tubbee, 555

Nock e sha, 450

Nock es ti yea, 137

Nock e ti ya, 113

Nock e wa tah, 375

Nock e wa tubbee, 442

Nocke way tah, 442

Nock ewny ho nubbee, 198

Nockey stiah, 110, 761, 781, 791

Nockey stiar, 711

Nockey stiare, 699, 710

Nockey stut tah, 708, 761

Nockey styer, 703, 704, 706, 708

r.c.*Nock hah tah, alias Yok hah tah, r. c. 627, *190

Nock ha tah, 140

Nock homa hajo, 198

Nock ho mah hah cho, 376, 597

Nock ice stior, 700

Nock in e tubbee, 142

*Nock ish te yah, 84

r.c.*Nock ish tia, 781, 800, 801, r. c. 617, *140

r.c. Nock ish ti ah, 383, 459, 715, 760, 802, r. c. 616, 617

Nock ish to nubbee, 405

Nock ish toonah, 385

*Nock ish too wah, 118

Nock is tei, 941

Nock ko wah, 140

*Nock nam ba, 314

Nock ne chubbee, or Na chubbee, 497

Nock ne la, 385

Nock ne oon ti yah, 848

*Nockni ho nabbee, 264

Nock o iah hab cho, alias Antabi, 803

Nock o mah, 89, 697

Nock o mah hah cho, 761, 781

Nock o mar hatcher, 697

Nock o mer hatcho, 699, 803

R.C. Nock o nah hah cho, 379, R. C. 615

R.C. Nock o nah hah cho, alias An ta bee, 615

*Nock o nah hak che, 142

Nock o she, 138

*Nock o wa cha hobbe, 246

Nock o wah, 149

Nock pa la sah, 422

Nock pa tah, 148

Nock pe tubbee, 110, 137

Nock shun ubbee, 146

Nock un am be, 502

Nock un am bee, 375, 442

Nocky stul tah, 380

Nocky styer, 709, 711

Noc ne a che, 142

Noc ne o ka, 814

Noc ne tubbee, 145

Noc ne ty ah, 146

Noc on tubbee, 142

Noc o she, 85

Noc pa la sa, 169

Noc pe ba sa, 196

*Noc pe la sa, 234, 316, *290

Noc pe te sa, 191

Noc um mah ho ka, 590

Noeemyea, 316

R.C. No e ho yo, 464, R. C. 682

No e kes ti yah, 113

*Noel, 80

*Nognah, 52

Nogoa, 916, 1046

No go am tubbee, 100, 101

No go wah cha hubbee, 147

Noh ho lubbee, 84

*Noh mis teah, 144

*No ho sa, 70

No ho to ma, 191

No ka, 148

Nok a ba lah, 26

Nok a chooh ma, 218

Nok a chubbee, 387, 478, 522, 814

Nok a ha jee, 317

Nok a ha la jee, 267

Nok ah ne ah, alias Ah ka ne ah, 508

Nok ah pe sah, 509

Nok a man cha ha ba, 384

Nok a man che ha ba, 462

Nok a man che habe, 517

Nok an a cubbee, 885

Nok an a tubbee, 884

Nok an e la, 531

Nok an e tubbe, 269

Nok an e tubbee, 219

Nok any taya, 274

Nok a shubbe, 521

Nok a tah, 591

Nok au a tubbe, 561

R.C. Nok au a tubbee, 636

Nok a wa la, 872

Nok cha tu nah, 387

Nok chuk ma bee, alias Chok ma bee, 27

Nok chu nubbe, 545

Nok e chook ma, 227

Nok eenam be, 144

Noke e ne ubbe, 506

Nokee stah shah, 442

Nok e filla hona, 271

Nok e gla, 825

Nok e hal tah, 386

R.C. Nok e hat tah, 470, 541, 879, 880, 881, R.C. 636

Nok e meia, 238

Nok e mo nubbe, 508

Nok e mo nubbee 497

Nok e na bah nubbee, 570, 690

Nok e nah tubbee, 447

R.C. Nok e nam be, 580, R. c. 675

Nok e mambee, 1081, 1082

Nok e na tam bee, 508

Nok e na tubbee, 454, 455

R.C. Nok e neah tubbee, 1107, 1108, R. c. 679

Nok e ne ene lubbe, 501

Nok e ne fanah, 386

Nok e ne fe nah, 475, 523

Nok e ne ham be, 539

Nok e ne lah, 492, 563

Nok e ne tubbe, 531

Nok e sha, 386, 475

Nok e stah shah, 379, 497

Noke stas hah, 95, 146

Noke wam lees, 145

*Noke wa tubbe, 529, *110

Noke wa ya, 196

Noke weah, 436

Noke we ga, 169

Nok ha ne ah, or Ah ka ne ah, 382

Nok hat ter, alias Yock hatel, 772

Nok hat ter, or Yok hatter, 783

Nok ho ma, 383, 457, 580

Nok ho mah, 525, 817

Nok ho ma ha jo, 385, 469, 491, 572

Nok ho tubbe, 530

Nok in ta hubbe, 574

Nok ish tah ok la tubbe, 507

Nok ish tah shah, 522

Nok ish taim ba, 556

Nok ish tam bee, 144, 517

Nok ish te mah yubbe, 507

Nok ish te ubbe, 522, 564

Nok ish te ubbee, 493

*Nok ish ti ah, 445, 805, *204

Nok ish ti chubbee, 478

Nok ish ti shubbee, 386

Nok ish ti ubbe, 529

Nok ish ti yah, 382, 492, 543

Nok ish to nah, 380, 505, 580

Nok ish too nah, 471, 573, 826

Nok ish to yah, 562

Nok ish tubbe, 517

Nok is ni ubbe, 503

Nok is ti yah, 378

Nok is tom be, 533

Nok is tom bee, 379

Nok is tubbe, 564

No kis tubbee, 493

Nok nam be, 531

Nok nath lubbe, 525

Nok ne a tubbee, 270

Nok ne chubbee, 492, 559

Nok ne con tia, 267

Nok ne een tubbe, 540

Nok nee la, 472, 826

Nok neen tubbe, 523

Nok neen tubbee, 384, 462

Nok ne hah tah, 557

Nok ne hah tubbee, 561

Nok ne ho tubbe, 507

Nok ne hut tubbe, 518

Nok ne la, 531

Nok nem i yubbe, 265

Nok ne o ka tubbee, 387, 474, 573

Nok ne ok te ma, 224

Nok ne ti yah, 516

Nok ne to nubbe, 509

Nok ne tubbee, 102, 484, 542, 560

Nok ne ty ah, 97

Nok ne ubbee, 478, 814

Nok ne un tubbee, 824

Nok nin che, 388, 575

*Nok oa hona, 172

Nok oan tubbe, 544

No ko she, 517

Nok o un cha hubbe, 545

R.C. Nok o wa la, 499, 635

Nok pa la, 234

*Nok pa la chobba, 264

Nok se kah tube, 504

Nok ue oka tubbee, 242

Nok um che, 484

No kus a ha joe, 115

Nok wa ya, 191

Nok we a che, 570

Nok weah, or Ish tonahkueah, or Ish tonok
weah, 535

*Nok we tah, 529, 60

R.C.*Nola, 158, 163, 191, 197, 218, 274, 376, 397,
403, 439, 450, 535, 566, 689, 948, R. c.
630, *18

Nola hona, 219

Nola tubbee, 270

Nole ham be, 561

Nole ham bee, 388

*Noley, 28

*Nolubbee, 58

No mak ha, 525, 865

No mak ka, 866

Nom cha, 140

R.c. No mokka, 866, R. c. 634

No natchie, 920

No nbbey, 707

Nonch o hoka, 705

R.c. Non ish ma hoyo, 788, R. c. 616

Non ish mi poka, 723

No nok komba, 471

Noo ka, 497

Nook chin tubbe, 525, 386, 470, 817, 827

Nook fa lah, 378, 448, 679, 1108, 1111, 1112,
1115, alias, Nookpalah, 548

Nook file hiyah, 543

Nook fille, or Fille, 517

Nook lan te mah, 872

Nook la tubbee, 457

Nook o an tubbee, 375

Nook tah lubbe, 525

Nook tah lubbee, 816, 827

Nook tah tubbee, 88

Nook ta lubbee, 382

Nook wam be, 575

Nook wa tubbe, 517

Nook weah, 375, 442

Nook we an tubbee, 146

Noon chubbe, 564, 530

R.c. Noon chubbee, 389, 493, 889, 890, R. c. 637

Noon tubbee, 142

Nooquo ah tubbee, 376

Noo sa chubbee, 139

No po le, or Un um pole, chubbe, 581

No que ah, 398

No quoah tubbe, 592

Nork tah tubbee, 137

Norman, 276

Nor tubbey, 711

Nosa cubbe, or Ahnosa cubbe, 587

*Nosa cubbe, 72

Nosa cubbee, 376

Nosa ka, 141, 217, 228, 318, 689, R. c. 669

Nosa kah, 378, 456, 533, 540, 566, 1051

No se ho nah, 402

*Nose kah, Joseph, 92

Nosh ko bo tak colo, 468

No sho bah, 383, 459, 526, 813, 826

R.c. No sho ba no wah, 667

*No sho bar no wah, 254

No tak un lubbee, 191

*No uobe, James, 18

R.c. Noubbee, 380, 761, 806, 1041, R. c. 666

*Noutbee, Joseph, 18

*No ubbi, 50

No ubee, 380

No wa, 196

R.c. *No wah, 147, 375, 468, 511, 571, 717, 807, 808, R. c. 619, *80, 102, 202

*No wahaya, Thompson, 258

No wah cha, 280

No wah chubbee, 398

No wah he mah, 504

No wah ho cubbe, 548

No wah ho ka, 381, 498, 505, 580, 584

No wah ho nah, 18, 446, 544, 606, 1132, 1133

No wa ho ge, 143

No wa ho ka, 265

*No wa ho ke, 66

*No wa hona, 212, 298, 302

*No wah o tina, 104

No wa ho yo, 190, 194, 199

No wah ta kah, 376, 595

No wah tam be, 516

No wah te ka, 89, 140

No wah te mah, 493, 564

No wah to ka, 149

R.c. No wah to nah, 407, 464, R. c. 673

R.c. No wah tubbee, 806, R. c. 615

No wa hubbe, 532

No watchie, 924, 1039

No wa temah, 582

No wa to nubbee, 190, 197

No wa yah, 592

*No wayke, 24

*No way oke, 114

R.c. Nubbee, 623

Nubbey, 724, 723

Nubbey, O. N., 703

*Nuch chubbe, 224

*Nuchobi, 136

*Nuchubbee, 138, 258

Nuck we han tubbee, 143

Nuk a mun che ha bee, 825

Nuk fai la, 101, 145

Nuk far la, 97

Nuk fille, 580

Nuk ham be, or Nok ho ma, 580

Nuk ham e, 389

Nuk ko ah ho mah, 491, 582, 583, 506

Nuk ko ahhonah, 580

Nuk ko a homah, 559

Nuk she pa ubbe,

Nuk sho pubbe, 516

Nuk we tah, 101

Nu la, 854

N

Oackcheetemah, 721, 722

Oakahhokta, 745

Oakahookte, 112, 138

Oakalainchehaba, 93

Oakataha, 138

Oakaunwa, 139

Oakchahtintubbe, 604

Oakchanahajo, alias Chanahjo, 317

Oakchanehajoe, 112, 138

r.c. Oakchatubbee, alias Oakchubbee, r. c. 624, 742, 743

Oakchetubbee, 945

Oakchiah, Tomaha, 138

r.c. Oakchubbee, alias Oakchatubbee, 742, 743, [R. c. 624]

Oakchubby Higertnier, 741

Oakeleyhubby, 713

Oakfatchushoma, 139

*Oakha, 29, *282

Oakilleanne, 98, 138

Oakillenuwa, 98, 139

r.c. Oakishtahla, 606, [R. c. 653,] 974

Oakishtanne, 137

Oakishtallawahhonah, 389, 590

Oakishtanne, 103

Oakishtapne, 113

Oakishtime, 137

Oakistacha, 450, 608

*Oakka, Jim, *284

Oaklaba, 93, 137

Oaklahhoca, 780, 806

r.c. Oaklahhokah, [R. c. 619,] 717

Oaklahhomah, or Cunneahchubbee, 376

Oaklahhomah, 961, 962

r.c. Oaklahhubbee, 380, [R. c. 618]

Oaklahhubbee or Oakleyhubbey, 713

Oaklahoma or Cunneahchubbe, 597

Oaklahonah, 1045, 1046

Oaklahyubbee, 832

Oaklatubbee, 978

Oaklayubbe, 544

Oaklayubbee, 378

r.c. Oakleah, [R. c. 619,] 781, 792

*Oaklehubbee, 781, 800, *144

Oakleyhubbee, 761

Oakleyhubbey or Oaklahhubbee, 713

Oakleyhubby, 713

Oaklieah, 380, 714, 761

*Oaklinhar, *190

Oaklishtyah, 97

Oaklohah, 375

Oaklowonah, 922

Oakoolanguhubbee, 139

Oakshouenab, 851

Oaktakahajoe, 138

Oaktokahujo, 98

Oakubamustubbee, 137

Oakulainchehaba, 138

Oakulamustubbee, 111, 112

Oanerhamer, 711

Oatheah, 459

Oathlacha, 384

Oathlache, 461, 515, 824

Oathlanahhona, 113

Oathlanahhonah, 137

*Oathtuche, *66

Obatisha, 1027

Occanatah, 147

Occhochahtubbe, 507, 580

Occhockahtubbee, 381

Oche, 523

O

Ochee, 532

*Ochinchahoomah, Capt., *154

Ochinchihoma, 50

Ochla, 465

Ochmchehoma, 75

Ochopotubbee, 943

Ockaamubbee, 148

Ockliyahcubbee, or Lewis Brown, 382

Ockwahchicah, 146

Ococha, or Yococha, 192

Ocopa, 197

Ocoppa, 190

Oelatema, alias Ioglatema, 273

*Ofahoma, 521, *32

Ofahomah, 824

*Ofchoma, *94

Ogemiah, 146

Oglaema, 218

Oglahama, 264

Oglahambee, 421

Oglahhambe, 548

Oglahhambee, 395

Oglahhonubbee, 391

Oglahhotemah, 399

Oglahmahka, 605

Oglahnonnah, 392

Oglahhotonah, 389

Oglahoyo, 239, 1023

Oglahubbe, 265

Oglamaka, 452

Oglamistubbe, 263

Oglamistubbee, 316, 261

Oglanowahcha, 406

Oglaona, 252

Oglaontanole, 239

Oglaoh a tubbee, 242

Oplapissa, 235

Oglatimah, 1031

Oglatiya, 986, 987, 988

R.C. Oglatiyah, 597, [R. C. 658]

Oglatona, 942

Oglaubbee, 397

Ogleaboka, 908, 910

Ogleahchubbe or Immoglachubbe, 586

R.C. Ogleahona, 178, [R. C. 667, 668,] 923

R.C. Ogleahoyo, [R. C. 663.] 1023

Ogleapissa, Widow, 167

Ogleashubbee, 270

Ogleastema, 272

R.C. Ogleatema, 276, [R. C. 665]

Ogleatubbee, 271

Oglehoner, 142

Ogleisteia, alias Akwatochubbee, alias Tish-
umustubbee, (alias Hushtomubbee,) 275

Oglemia, 401

Oglemionah, 405, 976

Ogleonah, 392

R.C. Ogleonetemah, R. c. 663

Ogletubbee, 421, 422, 423, 436

Ogleusta, 242

Oglihalah, 392

Oglinahona, 141

Oglio, 399, 422, 465

Oglishtiyah, 388, 484, 541

Oglockkayo, 465, 603

Oglootubbee, 148

Oglyeubbee, 148

Oguishtemah, 604

Ogvahotenah, 18

Ohahahtubbee, 551

*Ohahtubbee, *74, *76

Ohelanetubbee, 402

Ohelintubbee, 451

Ohlemagubbee, 106

*Oh-fcc-his-hemah, *108, *110

Ohnnah, 523

Ohnahhuntubbee, 140

*Ohona, *146

R.C. Ohonah, 382, 457, [R. C. 614], 816, 827

*Ohoner, 696, 695, *142

Ohontubbee, 385

Ohoochee, 139

*Ohosnkama, Capt., *202

Ohoyohonah, 145

Ohoyon, 18

*Ohoyonah, *230

Ohtiechemah, 525

Ohtoogahlantubbee, 591

Ohtuguto, 100

Ohuiintubbe, 530

*Ohwemtobbe, *168

Okacheah, 419

Okachee, 141

*Okahcheah, 399, 418, 509, *56

Okahcheahhonah, 530

Okahfamahhonah, 510

Okahhookta, 788

R.C. Okahhooktah, R. c. 616

Okahotemah, 591

Okahinchukmah, 507

*Okahnoloah, *110

Okahnowa, 459

Okahnowah, 383, 813

Okahnullee, 442

Okahomah, 454

*Okahotimah, *108

Okahshomah, 442

Okahstahna, 442

Okahstamah, 533

Okahstanah or Okahstemah, 378

Okahstemah or Okahstanah, 378

Okahstemahebahpalubbee, 442

Okahtahonah, 531

Okahubbe, 524

*Okaiache, *320

Okainchinkmah, 553

Okaintola, 243

Okaishbalala, 275

Okaishtemah, 574

Okaishtiemah, 516

Okaknowah, 529

Okalaanchahubbee, 471

Okalaauchahubbe, 525

Okalacha, or Ishtopanubbee, 385

Okalache, or Ishtopahnubbe, 522

Okalache, or Ishtopahnubbee, 826

Okalahanchahubbee, 385

Okalahtubbe, 580

Okalainchehabee, 826

Okalaminyubbee, 147

Okalanchehubbe, 265

Okalanchehubbee, 316

Okanaah, 442

Okanowa, 1097

Okashahhonah, 1081, 1082

Okatolahonah, 530

Okayomah, 148, 567, 689

Okchah [for Emalle,] 381

Okchah, or Elahokchubbe, 505

Okchah, 580

O

Okchanehajo, 460, 461, 462, 475, 817, 825

*Okchameharjo, *258

R.C. Okchatubbee, 277, 385, 471, 514, 517, 525, 542, [R. c. 678,] 826, 1097, 1098

Okchatunah, 478, 542, 814

*Okchaya, Wincey, *210

*Okchaya, Capt., *240

Okchehatonah, 531

*Okchetimah, 503, *48

Okchilehoka, 501

Okchilla, 146

Okchitema, 108, 145

Okchubbe, 501, 580

Okchubbee, 146

Okchunehajo, 463

R.C. Okechatubbee, R. c. 646

Okechetubbee, 946, 947

Okechubbee, 442

Okehokhokta, 744

*Okehumma, *210

Okeelishtiah, 474, 814, 387

Okeinchuckma, 575

Okelahemah, 523

Okelahhemah, 384, 462, 824

Okelemiah, 814, 827

Okelenla, 29

Okelishtiyah, 517

Okemeia, 265

R.C. Okemiyah, 375, 528, [R. c. 633,] 862

*Okesteyah, *68

Okfocheshemah, 562

Okfoochishomah, 390, 446, 492

*Okfochush, *182

Okhahchetah, 384, 491, 558

*Okhataya, *280

Okiacha, 376

R.C. Okiacha, alias Tahnappehoja, 593, [R. c. 648]

Okiacha, alias Tahnuppehahja, 953, 954

Okilishtime, 935

Okimiyah, 862

*Okimiahona, *298

Okintimah, 580

R.C. Okintolahhonah, 580, [R. c. 678,] 1103, 1104

Okintolahonah, 507

Okintumlahonnah, 146

Okishmintah, 143

Okishtahna, 535

Okishtalohahhoka, 493, 565

Okishtamahhomah, 493, 565

Okishtambee, 145

*Okishtane, *278

Okishtantah, 533

Okishtemah, 508

Okishtime, 537

Okishtimah, 144

Okishtiyah, or Ishtiah, 524

*Okishtolla, *176

R.C. Okishtonah, R. c. 674, 1078, 1079

*Okishtulawahhonah, *60

Okishwakeia, 222

Okistille, 383, 459

Okistahbola, 497

Okistahchokmahoka, 525

Okistablahonah, 531

Okistambee, 553

Okistemonah, 547

Okistiah, 383, 459, 813

Okistiayh, 531, 826

Okkalah, 148

Okla, 145

Oklaba, 825

Oklabba, or Tuppenahoma, 319, 364

*Oklabe, *48

*Oklabi, *158

*Oklabi, Davis, *194

Oklache, or Ishtopanubbee, 471

Oklachehoka, 471, 530, 826

*Oklachehoyo, *246

Oklachekoka, 385

Oklachenoyo, 533

*Oklachi, *180

Oklachubbee, 145

Oklahala, 266

*Oklahambe, Impsy, *220

Oklahantubbee, 584

Oklahatubbee, 143

Oklahbe, 535

Oklahbee, 379, 454

R.C. Oklahche, [R. c. 675], 1085, 1086

Oklahchubbe, 583

Oklahchubbee, 553

Oklahelubbee, 501

Oklahemah, 492, 562, 572

Oklahhamah, 380, 508, 580

Oklahhemah, 491

Oklahhonah, 499, 695

Oklahhoonah, 517

Oklahhotemah, 580

Oklahhotubbee, 381, 442, 502

Oklahhoya, 538

Oklahimah, 498, 144

Oklahkahhoyo, 690

Oklahlea, 448

Oklahmeashah, 504, 584

Oklahmia, 448

Oklahmiah, 505

Oklahogo, 145

Oklahoka, 378, 549

Oklahoma, 503

Oklahomah, 378

*Oklahona, *250

*Oklahonah, 384, 516, 531, 554, *270

Oklahonubbe, alias Mukonubbe, 517

*Oklahotubbee, 224, 377, 507, 580, *56

Oklahoyea, 145

Oklahshehonah, 518

Oklahshubbe, 580

Oklahtimah, 561

Oklahtubbe, 504, 577, 579

Oklahtubbee, 381

Oklahubbe, 514

*Oklahunma, *210

*Oklahushta, *124

Oklahyahcubbe, 445

Oklahyahhonah, 520

Oklahyo, 379, 454

Oklahyoka, 448

Oklaishtiyah, 382

Oklakahhoyo, 569

Oklakatubbee, 270

Oklakinah, 571

Oklamba, 524

Oklamiah, or Ahmiah, 579

Oklamiyea, 145

Oklamyyea, 144

Oklanaka, 81

Oklanchehabee, 814

*Oklanowa, *266

Oklanowah, 242, 462, 523, 824

Oklaonah, 563, 592

O

*Oklarbommar, *202

*Oklashabbee, *316

*Oklashtubbee, *290

Oklatea, 243

Oklateaubbee, 146

*Oklatema, 228, *236

Oklatona, 277, 943

Oklatonah, 491, 530

*Oklattubbe, *208

Oklatubbee, 144

Oklaunchehabee, 825

Oklayo, 571

Okleaune, 524

Oklehheyubbe, 523

Oklehhonah, 696

Oklehoka, 271, 317

Oklemagubbee, 145

Oklemahcheahhonah, 520

Oklemahyubbee, 375

Oklemeia, 268

*Oklemeyubbee. *308

Oklemiubbee, 552

Oklemiyah, 387, 474, 529

Oklemonah, 566, 689

Oklemultah, 387

Oklemuttah, 474, 532, 814, 826

*Oklenowa, Capt., *288

Okletunah, 942

Okleubbee, 190, 197

Okliah, 384, 574, 824

Okliah by Okahookte, 461

Oklihoka, 523

Oklikhowich, 385

Oklimeubbee, 442

Oklishtia, 501

Oklishtiah, 146, 377

*Oklishtona, *284

Okliyah, 525

Okliyokubbe, 526

Oklockkayo, 147

Oklohah, 532, 567, 687

Oklohubbe, 542

Oklokintubbe, 523

Oklomanra, 196

Oklonetemah, 1023

Oklongehubbee, 469

Oklubbee, 144, 263

*Oklucla, *186

Okluhah, 377

Okluhantubbe, 509

Okluhantubbee, 382

Okluhubbe, 530

Oklumgeehubbee, 827

Oklungeehubbe, 523

Oklungeehubbee, 385

Oklungehubbee, 817

*Oklunla, *188

*Okmowahonah, *154

*Okohhotimah, *98

Okpeahubbee, 237

Okshowena, 319, 248

R.C. Okshowenah, R. C. 630

Oktahe, 143

Oktokahajo, 814, 825

Okulamustubbee, 825, 817

Olahhahucha, 587

Olahja, 834

Olahjah, 375

Olahla, 397

Olahlintubbee, 405

Olalatubbee, 192

*Olasechubbi, *22

*Olasechubi, *22

Olbiya, 117

Oleahhowkey, 801

Olioka, 499

Oliver, 50

Olubbetona, 219

Onnahhuntubbee, 690

R.C. Omahhoka, R. c. 634

Omahuska, 587

Omahteah, 465

Omaka, 139

Omalehona, 228

*Omehtubbee, *250

Omhtubbee, 690

Ommahteah, 395

Omolletubbee, 379, 455, 501

R.C. Omonubbee, R. c. 616, 788

Ona, or Nanomahona, 191

R.C. Ona, 197, 600, [R. c. 655,] 979

Onaaxta, 92

R.C. Onacha, 406, [R. c. 663,] 1014, 1015

Onache, 223

*Onachehoyoh, *226

*Onachehoyo, *234

*Onachihoyo, *92

Onachubbe, 520

Onachubbee, 190, 196, 393, 838

Onah, 148, 190, 594, 1052

Onahaambee, 163

Onahaga, 274

Onahago, 117

R.C. Onahajah, R. c. 630

Onahaker, 711

Onahamba, 1002

Onahambe, or Miyahtubbee, 593

R.C. Onahambee, 18, 157, 266, 389, 596, [R. c. 659,] 997, 998, 1000

Onahatubbee, 86, 137, 382, 520

Onahawbee, 159

Onahaya, 320

Onahayo, 238

*Onachale, *46

Onahchatubbee, or Icksanampulli, 398

Onahchehoyo, 523

Onahchetah, 384, 462, 825

Onahchetimah, 522

Onahchubbee, 392, 442

Onahema, 266

Onahhachubbee, 391

Onahhamah, 585

R.C. Onahhemah, 516, 521, [R. c. 617,] 803, 804

R.C. Onahhoca, R. c. 619, 791, 792, 737

Onahhoca, alias Elahtehemah, 738

Onahhoka, 866

Onahhokata, 1120, 1121

R.C. Onahhoketa, [R. c. 682]

Onahhotubbee, 816, 827

R.C. Onahhoyo, 380, [R. c. 619,] 781, 803

Onahhoyo, or Onahowior, 715

Onahhubbe, 560

Onahhubbee, 384, 405

Onahinlubbe, 501

*Onahinta, *312

Onahlahonah, 1031

*Onahlihokey, *274

Onahochubbee, 139

*Onahoga, 111, 139, *152

R.C. Onahoka, 139, 167, 169, 178, 191, 200, 209, 235, 237, 251, 271, 316, 382, 521, 525, [R. c. 667], 816, 827, 865, 1044

O

R.C. Onahoketa, R. C. 669

Onahhoketa, 1049, 1050

Onahokia, 139

R.C. Onahoma, 669

Onahona, 228

Onahookta, 542

*Onahota, *310

Onahowior, or Onahhoyo, 715

R.C. Onahoyo, 167, 192, 196, 265, 169, 319, [R. C. 662], 1009, 1010

Onahta, or Unatta, 580

Onahtah, 515

Onahteah, 377, 402, 442

Onahtenah, 535

Onahtemah, 510

Onahtickah, 587

Onahtomtubbee, 422

R.C.*Onahtubbee, 379, 402, 572, [R. C. 615,] [R. c. 672,] 761, 781, 1067, 1068, 1069, *62

Onahtubby, 698, 803

*Onahubbee, *202

R.C. O-na-ka, alias Im-ma-ka, 668

Ona ka, alias Immaka, 932

O-na-kah, 142

R.C. On-a-nak he mah, 614

On-a-nah-he-mah, 808

Onan che hubbe, 532, 542

Onanta, 169

O nan ta hoyuo, 137

Onantoonah, 568

Onantubbee, 491

*Onantubbee, 248

O na ok ta, 141

Ona pambee, 162

*Onarle hona, 202

Onas-koo-nah, 386, 470, 817, 827

Onata, 167

Onata-cha, 389, 1001, *134

O-na-ta-ha, 148

Onata hoyo, 273

Onatambee, 18

Onatea, 184, 186, 191, 196

Onateah, 535

Onat ho ka, 436

*Onatima, 122

*Onatina, 122

Onatona, 269

Onatona, alias Matona, 276

Ona ton tubbee, 200, 209

Onatubbe, 593

*Onatubbee, 85, 139, 167, 169, 190, 194, 196, 222, 234, 273, 316, 610, *214

Onatubbee, alias Jack, 235

*Onchale, *134

On-che-le, 146

*Onchetubbe, 40

O-ne-ah-chubbee, 838

Oneche, 184, 186

Onechehoyo, 1061

One ho te mah, 401

Onemiyah, 528

On er Hamer, 708, 711

One tamba, 1051

O-nia-chubbee, 838

*Onish tubbee, 202

Onnah hoyo, 690

*On narka, 232

*Onnatachi, 110

On-no-namer, 694

Onntambee, 690

Onnubbee, 184

Onoche, 243, 225

*Onochi, 176

*Onochitobi, *152, *186

R.C. O no che ho yo, 671

ONE CHE HUBBE, 523

*Onohambi, 134

Onohhoyo, 419

Onokfullatubbee, alias Fillatubbee, 317

Ono la hoyo, 1049

R.C. O-no-le-ho na, 665

Onoocha, or Chubbee, 464

Onook cha, or Onookchubbe, 608

Onook chubbe, or Onookcha, 608

Onopoko, 196

On Or Timer, 707

*Onotambe, 162

Ono-tub-bee, 148

Ontacubbee, 569, 690

*On ta hi kubbe, 28

Ontah e mah, 522

*Ontahikubbee, 322

Ontamba, 282

Ontei tubbe, 522

Onte mah ka, 742, 743

Ontemahoyo, 525

*Ontes he habbee, 232

On-ti o mah, 383, 459, 520, 530, 813

On to bah na, 514

O-nub-bee, 141, 186, 192, 198, 393, 417, 418, 419, 979

Onubee, 586

*Onut ok cha ya, 248

*Onutechehubbee, 280

On wah ka, 178

Onwakubbe, 565

Onx ha tubbee, 457

Oohah tubbe, 528

R.C. Oo-kah-hubbee, 679, 1107, 1108

Oon-a-chub-bee, 138

Oo-na-ha-ga, 853

Oon-a-ha-gah, 138, 814, 825

Oonahaka, 212

Oon aham ba, 517

Oon-ah-cha-hubbe, or Al moon Tubbe, 579

Oon ah cheah tubbe, 505

Oonahcho hambe, 513

Oonah chubbe, 502, 504

Oon-ah-ha-tubbee, 381

Oonahhe chubbe, 575

Oon ah he mah, 492, 512, 563

Oonah he tubbe, 504, 580

Oonah hookta, 493, 565

Oon ah hook tah, 390, 571

Oonah ho nah, 484, 540

Oonah hubbe, 559

R.C. Oon ah ta cha, 660

Oonah ta che, 596

Oonah tubbe, 501, 538, 580, 596

Oonah tubbee, 402

*Oonah huttubbee, 80

Oo-na-in-chi-ha-bee, 139

Oonannchetubbee, 690

Oon a tam bee, 404

Oon a tom bee, 140

Oo na tubbe, 525, 562

Oonanche tubbe, 568

Oon both tubbe, 597, [R. c. 660]

Oon both tubbee, 999, 1000, 1091

Oon cha la, 501

Ooncha le, 376

Ooncubbee, alias Aueubbee, 276

Ooncubbee, alias Ancubbee, 317

Oone mi yah, 471

Oonge tubbee, 139

Oon hah tubbe, 501

Oon he kub bee, or An cubbee, 814

Oon hick ah, 518

Oonishe ho yo, or Oontishehoyo, 598

Oonkahubbee, 270

Oon nah, 394, 439

Oon nah chubbee, 377

Oon nah ho ka, 404, 405, 424

Oon nah ho nah, 388

Oon nah tone tubbee, 394

Oon nah tubbee, 378, 442, 492

*Oon nah noke, *72

Oon nan che ah tubbe, 584

R.C. Oon nish e ho yo, or Oon tish e ho yo, 649

Oon ish e ho yo, 960, 961, 962

Oon nock a mah, 598

Oon noh toon tubbee, 423

Oon nubbe, 584

Oon nubbe, or E lo nubbe, 579

Oon nubbee, 381, *52

Oon tacha, 271

*Oon tachea, 206, 208, 223, 316, *90

Oon tah hah yo tubbee, 393

Oon tah hoyo, 395

Oon tah yubbee, 401

Oon ta ka, 138

*Oon ta kah, 377, 448, 501, *72

Oon ta mah chubbee, 395

Oon tan te mah, 891

Oon tan tubbee, 192, 193, 243, 330, 407, 408, 435

Oon ta tubbe, 507

Oon teah tubbe, 503, 530, 537

Oon te ah tubbee, 386, 476, 825

Oon te ah ubbee, 223

Oon te ka ah, 381, 510

Oon te mah, 530, 540

Oon tem e yah honah, 379

*Oon ti ah tubbee, *56

Oon ti e mah, 523

Oon ti kah, 584

Oon tim mi hoka, 422

Oon ti o ma, 461

Oon ti o mah, 383

R.C. Oon tish a tubbee, 642

Oon tish e hoya, or Oon ish i hoyo, 598

Oon tish e hoyo, or Oon nish e hoyo, 649

Oon tish e hoyo, 961, 962

Oon tish e tubbe, 256

Oon tish e tubbee, 916, 917, 918

Oon tock ah ne ubbee, 595

Oon to tubbee, 1030

Oon ubbe, 507, 518, 531

R.C. Ooon ubbee, 616

Oon wack ah tubbee, 389

Oon waka, 273

Oonwa tubbee, or Watubbee, 493

Oo thah, 383, 515, 813, 826

Oo ush nahhoka, 586

Oou tun ioka, 391

Opacaga, 211, 214

*Opa hullo, 12

O paish ta lubbee, 661

O peah kubbe, 531

O peah tubbee, 399

O pe ni chubbe, 204

Oppa sah he mah, 397

Oppo ca nah, 190

*Opum e chubbe, 228

O quah ha nah, 593, 610

Oquah tan, 396

Ora hoka, 457

Or la la ubbee, 197

*Orley, Davis, 50, 52

Os cuma, or Iscuma, 207

Oshe hona, 138

Oshe unwa, 139

Osh he homa, alias Atokolia, 925

Osh ka na homa, 34

Osh ta hah ba, 514

Os tubbe, 527

O tah hoka, 138

O ta kubbe, 522

O tam bee, 899

O ta nubbee, 231, [R. c. 640,] 905

Ota she mah, 535

Ota ta homa, 190

Ote ah tubbee, 522

Oteman sha, 18

Oth, William, 28

*Othla, 170, 196, 236, 1014, *100

Oth la chubbe, 501

Oth lah honah, 504

Oth lack a hoyo, 497

Oth te yea, or Ho tan yah, 388

Oth ti ya, 580

Otim po nubbee, 400, 451

Oti nah ough, 139

Otish te mah, 580

Oto la tubbee, 141

*Ott, William, 88

Ott, Willie, 88

Otubbee tonah, 397

OUN A CHUB BEE, 148

Oun ah hantubbee, 569

Oun ah hoyo, 569

Oun a tone tubbee, 209

Oun ka ha jo, 140

Oun nah ta, 389

Oun ta cha yah, 141

Oun tah cheah, 544

Oun tam be, 568

Oun tea tubbee, 140, 147, 149

Oun toa tubbee, 85

Oun wak hubbee, 390

Oun wak ubbee, 445

*Ourtier, 68

Oute kah, 522, 813, 826

Outh la hubbee, 513

Ou ti o mah, 826

Outeah, 141

Ou wak ubbee, 493

O wa chee, 141, 419

O wah teah, 419

*Owaka, 294

Owan tubbee, 100, 147

Owatea, 192

O wa teah, 141

O wa to ka, 148

Owa tubbe, 528

Owa tubbee, 28

Oweeche, 440

Ownah, 1051

Own ah hoyo, 1009

O

Pa ah le che, 144

*Pacamah, Capt., *160

Pa chubbe, or Lahpa chubbe, 528

Pa Co Chub bee, 146

Pa co nubbee, 179, 180

R.C. Pa e than tubbee, alias Pul kin tubbee,[R. c. 614,] 696

Paetha Tubbe, 695

Page, Nehemiah, 423

R.C. Pa ka la tubbee, [R. c. 617,] 804

Pahaley tubbey, 711

R.C. Pa ka lin go, 665

Pah bubbee, 378

Pah cha, 1070

Pah ha cho, 393, 414, 415

Pah ha mah, 394

Pah his tiah, 141

Pah ko ke ta, 421

Pah ho timah, 1011, 1012

*Pahima, *184

*Pah lah, 147, 376, 547, 448, *48

Pah lah nalthlubbe, 448

Pah lame tubbee, 1032

Pah lam ma, 397

*Pahle, *220

Pah la cha, 580

Pah lubbe, 456, 536

R.C. *Pahlubbee, 157, 166, 193, 197, 215, 218, 232, 316, 437, 464, 467, [c. c. 622], 717, 760, 762, *78, 140

Pah na, 192, 193, 199, 242, 393, 379, 418, 435, 439, 448

Pah nah, 500

*Pah ne, 87, *94, 178

Pah nee, 419

Pah nete, 591

Paholema, 319

Pa ho nah, 109

Pa ho ta ma, 169

Pa ho te ma, 192, 238

Pa ho to ma, 196

Pah sah che mah, 552

Pah sah ho nah, 505

Pah sha co no, 382

R.C. Pah shah ho te ma, 400, 599, [R. c. 657], 982

Pah sha ho to na, 568, 690

Pah sha im is ha, 141

R.C. Pah shan nubbee, R. c. 624

R.C. Pah shan nubbee, alias Pah sho nubbee, 624

Pah she ca nah, 387

Pah sho nah, 398

Pah sho mubbee or Pars Han Mubbey, 741

Pah sho mubbee, 761

*Pah sho nah, 593, *52

R.C. Pah sho nubbee, alias Pah shan nubbee, 624

Pah sho nubbee, 380

R.C. Pah shishtam bee, 605, [R. c. 653]

Pah shish to mah, 937, 938

R.C. Pah shish wah ki ah, 380, [R. c. 622,] 718, 719, 761

Pah shish wah me ah, 718

Pah shish wak ki ah, 783

Pah shis wak ki ah, 780

R.C. Pa ho ta ma, 167, [R. c. 662]

Pah ta tubbe, 530

*Pah te chubbee, *78

Pah tubbee, 191

Pahua, 319

Pahyah, 377, 554, 591

Paia sha tubbee, 474

*Pain, Robert, *280

P

Pakeli, 934

*Paknobi, *184

Pa la chubbe, 535

R.C. Pa la ha tubbee, [R. C. 619,] 803

Pa lah ha tubbe, 599

R.C. Pa lah ha tubbee, R. C. 657

Pa lah ho tubbee, 984

Pa lah hubbe, 530

Pa la ka tubbe, 509

Pala ma hoka, 274

Palan tubbee, 281

Palasa, 117, 139, 167

Pa la sa honah, 562

Pa la sah honah, 492

Pa le chub bee, 137

Pale sa hoka, 276

Pa lin go, 1033

R.C. Pal lan tubbee, [R. c. 671,] 1063

Pallas, 50

Pal lum e kab ba, 877

Pal lum e kub bee, 878

*Pally, *142, 186

Pal ma, 142

Palm tam be, 389

Pa lubbee, 108, 145

Pam bohla, 143

Pam filla, 190, 197

Pam fille, 184, 216

Panacha, 220

*Panah, *46

Pana linge, 229

Pan che michi, 179

Pan er tub by, 803

R.C. Pan es tub bee, R. C. 615

Panes Tubey, 697

Pan ney, 145,

R.C. Pan sha chubbee, R. c. 668

Pan sha cona, 117, 138

Pan sha misha, 251

*Pan sheoka, *66

Pan she tubbe, 252

Pansh ik ish o, 386, 470

Pansh ish to nah, 825

Pan shis tonaho yo, 1023

Pansh ish to nubbee, 474, 827

Panshish tuna, 212

Panshisktuna, 317

Pansh lock a nah, 591

Pan sho ak chiah, 110, 117, 138

Pansh oak chi ah, Senior, 137

Pansh oak chiat, Jr., 111

Pan sh ok chi, 472

Pansh ok chi ah, 383, 385, 470, 471, 473, 523

Pan so ak chiah, 111

R.C. Panth la chubbe, 597, [R. c. 658]

Panth la chubbee, 385, 389

Panubbee, 242, 514

*Paple, *220

Parah a chubbee, 922

Par han nubbee, or Par sha nubbee, 783

*Parker, Johnson, *28

Parkin tubbey, 703

Parlubbee, 792, 793

Par lubbey, 781, 785

Parlubbi, 117

Parluby, 379

*Parnubbe, *42

Parres, Antony, 18

Parsh ok chi ah, 457

Pars ham mubbee, 742

Pars han mubbee, 743

Pars Han Mubbey, or Pah sho mubbee, 741

Pars Han Mubbey, 741

Pars han nubbee, alias Par sho nubbee, 742

Pars han nubby, alias Pa sho nubbee, 743

Par sho uubbe, 780

Par sho Nubbee, alias Pars han nubbee, 742

Par sho nubbee, alias Pars han nubby, 743

Par sho nubbee, or Par han nubbee. 783

Par Tubbee, 698

*Paruxte, *210

Pa sa cha hoyo, 459

Pa sa che ho yo, 383, 826, 813

Pa sa chubbee, 502, 547

Pa sa chubbee, 406

Pas ah bam be She tam be, 581

Pa sah chee nah, 982

Pas ah ho mah, 459

Pa sah ho nah, 383, 394, 492, 518, 564

*Pas a hoka, *172

*Pas a honah, *70

Pa sah te mah, 525

Pa sah tom ba, 517

R.C. Pasah tonah, 599, [R. C. 657,] 982

R.C. Pasah tubbee, 602, [R. C. 650,] 964

Pasalukanubbi, 50

Pasamba, 1005

Pa sam bee, or Ah pa sam bee, 464

Pa san tubbee, 178

R.C. Pa sa tubbee, 405, 463, 516, [R. C. 631,] 859

Pas cumme, 518

Pashah honah, 544

Pash ah thlocco, 817

Pash a ma ta ha, 574

R.C. Pa sham ba, alias Co pah sha, [R. C. 617,] 798, 803

Pa sham ba, alias Cop a sah, 791

Pash am ba, alias Cop a sa, 718, 719, 720, 806

Pasham ba, 781

Pa shan ge hobbee, 108

*Pas hat tubbee, *314

Pash co chubbee, 401

*Pas hea hook ta, *90

*Pashe banowah, *264

Pashe mah, 690

*Pashemastubbe, *42

*Pas heonah, *64

Pash homah, 587

Pash i o nah, 387, 478, 827

*Pashish foiah, *118

R.C. Pashish toniah, 258, 319, [R. C. 645]

Pash min ja, 26

Pashone sha ubbe, 580

*Pash po ko ba fa, *298

Pash she co nah, 827, 478, 814

Pashubbee, or Muskogee, 319

Pa shun ge hub bee, 142

Pashuthloko, 317

Pas it ti yah or Choktahhomah, 515

Passahhonah, 813, 826

R.C. Pasubbee, or Muscogee, 250, [R. C. 666]

*Pasubbee, 275, 141, 403, 421, *172

Pa subbee, alias, Muscogy, 1037

*Patcha, *310

*Paterson, Hamon, *260

R.C.*Patsey, 239, [R. C. 663,] 1024, *30

*Patterson, Harman, *232

Patterson, James, alias Kanaintubbe, 255

R.C. Patterson, James, alias Canantubbee, R. C. 641

Patterson, James, 908

*Patterson, Mrs., *232

Patubbe, 514

*Patubbee, 497, *112

R.C. Paunch e ko no, 390, 445, [R. C. 683,] 1129, 1130

Paunch hi o nah, 445

Paunch ish tubbee, 445

Paunch tunab, 507

*Pausha hoyo, *30

Paushamisna, 319

Pau she chubbee, 922, 923

Paush ik isho, 573, 817

*Paushi meshi, *266

Pau shi ona, 275

Paush ish to nub bee, 814

Paushistuna, 312, 274

Paush ok chia, 515

Paush ok chi ah, 817, 826, 828

Paushonubbee, 270

Paush u nub bee, 139

Pauth la chubbee, 986, 987, 988

Paw shish tam bee, 973

*Paxton, William, *82

*Pa ya ha ke, *44

Pay a ta, 111

*Paya tubbee, *300

*Payne, Robert, *138

*Payne, Thomas, *22

*Payostobi, *128

Paysubey or Muegey, 1037, 1038

*Payton, Tecumseth, *212

Pe ah hubbe, 504

R.C. Pe al la, R. C. 644

Pealle, 257

Pealley, 141, 929

Pealy, 89

Peas a chim ma, 95, 146

Peas tubbe, 533

*Pebnorth, Henry, *184

Pebworth, Henry, 18

Pe ci timah, 887

Peelah tubbee, 567, 689

*Peggy, 140, 405, 403, *30

Pe ha tubbe, 516

Pe hele tubbe, 561

Pe he tubbee, 384

Pe his tubbe, 544

Pe lan ah che, 505

Pe la tubbe, 529

*Pe la tubbee, *314

Pe le chubbe, 560

Pe le ham be, 504, 584

Pe le ham bee, 381

Pe le ma, 1052

Pele tub bee, 138

Pella, 401

Pel le sah ho nah, 581, 504

Pelubb, 497

Pe lubbee, 385, 497

Pennis sah, 396

Penola, Perry, 248

*Perkins, Davis, *206

*Perkins, Mrs. Elcy, *206

*Perkins, Jane, *234

*Perkins, Mary, *246

R.C. Perry, Amy, 254, [R. C. 669,] 1045

Perry, Anoba, 203

Perry, Anola, 173

*Perry, B. F., *292

*Perry, Benj. F., *312

Perry, Berriman, 247

Perry, Betsy, 247

*Perry, Edmond, 247, *292

Perry, Edmund, 178, 245

*Perry, Elba, *262

*Perry, Eli, *218

*Perry, Emily, *68, 70, 72

*Perry, Fany, *36

*Perry, Forbis, *122

*Perry, Hardy, 179, 172, 174, 249, *38, 44

Perry, Haslin, 899, 900

*Perry, Isaac, 28, 178, 247, 899, 900, *88, 242, 292

Perry, James, 46, 47, 49, 50, 77, 140, 142, 170, 171, 172, 174, 179, 247

Perry, Joe, 176, 177, 179, 249

Perry, John, 27, 47, 170, 172, 177, 178, 179, 245, 249

Perry, Johnson, 247

*Perry, Joseph, 140, 141, 170, 171, 172, 179, 202, 203, 247, *292

Perry, Levi, 171

*Perry, Lewis, 179, *36

*Perry, Moses, 46, 50, 78, 140, 170, 172, 174, 254, 319, [R. C. 669,] 1048, *218, 232, 254

*Perry, Nail, *44

Perry, Nat., 178

Perry, Ned, 27, 171

Perry, Penola, 319

Perry, Polly, alias Frazier, 179

*Perry, Rhoda, *38

Perry, Sampson, 254, 899, 900, 901

Perry, Sarah, 170

R.C. *Perry, Sinah, 245, 254, 319, [R. C. 639], 889, 900, 901 1047, *256

Perry, Siney, 137

*Perry, Solomon, *38

Perry, Stephen, 247

Perry, Susan or Widow, 27

Perry, Widow or Susan, 27

Perry, Susan, 170, 172, 174

*Pesalitubi, Basil, *182

*Pesatukuppy, Ellick, *230

*Pesachatubbee, *94

Pe sa che honah, 500

*Pes achobi, *128

Pe sah chick e mah, 873

*Pe sah o chobbe, *320

Pe sa hock lah, 141

*Pe sah onubbee, *274

Pe sah hoonah, 804

*Pesali hoke, *146

Pe sa mock tubbee, 140

*Pesatachahubbe, *212

*Pesatener, *310

Pe shubbee, 111

*Pesotabbee, 286

*esotobby, *210

*Pessoe he hoyo, *96

Pestage, 266, 319

*Peta, Laite, *282

Petah, 587

Petah ah mah, 539

Pe tam o tubbe, 455, 536

Pe tam o tubbee, 378

R.C. *Peter, 27, 178, 250, 279, 405, [R. c. 665,] [R. c. 672,] 1071, 1072, *278

*Peter, Sarah, *320

*Peter, Simon, alias Nakintahubbe, *2

*Peter, Simon, *30, 194, 296, 304

Pe yah hoka, 525

*Peyton, Tecumseh, *136

Phal a mah, 147

Phal a mo ah, 147

Pha lummatemah, 916

Pha nubbe, 521

Phebe, 279

Phe la che hoka, 510

Phe la ti ah, 27

Phe lim tah, 580

Phe line tah, 382

Phe lin tah, 507

Phila moon tub bee, 142, 1018

Phila tah, 149

Philatub, 89

Phil e ah ho yo, 499

Phil l cut che, 825

*Philee k gee, *56

Phil e ma hubbe, 517

Phil e mah hubbee, 826

Phil e ma tub bee, 142, 385, 92

*Phile Montubbee, 82, 469, 817, *224

Philemohtunah, 540

Phil e moon te kah, 383, 529

Phile moon tubbe, 542

R.C. Phile moon tubbee, 383, 385, 456, 457, 512, 517, [R. c. 634,] 817, 827, 828, 869, 870, 871

*Philemoon tukah, *102

Phil e mo yah, 382, 457, 52, 5, 816, 827

*Philintah, *60

Phila moon tubbee, 101, 147

Phil la mo to nah, 862

Phil la tah, 140

Phille ah, 397

Phil le kah ja, 424

Phille ka jah, 401

Phillemah, 417, 418, 419, 394

*Phille mah hayo, *280

Phille ma hobbe, 93, 139

Phil le mo ah, 93, 137

Phil le mon tubbee, 106, 138

Phille moon tubbee, 93

Phille te ah, 440

Phille ti ah, 402

Phil lin tah, 143

Phillis, 223

Phill ma hobbee, 110

Phil lubbee, 468

R.C. Phillum ma tubbe, 596, [R. c. 659,]

Phil lum ma tubbee, 997, 999

Phil lu moon tub bee, 137, 139

Philo man tubbee, 1016

Phi te ti yeh, 141

Phlo pul la, 381

R.C. Phoebe, 257, [R. c. 644,]

Piahoma, 184, 185, 186, 216, 217

Pialle, 319

R.C. Pianeta hubbe, 596, [R. c. 659,]

Piane ta hubbee, 997, 979

Pic ci te mah, 887

Pic ci tomah, 499

Pick a bah, 379

*Picken, Rachel, *224

Pickens, Capt., 159, 282, 296, 298, 297

*Pickens, B. J., *224

*Pickens, Ben, *20

*Pickens, Benj., *236, 304

Pickens, James, 18, 168, 232, 287, 343, *224

Pickens, John, 18

*Pickens, Joseph, *20

Pickens, Rachael, 403, 464

*Pickens, Vicey, *22

*Pickin, Vicey, *304

R.C. Pie c te mah, R. C. 637

Pie yah, 546

Piga, 178

Pilah tubbe, 541

Pilah tubbee, 385, 471

Pil an tub bee, 826

Pi la tub bee, 146

Pil e honubbee, 517

Pil e mah hubbee, 471

Pil le sa ho nah, 580

Pil ubbe, 100, 147

*Pin sah im mah, *232

Pinson, Betsey, 18

R.C. Pio sah ni o ka, or Pis sah ni ya, 649

Pir sah ho nah, 457

*Pis abanabi, *128

Pis a cha hubbee, 813

Pis a cha tubbe, 518

Pis a cha tubbee, 386

*Pisa chayahe, *196

Pis a che tubbee, 137

Pis ach honer, 711

Pisah, 983

Pisaha, 264

*Pisan aiya, *8

R.C. Pis a ham ba, [R. C. 643,] 919, 920

Pis a ham bee, 256, 525

Pis ah cha honah, 548

Pis ah cha hubbe, 529

Pis ah chan tubbe, 507

R.C. Pis ah chee ho yo, [R. C. 620,] 796

Pisah che honah, 690

Pisah che ho yah, 570

Pis ah che ho yo, 492, 563

Pis ah chek e mah, 874

Pis ah che lubbee, 826

Pis ah che tubbe, 504, 580

Pis ah che tubbee, 143, 382

Pis ah chick e mah, 874

R.C. Pis ah chike mah, 540, [R. C. 635,] 873

Pis ah chimah, 535

Pis ah ha chubbe, 577, 579, 583

Pis ah ha mah, 552

Pis ah hambe, 537

Pis ah haw tub bee, 144

Pis ah he chub bee, 144

Pis ah ho chubbe, 508, 580

Pis ah ho chubbee, 380

Pis ah ho ka ta nah, 568

Pis ah hoka timah, 536

Pis ah hokah timah, 556

Pis ah ho katona, 690

Pis ah ho ka tubbee, 497

Pis ah hom be, 501

Pis a honah, 524, 689

Pis ah ho nim ah, 533

Pis ah ho tim ah, 559

Pis ah ho tuna, 535

Pis a hi ah, 140

Pis ah ish no wah, 518

Pis ah jah, 569

R.C. Pis ah la ho kah, [R. C. 616, R. C. 627]

Pis ah le ho ka, 381, 498

Pis ah man tubbe, 525

Pisah mak in tubbee, 556

R.C. Pis ah no wah, 448, 480, 481, [R. C. 680,] 1110

*Pis ahnowubbe, *18

P

Pis ah ogla, 514

Pis a ho ka, 190

Pis a ho kah timah, 501

*Pisahoka tubbee, 242, *46

Pis a ho keta, 198

*Pisah okotima, *172

*Pisahona, *198

Pis ah on te mah, 526

Pisah otema, 224, 273

Pis a hoyo, 147

Pisah she temah, 537

Pis ah ta cah, 377, 442

Pis ah ta cubbe, 512

Pis ah tambe, 509, 864

Pis ah tambee, 381

Pis ah temah, 569, 690

Pis ah ti ah, 377, 501, 507, 560

Pis ah timonah, 535

Pis ah tin lah, 501

Pis ah tish a, or Pis ah tish abbee, 442

Pis ah tish a, or Pis ah tishubbee, 376

Pis ah tish abbee, or Pis ah tish a, 442

Pis ah tish ubbe, 535

Pis ah tish ubbee, or Pis ah tish a, 376

Pis ah to cubbee, 567, 689

Pis ah to ke mah, 497

Pis ah tonah, 523

Pis ah took im mah, 442

Pis ah to she mah, 515

Pis ah tubbe, or Sahtubbee, 507

Pis ah tubbe, alias Ah po sa tam be, 525

Pis ah tubbe, 541

Pis ah tubbee, 137

Pis ah tu nah, 506

Pis a la hema, or Tahomba, 226

Pis a la he ma, 1015

Pis ala ho ca, 789

Pis ala homa, 193, 199

Pis ala ho na, 192

Pis a la tubbee, 233, 167

Pis alle ho wah, 767

R.C. Pis ama tubbee, 228, [R. c. 665]

Pis am be, 491, 558

Pis am bee, 384

Pis a me tub bee, 137

Pisamik an tubbi, 50

R.C. Pis a mok ain tubbee, 642

Pis a mok an tubbee, 237

Pis am tim er, 695

Pisam ukain tubbee, 256

R.C. Pis an te mah, 614

Pis an tub bee, 145, 379

Pis a po ka, 197

Pisa poketa, 192

Pis atam temah, 540

Pis ate a, 236

Pis a te ga, 105, 145

*Pis a tekabee, *264

R.C. Pisa tema, 251, [R. c. 667,] 1043

Pi sa te mah, 138

Pisatiah, 569, 690

Pis a tik cubbe, 500

*Pisatima, *188

Pisa to cubbe, 259

R.C. Pis a to cubbee, 926, 928, [R. c. 648]

Pis a to ka mah, 148

Pis a tom ba, 863, 864

Pis a tom be, 512

R.C. Pis a ton bee, [R. c. 633,] 864

*Pis a ton ubbe, *269

*Pis ato shenia, *30

Pis a tubbe, 266

Pis a tubbee, 273

*Pis au tubbe, *32, 34, 36

Pis awa tubbee, 1031

Piscley ho kay, 703

Pis e ho tanah, 522

Piser Timer, 695

Pish ah chi tub bee, 142

Pish ah ge, 145

R.C. Pish ah han lah, [R. C. 620,] 717

Pish ah han lar, 781

Pish ah han ler, 799

R.C. Pish ah hen lubbee, 616

Pisher hen lubbey, 702

Pisher hen lubby, 791

Pis hom bee, 115

Pish tan ta tubbee, 399

Pis s tubbe, 536

Pisite mi ah, 114

Pis i to cubbee, 388

Pis i to kubbe, 542

Pis i to kubbee, 484

Pis it ti yah, 478

Pis it ti yah, or Chok tah ho nah, 814

Pis it ti yah Chok tah ho mah, 827

Pis it yah or Chock tah ho mah, 387

Pis o cha tubbee, 826

*Pisohona, *128

Pis on tin er, 696

*Pisotaya, *114

Pissa, 169

*Pis sabbe, *220

Pis sa che hoyo, 530

Pis sa ham la, 90

Pis sa ham ba, 137

Pis sah cha, 420

Pis sah cha hubbe, 471

Pis sah cha hubbee, 385, 1073

Pis sah che hubbee, 387, 478, 540, 814, 827

Pis sah che temah, 516

Pis sah e kah, 519

Pis sah hah tubbe, 592

*Pis sah hah tubbee, *52

Pis sah ha mah, 404

R.C. Pis sah ham ba, 388, 484, 540, [R. C. 618]

Pis sah ham bee, 531

Pis sah hoke ate mah, 392

Pis sah hoke ta, 393, 422

Pis sah hoke a tubbee, 391, 414, 1126

Pis sah ho nah, 382, 520, 816, 827

Pis sah honubbe, 531

R.C. Pis sah hoo nah, 617

R.C. Pis sah hote mah, 542, [R. C. 673,] 1073

Pis sah ho timah, 492

Pis sah ha to rah, 575

Pis sah la ho ka, 607

Pis sah la he mah, 522

Pis sah mock in tubbee, 401, 450

Pis sah muk in tubbee, 916, 917

Pis sah nah honah, 589

R.C. Pis sah ni ya, or Pio sah ni o ka, 649

Pis sah niyah, or Pissa mioka, 598

Pis sah ni yah, 960, 961, 962

Pis sah nowah, 467

Pis sa hoka, 530

Pis sah hoke a tubbee, 415

Pis sah tekah, 321

Pis sah te mah, 597, 529

Pis sah to mah, 393

Pis sah tubbe, 596

Pis sa la ha ma, 392

Pis sal atubbee, 464

Pis salle tubbee, 421, 422

Pis sallitubbee, 436

Pis sam ma tubbee, 1031

Pis sa mi oka, or Pissah niyah, 598

*Pis sar tubbee, *192

Pis sha tim ah, 1043, 1044

Pis shub bee, 146

Pisson o wah, 468, 469

Pis so oon tub bee, 148

Pis subbe, 547

Pis subbee, 397, 440, 587

Pis ta cha homah, 589

Pis ta cha ho nah, 567

Pis ta ga, 212

Pis ta gee, 814, 825

Pis tah onah, 539

Pis ta ko cha, 142

*Pistambe, Capt., *10

*Pistambe, Forbis, *32

Pis tam bee, alias Tambee, 503

*Pistambi, Capt., *116

R.c. Pis tan o le ha na, 661

Pis tan ole hona, 1004

Pis tan Temerded, 694

R.c. Pis te ah, 378, 545, [R. c. 677,] 1092, 1093

Pis te ah tubbe, 505

Pis te ke yea, 865

Pis te ock a ny, 785

Pis ti ackaney, 785

Pis ti ak o noy, 748

Pis tick e ah, 396

Pis tik atubbee, 236

Pis tike ah, 525, [R. c. 634, 679,] 866, 1109

Pis tik e ubbe, 502

Pis ti ock a na, 379

Pisti Ockaney, 747

R.c. Pis ti ok o na, 625

Pis ti ok o nay, 749, 780

Pis ti ok o ney, 783

Pis ti ok onoy, 748

Pis ti owah, 451

Pis toh ho koh, 906

Pis toh punne, 478

Pis toh onah, 1111

*Pis tok cha, *204

*Pis tok cha, John, *204

Pis toke cha, 197

Pis took cha, 391, 414, 415, 523

Pis took chah, 571

Pis took chubbee, 551

Pis to punne, 387, 520, 814, 827

Pis tub bee, 137

*Pis ubbe, *50

Pis ubbee, 167, 169, 192, 196, 233, 316

Pitchlyn, J., 10, 12

*Pitchlynn, Alix,, *268

*Pitchlynn, E. J., *268

Pitchlynn, Ere, 29

Pitchlynn, John, 26, 62

Pitchlynn, Peter P., 28

Pitchlynn, Silas, 26

*Pitchlynn, Sophia, 18, *130

*Pitchlynn, W. B., *80, 82

Pithele, 504

Piyah, 604

Pi yah hoc ta, 814, 826

Pi yah hoe ta, 387

Pi yah hooc ta, 499

Plumer, F. E., 76

Po cham bee, 219

Poch nah, 141

Pock ah ma, 503

R.C. Pock ah mah, 376, 587, [R. c. 649,] 962, 963

Pock a na yah, 592

Pock in ambee, 389, 588

Pock om e chubbe, 503

Po hah mah, 85

Poh lubbee, 438

Poh lumma, 422

Poh na, 417

Poka, 530

Pok ah la ho nah, 569, 690.

Pok ah mah, 149

Pok ah tah ho mah, 832

Pok a mah, 140

Pok o chubbe, 501

Pok o la tubbe, 515

Po lah, 102, 145, 147, 548

Po lah, sometimes Ah no po lubbee, 377

Po la lah, 442

Polio, 147

*Polk, J. K., or Eyabanolubbe, *2

*Polk, J. R., or Ey abanatubbe, *2

Polla, 406

Polla chubbee, 385

Pollume kubbe, 499

R.C. Pollum e kubbee, [R. c. 635,] 878

Polly, 542, 614, [R. c. 652,] 970

Polly Ann, 50

Polum a chubbee, 393

Pom fillah, 391, 414, 415

Ponah, 465, 517, 602, [R. c. 651,] 966, *270

Pon chis tubbee, 94

Ponelah, 569

Po nok to chubbe, 508

Pon shese tubbe, 563

*Pon shese tubbee, 382, 390, 492, *84

Ponsh ish to nah, 543

*Ponsh ish to nubbee, 387, *68

Po nubbee, 397

Poo ah loop ka, 569

Poo co nah, 148

Poon tah, 540

Poore, Arckler, 707

Poo she mah, 147

Poo tah, 515

Portupey, 785

Posah slock co, 86

Po sha at tah, 85, 140

Po sha bo tubbee, 162

Po sha hee na, 148

Posh ah ho yo, 525

Posh ah mus tubbee, 825

Posha hoke ta, 464

Po shah hoke ta, or Po shockta, 607

Posha ho mah, 94

Po sha hon ah, 381, 385, 580

Po sha ho tim ah, 147

*Posh ahoyo, *62

Posh ah slock co, 137

Po shah tah, 389

Posh ah thloe co, 825

Po shah tubbee, 401

*Posh ambee, *54

Posh am us tubbee, 276

Poshan o wabbe, 518

Poshan o wabbee, 386, 817, 827

P

Posh an o wah bee, 470

Posh athloke, 268

Po sha to nubbee, 404

Po shat tah, 448

Poshatto locko, 213

Po shem a, 1026

Po shemah, 517, 569

Po shi aka, 983

Po shi oka, 984

Posh i onah, 542, 814

Po shish teia, 186

Posh ish te ubbe, 542

Posh ish te ubbee, 384, 461, 824

Poshish tiyah, 417, 418

Po shish tua, 184

Po sho at tah, 148

Po shoa tubbee, 220

*Poshobi, *180

Po sho bo tubbee, 190

Poshock ta, or Posh ah hokte, 607

Po shon she hubbe, 509

Po shon chubbee, 388

Poshubba tubbee, 218

Poshubbo tubbee, 197

Po shun che ab bee, 143

Pos huth loko, 211

Posh ut tah, 148, 377, 554

Posish teah, 419

Posis ti yah, 391

Post Oak, Capt., 56

*Post Oak, Red, 59, 458, 809, *116

Post Oak, Capt., or Ches ha Homah, 111

Post Oak, Red, alias Che sha ho ma, 137

Post Oak, Red, [Chisha homa,] 181

Post Oak, Capt. Red, alias Chishehoma, 316

Post Oak, Red, alias Chish a homah, 809, 810

Post Oak, Red, alias Chesh ah ho mah, 818

Po tah, 397, 517, 521. [R. C. 617,] 738

Po ta mah, 523

*Po tho tah, 398, 452

Po to honer, 709

Po to le chubbe, 505

Po to tubbe, 540, 586

*Po to tubbee, *76, 100, 115, 148, 378, 381, 484

Po tubbee, 503, 567, 689, 826

Po tubbee or Brandy, 472

Po tubby, or Brandy, 385

Pouchis tubbee, 141

Poush ik isho, 827

Poush is tonah homah, 523

Poush is to nubbe, 516

Poush ok chiah, 482

Pow show e sha ubbee, 381

R.C. Po yoh, [R. C. 683], 1130

Price, 155

Price, John F., 430

Pri zah hoc ta, 474

Puckchenubbee, 317

*Puck nahan ubbee, *52

Puck she nub bee, 139

*Pudloom, Chas., *188

Puk an ah hoka, 525

Puk ho mo, 115

Puk she nub bee, 825

Pulah, 393

*Pulhetubbe, *110

Pul he tubbee, 381

Pulka, 573

R.C. Pul ka tubbee, 555, [R. c. 617]

Pul ker, 145

Pul ke tubbe, 509, 584

Pul key tub bee, 801

Pul kin tubbee, 91, 138, 695, 825

R.C. Pul kin tubbee, alias Pa e than tubbee, [R. c. 614,] 696

*Pulleeha, *280

Pulle honah, 530

Pun ah, 381, 505, 580

Pun a pish ubbee, 101

Pun nah, 144

*Punnissah, *254

*Puns hok chiah, *96

Pun ubbe, 522

Pup a mah, 100

Pus a ca, 95, 145

Push ah ho mah, 93

R.C. Pus ah ka, [R. c. 680,] 1110

Pus ah kah, 377, 448, 549

Pu sa la, 107

*Push, Simon, *168, 170

*Push, Stewart, *222

*Push, Elom, *286

Push ah ho mah, 382, 445, 564

Push ah ho nah, 141

Push ah mus tubbee, 91, 138

*Push a honah, *70

Puskey Tubby, 710

Pusley, 402

*Pusley, Calvin, *90

*Pusley, Edmund, *86

*Pusley, George, *86

Pus sah hah, 403

Puth kin tubbee, 211, 214, 273, 317

Put tah, 142

*Pujah, *206

*Pytchlynn, *264

Qtamba, 1032

Quachenu, 147

Quahna, 403, 465

Quiematah, 148

Quina,

Quishtubtah, 394

R

Rachael, 406, 970

R.C. Rachel, 604, [R. C. 652]

Radford, Widow, or Heacatenah, 26

*Randolph, Sebeon, *56

*Randon, James, *56

Rayburn, 607

Rebecca, 81

*Red Cedar, *208

*Red Dog, *310, *312

*Red Knife, *264

*Red Man, *110

Red Pepper, 65

*Red Squirrel, 40

*Red Turkey, 27, *270

Reyley, Patrick, 18

*Rhoda, *244

*Rhody, *72

*Riddle, George, *16

*Riddde, John, *16

*Riddde, Wm., *238

*Riddle, Jr., Wm., *238

Riley, Patrick, 171

*Rince, Josiah, *254

R.C. Ripley, Ezra, 206, 208, 230, 318, [B. c. 640,] 901, 902, 979

*Robbe, *318

Robert, 50

*Robert, Lawry, *288

*Robert, John, *278

*Roberts, Lucy, *88

*Roberts, Mary, *234

Robertson, Lewis, 18

*Robinson, Amzire, *236

*Robinson, Elvira, *236

*Robinson, James, *42

*Robinson, John, *20

*Robinson, Sam, *194

*Robuck, *196

*Robuck, Maryann, *240

*Roebuck, Sophia, *196

*Roebuck, Wm., *250

*Roebuck, Z., *250

Rodgers, Philip or dhil., 27

Rosseau, 432

Ruthey, 50

Rowle, 398

Sach-an-tub-bee, 143

Sah-chah-ho-nah, 394

Sah hoba, 537

Sah ho te nah, 597

Sah-im-me-ho-ka, 381

Sah-im-me-ho-ka. or Tah-im-me-ho-ka, 581

Sah-in-e-ho-ka, 584

Sahla, 401

Sah lah ma, 588

Sah mah ha chubbee, 516, 824

Sah-ma-ho-chubbe, or Yok-ash e mah, 384

Sah-mah tah, 462

Sah-man tah, 384

R.C. Sah-me-ah-ho-nah, R. c. 675, 1081

Sah-meoka, 592

Sah-na-che-hoenah, 459

Sah-nah-che-ho-ma, 826

Sah-nah-che honah, 520

Sah-nah-che-hoo-mah, 813

Sah mah tah, 824

Sa ho te mah, 547

Sa hoyo, 236, 245, 263

Sah-sin me hoka, 506

Sah-tubbe, or Pis-ah-tubbe, 507

*Saiema, *14

*Saikitambi, *178

*Saikatubi, *176

Sa im nu ho ge, 144

Sak ah tiah, 146

Sak a tiyah, 690

Sak a tubbee, 469

*Sak e tabe, *224

Sak e tiah, 449

Sak e timah, 497

*Saki, *150

Sak ka tubbe, 540

Sak kee, 144

*Sak-ki, *220

Salah m ha, 18

R.C. Sa-lam, 640

R.C. Sal am ah, [R. c. 680,] 1110

*Sale, *318

*Salina, *88, *92

*Salitobi, *166

Salla, 395, 424, 502, 601, 1013

Salla honah, 591

Salla hoyo, 406

Sal-lee, 384, 825

Salleoka, 568, 690

*Sallie, 462, 517, 537, *70

R.C.*Sally, 225, 239, 280, 406, 542, [R. c. 617,] [R. c. 662,] [R. c. 665,] 796, 1013, 1029, *120, 302, 310, 312

*Sally Ann, *128

*Sam, 402, 591, *296

*Sam Bill, *80

*Sam Billy, *140, 148

*Sam, Mary, *38

Sam ma ha chubbee, 462

Sam me, 504

Sam pa, 843

R.C.*Sampson, 233, 250, R. c. 665, *232, *280

*Samuel, *74

Sa na che hoo nah, 383

San amp a chah, 376

San-no-ti-ka, 143

*Sapin, *4

Sarah, 401

Satowa, 316

Savell, James, 423

Saw-wa-che-ho-yua, 99

Saw-win-cha, 89

Scah-ham-ba, 788

Schap-bam-be, 581

Schap-pa-ho-mah, 148

Scott, Charles, 27

Se-ah-po-le, 377

*Seama, *64

Seanola, 235

Se-ap-po lo, 142

*Sela, *56

*Selfe, *296

*Selina, *320

R.C. Selis, 604, R. c. 652

*Selsa, *86

Semmony Wm., 78

*Senis Mary, *96

*Sexton Charles, *88, 90

*Sexton Dauy, *78

*Sexton Jessee, *40

*Sexton Mahah, *36

*Sexton Thompson, *40, 78

Sha-a-bea-cha, 85

Sha am pi ah, 157

*Sha ba we ca, *284

Sha co pa na wa, 212, 213

Sha-coppa, or Shah co po, 712

Sha co ya, 204

Sha-fam-bee, 144

*Sha-fam sha hobbe, *142

Shah-ah-ba-cha, 149

Shah-ah-bea-cha, 140

R.C. Shah co po, [R. c. 618,] 761, 781, 799

Shah co po, or Sha coppa, 712

Shah-hook-ta, 581

Shah-hubbee, 769

Shah la tab, 399

Shah-ma, 586

Shah mah, 594

Shah nah, 378, 399

Shah-ni otubbe, 571

Sha ho ka, 402

Shah oka, 1068

Shah pah-ho-mah, 376, 595

Shah pa ja, 591

Shah-pa-jah, 376

Shah-tubbe, 768

R.c. Shah-tubbee, 627

*Shainitubbee, *44

Sha-ka-ho-mah, 385, 472, 499

*Shak-a-honah, *112

*Shak a honeah, *60

Sha ka pa honah, 500

Shak-co-po, 380

*Shak op li cha, *168

Shak owa, 229

R.c. Sha-ko-way, R. c. 665, 1032, 1033

*Sha lake hona, *212, 214

*Shalalle, *294

*Shalaube, *22

*Shal copo, *140

Shal lacka, 908

Shal lahoka, 218

R. c. Shal li o ho-ka, R. c. 668, 923

Sha lin hoka, 252

Shal in tubbe, or Ah shal in tubbe, 579

Sha litta, 1026

*Sha litubbe, *2

R. c. Sha ma, R. c. 668, 926

*Shamah, *8

Sha-mah-ho-yo, 497

Sham bee, 540

Sham pah no-ka, 503

*Sham pia, *176

Shampiaya, or Champaya. 219

Sham-pie, 389, 536

Sham pionah, 595

Sham pi ya, 437

Sham pi yea, 137

Sham py ea, 86, 87

Sham to nah, 397

Sha na ho tubbe, 446

Sha-ne-kah, 148

Sha ne kia, 554

Shaniotubbe, 548

Shan nah tah, 385

Shan-nan-tub bee, 145

Shan nan tubbe, 105

Shan tah ho ka, 455, 493

Shan tah oka, 378, 382, 455, 501

Shan ti yo, 445

*Shap emas tobi, *150

R.C. Sha pon sha ha, 623

Sha pon sha hah, 788, 806

Shap po-ho mah, 85, 140

*Sharkarbe, *272

*Sharney, *32

*Shauke, *208

*Shau tubbe, *22

Shaw, Joseph, 26

Shaw-wa-am pa, 457

*Shaw a homah, *64

Sha wa i yah, 386

Sha wak i yah, 827

*Shawana, *92

Shaw tah ho ka, 565

She a pam bee, 142

She co pa ha joe, 99, 138

She-co-pah ho-mah, 581

She co-pah lok nah, 386, 476

She copa homa, 112, 138, 383, 461, 824

She co-pa hoom ma, 142

She co-pam be, 92, 542

She-cop-an-cha ab bee, 143

She co pan she ubbe, 382

She copom ba, or James Na kon sha, 382

She cubbe, 581

She he ma, 145

She in don na, 145

Shek a pa no wa, 817

She ko pah ho mah, 380, 507

She ko-pah lok nah, 825

She ko pan she hubbe, 528

She ko pan she-ubbe, 581

She ko pom ba, 445

Shek o yah, 1032

Shelah hocah, 922, 924

She le tah, 968

*She lop ambe, *96

*Shema, 208

Shemaah, 436

*She mah, 385, 471, 499, 517, 777, 826, *114

She mah hoyo, 526

She mah la tonah, 501

She mah la too-nah, 379, 454

*Shemahoke, *112

She-ma-ho-tubbee, 92

She ma ho yo, 387, 478, 814, 827

Shema ka Cole, 203

*Shemar, *264

R.C. She maya, 167, 191, R. c. 628, 839

She me ah, 92

She me ho ka, 493, 565

She mi ah, 387, 446, 926

She mi yah, 234, 318, 474, 522, 814, 826, 838

*She miyeh, *136

She mya, 111, 118

She-na-ho-tubbee, 142

She ne po-tubbe, 509

She nu ah, 142

She pan ee, 184

She tah, 436

She tam be, alias Pasah bam be, 581

Sheway, or Cheway, 28

Shiah kah, 689

Shiah kak, 567

Shia hoka, 200

Shia poka, 210

*Shields, Capt. James, 42, *242

*Shields, Martha, *276, 284

*Shika, *28

Shik-a pa nawa, 319

Shik o pa no wa, 260, 266, 825

Shimah, 776

Shimamble, 1037

Shimeia, 194

*Shimiah, 243, 316, *176

Shim ma ya, 170

Shim mya, 199

R.C. Shimolaka, 256, R. c. 643

Shim tonah, 536

Shi ner hoo ker, 803

Shinn pika, 77

Shin to nah, 377

Shi yah, 592

Shoat, alias Hiotubbe, or Utubbe, 271

Sho-ah te ki ah, 379, 454

Sho-ca yo, 213

Shock a yo, 212

Shock-ko-yea, 392

Shock ti yah, 594

Sho copah honah, 530

Sho coyo, 207

R.C. Shoe maker, [R. c. 626,] 764, 765, 766

Sho-ho-meia, 252

R.C. Sho ho mi ah, [R. c. 668,] 926

Sho hotta, 911

*Shok a homah, *92

R.c. Shokaio, 267, 319, R. c. 630

Shoke tah, 1031

Shok kai o, 852

Shok kai yo, 817, 825

Shok ola yah, 140

Shok ta, 224

*Sho lika chahabe, *194

*Sholush huma, *150

Sho ma ha ka, 470

Sho ma ha kah, 386

Sho mah hoketa, 402

*Sho mah hoyo, *108

Sho mah-la-tubbee, 525

Sho ma ho ka, 541, 817, 827

Shomaka, 319

Sho ma loh ka, 925

Shomantah, 422

Shomantohr, 423

*Shomartuchar, *238

Sho mo lah ka, 399, 464

Sho moon tah 524

Shomp ka, 191, 199

Shom pul lah 461

Shom ula tubbee, 280, 320

R.C.*Sho mul la tubbee, R. c. 662, 1013, *282

Sho na, 376, 442, 553

R.C.*Shonah, 274, 380, 381, 505, 581, R. c. 622,
    *30, *102

Sho nah ho ka, 389

Shona hoka, 198, 899

Sho nah tah, 786

*Shonaichey, *10

Shone, 95

Sho-ner, 717

Sho-ney, 146

Sho ni-yah, 403

Shon ka ha yo, 140

Shon ka ho yo, 89

Sho-nooka, 523

*Shonoparlae, *158

*Shook a homa, alias Am ba la tubbe, *4

Shook o pan o wa, 853

Shoom pal la, 825

R.C. Shoom pal lah, 278, 320, R. c. 647, 948, 949

R.C. Shoom pi ka, 50, R. c. 642, 907

Shoom pi kah, 915

Shoom pulla, 211, 214

Shoo nah, 148

Shoon-pi-ga, 178

*Shopallubee, *18

Sho-po-le-ka, 148

Sho pon sha, 797

Sho pon sha ha, 723, 724

R.C. Sho pon sha hah, 380, R. c. 619, 761, 781,
    788, 795

Sho-pon sha hak, 788

Sho-pon sha her, 713, 714

Sho se, 561

*Sho ta, 167, 169, 190, 194, 233, *178, *182

Shotah, or Shoto, 415

*Sho tim ah, 507, 535, *60

Sho tubbe, 502, 518, 538, 540

*Sho tubbe, Isom, *28

*Sho tubbee, 242, 442, *298

*Shou ta, *202

Showa, 243

Sho wak iah, 817

Sho wak i yah, 469

Show e na, 179

Show e to nah, 148

Show ka ho yo, 148

R.C.*Show nah, [R. c. 621,] 717, 761, 781, 788,
    *140

Show wa am pa, 383, 817, 828

Show wa no, 519

Shu a tubbee, 105, 145

Shubbey, 778

Shuck co pa no wa, 139

Shuk a tubbee, 270, 317, 825

Shu ka ubbe, 78

Shukaubbi, 50

*Shuk ha homa, *190

Shu lap, 142

Shul la, 140

*Shulush hom ma, *122

Shu ma, 252

Shu mah lock ka, 436

Shu mak a, 844

Shu ma laker, 1035—6

*Shu mar harky, *174

*Shu mayi, *148

Shum ka, 111, 117

Shum pa, 139

S

Shum pa la ka, 377, 442

Shum pa la ka, or Chumpulaka, 535

Shum pi kah, 256, 319

Shum put a ca, 146

Shu-na, 147

Shun ah ka, 844

R.C.*Shunaka, 248, R. c. 629, *198

*Shu tik a cha hubbee, *244

Shu wak ki yah, 521

Si a na, 392

*Si an ta hubbee, *232

*Sid ney, *84

Sie a nah, 1005

Siela, 218

Siel la honah, 497

Si e mah ho nah, 696

Siena, 275

*Sigea, *34

Sila, 404

*Silas, *58

*Siley, *28

Silis, 401, 970

Silles, 748, 749

*Silmon, Gains, *136

*Silney, *244

*Silwah, *76

*Simeon, *64

Simmons, Willam, 51, 52

*Simon, 50, 253, *74, 78

*Simon, Mary, *308

Simpson, 1050

*Simpson, Sally Ann, *26

Sims, Thomas, 282

R.C.*Sina, 225, 242, 393, R. c. 661, 1005, *204

R.C. Sinah, 256, R. c. 642, 916, 917

*Siney, 50, *192

*Sip-pubbe, *38

*Sish shimah, *24

*Siston, Lucy, *198

Sives Martin, 279

Skatena, 600

*Skelton, Wincey, *298

Skonche, alias Stemaya, alias Stancha, 275

Sliwash, Thomas, 77

*Smallwood, Anna, *282

*Smallwood, Benj., *266

*Smallwood, Betsy, *244

Smallwood, Mary, 27

*Smallwood, Mrs. Mary, *266

*Smallwood, Pusley, *244

Smith, 223, 605

*Smith, Choate, *118

Smith, John, 142

*Smith, Melly, *118

Soca, 170, 191

Soca, Tona, 1029

*Soc a tubbee, 166, 167, 169, 191, 232, 233, 318, 834, *134

Socca, 199

Socka, 237, 316

Socka, or Imiachubbe, 580

Sock-a tah tubbee, 142

Sock-a tubbee, 146, 189, 194, 438, 464

*Socka tubbee, Capt., *118

Sock-e tubbe, 544

*Sock e tubbee [R. c. 628] 835

Sockey, John, 142

*Sockey, William, *178

Sock-key, 81

Sock kia 393,

Soc la ho na, 178

Sofa, 399

So ho me tubbe, 562

Soka na, 190

Soka tonah, 544

So kin nah, 391, 414, 415

Sok ka tiah, 570

*So kubbee, *290

So kut che, 573

Sollem, 905, 906

*Solomon, 50, 586, 971, *246

R. c. Soma, R. c. 665

Somet-egee, 97, 101

*Som mar tubbee, *290

Son-ah-tubbee, 144

Son-e-ha jahor, Ton e ha jah, 27

Son wah-tubbe, or Watubbe, 565

Son we, 107

Sooc sa, 461

Sook immah, 190

Soo sa, 138, 384, 524, 824

R. c.*Sopha, 607, R. c. 654, *120

*Sophy, 223, *24

Sosa, 978

Sota, 196

Sotimiah, 144

Sotcwa, 265

So tow wa, 825

Spa la ta, 190

Spa lo te, 581

Spam ba, or Es mam ha, 26

Span a ha ga, 111

Span a hojo, 191, 197

Span a mingo, 260, 262, 263, 316, 825

Span ha cha, 437

Span tubbee, 140

*Speaker, Thomas, *196

Spears, Nice, 142

R.c. Spi sah tubbee, R. c. 616

Spis en tubby, 803

Spis er tubbey, 704

*Spring, Mrs. Janes, *278

Sta ah nub bee, 402

Stabohla, alias Stab ole hona, 272

Stabole hona, alias Stabohla, 272

Stafana, 269

Sta ge hoo nah,

Sta ha ga, 269

Stah honah, 531

Stah ka, 196

Stah lubbee, 402

Stah ma, 397

Stah nah to nah, or Stam mah han to nah, 394

Stah nubbee, 551

Sta hoketa, 272

Staia, 198

Stala he ma, 270

Sta lubbee, 197, 219

Stam a chubbee, 1005

Stama hatona, alias Ta ma hatona, 272

Stam mah han to nah, or Stah ha to nah, 394

R.c. Stam a le yo, R. c. 657

Sta miah, 950

Stan a hah, 773

Stan cha, alias Siemaya, 483

Stan cha, alias Stemaya, alias Skonche, 275

Stanche, 108, 139

Stanche, or Stemanche, 814, 825

Stan chubbee, 376

Standley, James, 161

Stan ho ka, 907

Stanley, James, 27, 160

Stantima, 234

Stanton, 18

Stan tubbee, 87, 137

Sta pe sa, 186

Starnes, Jane, or Jane **Starrer**, 26

*Starns, Widow Jane, *18

Starrer, Jane, or Jane **Starnes**, 26

Ste ah hopa, 601

Steah kiah homa, 972

Stea hotema, 270

Ste ah sha che, 142

Steale, 517

Stea tubbee, 221

*Ste hil cha, *104

Steia, 237

Steimetubbee, 237

Stem a chubbee, 27

R.c. Ste ma ha ya, R. c. 666

Ste mah ka yo, 828

Stemahogu, 50

R.c. Stema ho ya, [R. c. 667,] 1037, 1038, 1045

Stema hoyohona, 235

Ste mak ka yo, 437

*Stem ala, 211, 214, *266

Ste ma lah, 514

Ste ma le hogah, 142

Stem a leyo, 599

Stema li ha gah, 845

Stemanche, or Stanche, 814, 825

Stemanola, 1041

Stemaya, alias Stanche, alias Skonche, 275

Ste ma ya, 1061

Stemi ha ya, 1018

Ste mi la ha jah, 99

Ste mok ka yo, 383, 525, 817

Stemonah, 114

Stemonahaka, 50

Stemona hoka, 77, 79, 174

R.c. Ste nah hoo kah, R. c. 615

*Stephens, Simon, *138

Ste pis sah, 145

*Stern, Jane, *8

Stete mah, 525

*Stewart, Charles J., *156

*Stewart, Hannah, *310

*Stewart, Henri, *236

*Stewart, Jackson, *208, 218, 280

*Stewart, Mulcie, *132

*Stewart, Mrs. Nancy, *236

tSewart, Thomas, 58

*Stiami leche, Capt., *254

Stiare, 710

*Stier, Capt., *180

Stil a bo la tubbee, 190

Stile a tubbe, 89

Still a tubbee, 140, 149

Stim a hal ubbee, or Holah, 1073

R.c. Sti ma ha ya, 244, [R. c. 663]

Stim ah ha lubbee, 402

Stim a ho ya, 186

Stim a ho yo, 271

Stim ala, 272, 273

*Stim ala ha jah, *134

*Stima lahajah Joseph, *134

R.c. Stim alih ajah, 279, 320, [R. c. 629]

Stim eah, 393

Stim e li yo, 982

Stim elyo, 983

Stim mi yah, 435

Stim mul le hachah, 415, 416

Sto bub bee, 141

Sto mah chubbee, 407

Stona, or Ah tone, 388

Stona cha, alias Sto na hoc-ga, 142

Stona ha cha, 87

Stona ha je, alias Apelatubbee, 281

Ston ahaje, alias Apellatubbee, 320

R.C. Sto na ha jo, alias A-pel a tubbee, R. c. 671

Sto na ha jo, 1060

Sto nah cho, 973

*Stonah hok tah, *88

Sto na-hoc-ga, alias Sto na cha, 142

Stonaje, 185

Stone ha, 716, 717

Stoo roka, 514

Sto-po-nubbe, 516

Sto po nubbee, 385, 469, 817, 827

Sto pun nubbee, 115, 139

Stub ba hat ta, 484

Stub ba hat tah, 388

Stulah, 380

*Stull, Tan honah, *216

*Stull, Capt. Willis, *216

Stu na, 516

R.C. Stut ah, R. c. 616, 761, 780, 797

Stut ah, or Stut Hir, 703

Stut Hir, or Stutah, 703

R.C. Stut tah, [R. c. 619.] 797

Sty cha, 148

Suc ka tubbee, 86, 111, 118, 139

*Suckey, *110

Suckey, or Mahla, 591

Suck ke tu nah, 146

Sucky, 403, 1024

Suee, 99

Suk a tubbe, 521

Suk a tubbee, 385, 817, 827

Suk ena, 197

R.C.*Sukey, 220, 227, [R. c. 664,] *98

*Sukutubbee, *122

Su man tuk abbee, 146

*Suma tubbee, *82

Sume hah chubbe, 533

Sum me chubbee, 144

R.C. Su pe sah, [R. c. 679,] 1106

R.C. Susa, 234, 539, [R. c. 666,] 1042

*Susan, *74

*Susanna, *62

Sush ho nah tah, 507

Suska, 503

R.C. Susy, 250, [R. c. 665]

Sutte, 394

Suzan, J., 10

Syla, 220

Syloa, 926

R.C. Sylva, 252, [R. c. 668]

Systla, 1032

Tabacha, 400

Ta boh kah, 461

Ta-bo-kah, 383, 575, 824

Ta-bo-ko-h, 851

Tabole hona, alias Bolehou, 272

Ta-cha, 141, 581

Tach cubbee, 492

Tach cubbe, 562

Tackah lam be, 505

Tack kala, 446

Tac-te-ho-ma, 137

Tacubbe, 535

Tacubbee, 403, 452, 1028

R.C. Tahaka, 244, 319, [R. c. 663,] 1018, 1019, 1020

Ta-ha-nah, 385

Tah-ba, 825

Tah-bo-kah, 381, 508, 581

*Tah cheah, *52, *54

Tah cubbey, 921

*Tahe kubbe, *20

Tah e min tubbe, 522

Tah-e-yabbe, or Tambee, 869

R.C. Tah fah mah, 436, 602, [R. c. 631,] 856

Tah-fam-ah, 142, 514

Tah ha cubbe, 263

Tah-ha-ba, 380, 508, 581

Tah hah kah, 422

Tah-hah-lo-co-nah, 603, 651, 967

Tah ha na tubbe, 597

Tah he kah, 507

Tah ho ba, 797

Tah hobah, 517

Tah ho ba tubbee, 397

Tah hock a ma tubbee, 402

Tah-ho-ka, 397, 398, 813, 826, 1095

Tah hol ba tubbee, 465

*Tah hona, *98

R.C. *Tah ho nah, 148, 396, 499, 503, 517, 520, 531, [R. c. 650,] 894, 1044, *66

Tah ho nan, 602

Tah-ho-pe-ah, 378

Tah ho vah honah, 506

*Tah-ho-ye, 379, 533, *54

Tah hoyo, 395, 561

Tah hubbe, 520, 529, 530, 531

Tah-im-me-ho-ka, or Sah-im-me-ho-ka, 581

Ta-hi-obbi, 80

Tah ish cam be, 501

Tah-ish-ham-bee, 378

Tah-ish-ka, 145

Tah ish kam be, 455

Tah ka la tonah, 530

Tah la ho lubbe, 589

Tah-la-ho-lubbee, 376

*Tah la ho tubbee, *70

Tahla howah, 969

Tah liya, 601

R.C. Tah-lo-ah-to-nah, R. c. 676

Tah lo ah tun ah, 1091, 1092

Tah loo nah, 770, 771

Tah lowah, 535

Tah mah ha lubbe, 522

Tah-mah-hoke-chiah, 474, 522, 814, 826

*Tahm honah, *54

Tah min tubbee, 391

Tah mi Tubbee, 706, 709, 712, 714, 716, 722

Tah mi tubbe, 706

Tah-mo-ho-nah, 581

*Tah mustubbe, *114

Tah nah ho nah, 554

Tah nah inpo, 585

Tah nam pish tia, 965

Tah nam pish tiah, 602, 650

Tah nap ha cubbe, 532

R.C. Tah-nap-pe-jo, alias Ok-i-a cha, R. c. 648

Tah nap pe hoja, alias Okiacha, 593

Tah-na-tubbee, 679, 1107, 1108

Tah neen cha, 530

Tah ne honah, 520

Tah ne ho yo, 516

Tah nene tubbe, 535

Tah nin tonah, 532

Tah nin tubbee, 414, 415, 417, 418

Tah-no-ah-ho-ka, 581

Tah no le, 378, 455, 456, 533

Tah-no-wah, 387, 389, 478, 497, 521, 814, 827

R.C. Tahn-te-mah, [R. c. 672,] 1069, 1070

Tah nubbe, 542

Tah nu wah honah, 521

Tahcba, 546

Tahcka, 192

Tahcl batubbe, 605

Tahcltha, 50

Tahcma, 224

Tahcmba, (or Pisalahema), 226

Tahcmba, 1015, 1057

Tahcmbe, 420

Tahcmbee, 464

R.C.*Ta hona, 50, 190, 249, 259, [R. c. 667,] 941, *188

Ta ho nah, 137, 148, 544, *220

Ta-hon-na, 146

Ta hopeah, 538

Ta hote ma, 903

Tah palah, 548

Tah panah, 465

Tah-pa-nan-che-ha-bee, 817

Tah pa nanche hubbe, 525

R.C. Tah-pa-nan-che-hubbee, [R. c. 634,] 865, 866

R.C. Tah-pa-nan-nubbee, R. c. 619

Tah pah nis sto nah homah, 593

Tah pa nis sto nah homah, 595

Tah pa nis sto nah ho nah, 610

Tah pe chubbe, 498

Tah-pe-nah, 381, 536, 581

Tah pe nambee, 587

R.C. Tah-pe-ne-hubbee, [R. c. 667,] 1095, 1096

Tah pe oon cheah, 473, 474

Tah-poo-tah-tub-bee, 138

Tah sa hoh, 912

Tah-she-co, 382, 387, 390, 474, 491, 572, 814, 826

Tah temah, 544

Tah the ho nah, 573

Tah to bah, 507

Ta hubbe, 532

Ta-hub-bee, 140, 204, 224, 316

Tahu temah, 403

R.C. Tah-ya, alias Tambee, 525 [R. c. 634,] 868

Taishka, 105

Taka, 192

R.C. Takah, 417, 418, 198, 420, 400, R. c. 618

Taka hajo, 270

*Takah honah, *106

Takalah tim ah, 492, 559

*Taka lambae, *50

Take-a bot tah, 147

Take-ah-chaffa, 581

Take ba honah, 867

T

Take-ba-too-lah, 377

Take-ho-yo, 386, 470, 521, 817, **827**

Take Hoyus, 114

Taker, 80, 712, 799

Take ubbee, 399

Take-un-i ye, 389, 542

*Tak lan tobi, Jessee, *160

*Tak nubi, *174

Tokona, 250, 251

*Talahoma, *26

Talahona, 270

R.C. Tal-ah-po-nah, R. C. 615

Tal a hubbee, 234

Tal-a-min, 838

*Talapoosa, Saly, *100

*Tala poose, John, *84

*Tala poose, W., *66

*Tala poose, Washington, *100

Tal-a-push, 141

Tal a wah, 448

Tala watona, 192, 198

Talematema, 50

Taler honer, 697

Taler pro ner, 803

Ta leva tona, 190

*Tal hool lubbee, *310

*Tali hona, *150

*Talio tima, *136

Talla-ho-la, 89

Talla-ho-lo, 140

*Talla poose, Sampson, *106

*Talla poose, John, *106

*Talla poose Mary, *106

Talla o homa, 255

Talla-wa hona, 236, 1014, 1015

Talla wa honubbee, 218

R.C. Tal-li-a ho-ma, R. C. 641

Tallo ah ham be, 689

Talloah ham bee, 568

R.C. Tal-lo-ah-ho-ka, 597, [R. c. 658,] 987, 988

Tallo wah honah, 530

Tal mah hoketa, 1067, 1068, 1069

*Taloa wahona, *10

Talowah, 767

Talowah hoketa, 422

Tal o wah honah, 517,

Tal wah, 387, 474, 814, 826

Tal wah chubbee, 394

Tal wah ham bee, 405

R.C. Tal wah hoke ta, 402, 407, R. c. 672

Tal-wah-ho-nah, 386, 475, 528

*Tal wah to nah, 399, 463, *310

Tamache, 316

*Tamah, *114, *150

Tamah aeen lubbee, 274

Tamahatona, or Sta ma hatona, 272

Tamah le lubbe, 522

Tamai oka, 269

*Tamalahona, *94

*Tamba, *62

*Tambar, *64

*Tambe, 752, 753, *54

Tambe, alias Tahya, 868

R.C. Tambee, 145, 377, [R. c. 617, R. c. 625,] 806, 867

R.C. Tambee, or Tahya, 525, R. c. 634

Tambee, alias Tah-e-yabbe, 869

Tambee, alias Pistambee, 503

*Tame hayo. *98

Tam-it-u-nah, 143

Tam-mah, 143

Tammo, 574

Tam-mo-ah-hon-na, 143

Ta moa hona, 243

Ta-nabbee, or To nubbee, 26

Tan a be staga, 169

Tan a bo nobbee, 163

Tana bonubbee, 158, 197, 219, 316

Tanacha, 162, 207, 843

Tanache, 156, 204, 223

Ta-nah-pish-wak-i-ah, 581

Ta-nah-pis-no-wah, or Ah-pis-ah tubbe, 579

Tan-a-jah, 147

Tana kona, 269

Tanam pacha, 535

Tanam pachah, 448

*Tanam pachi, *60

Tanam pa staka, 534

Tanam pa stakah, 448

Ta-namp-ha-cubbee, 377, 570, 690

Ta-namp hee cubbe, 449

Tan-amp-ish-no-wa, 144

Ta-nam-pish-te-ubbee, 816, 827

*Ta nam pish tiya, *134

Ta nam pish ubbe, 528

Ta nam pish ubbee, 375, 467

Ta nam piste ubbe, 540

Tan amp o tubbee, 389, 557

Ta-namp-pa-sta-kah, 377

Ta nan bon ubbee, 420

Ta nan pish ti ah, 465

Tan-ap-a-ge, 95

*Tan ap eah homah, *14

*Tan ap ia holatta, *226

*Tan ap ia humma, Liza, *216

Tan-apish-ub-bee, 147

Tana pistaia, 196

Tan-ap-is-wak-iah, 144

Tan a pornubbee, 191

Tan-ap-pish-ubba, 155, 156

Tanatona, 919, 920

Tana tubbee, 185, 270

Tancha honah, or Canchahonah, 589

Tanecha, 220, 316

*Taneche, *166

Tanechubbee, 569, 690

Tan-e-too-nah, 381

Tane tubbe, 569

Tane tubbee, 690

Tan-he-nah, 148

Tan hubbee, 207

Tank-ah-ha-jo, 389

Tan-ke yo, 522

Tan-ke-you, 383, 459, 813

Tan-mam-pi-ga, 145

Tan-nam-pe-ge, 105

Tan-nam-pis-te-ga, 145

Tan-nap-ha-gub-bee, 144

Tanna pish wa, 243

Tan ne too nah, 509, 581

Tan-net-tu-nah, 145

Tan-nit-tu-na, 105

Tan-no-ly, 146

Tan-no-wah, 146

R.C. Tanole, 228, R. c. 669

Tanole hona, 225

Tan oon i o cubbe, 525

Tan oon i o cubbee, 382, 827

Tan oo wah ho nah, 386

Tan o wa tubbe, 528

Tan-pa-na-ish-tan-no-ho-mah, 140

Tan-pa-na-ish-tan-no-ho-no, 149

Tan pe nah hubbe, 563

Tan-pown-ah, 148

*Tan tah *142

Tan-te-nah, 145

Tan tima, 236

Tan tubbe, 509

Tan ulth la che, 523

Tan-un-chub-bee, 139

Tan up pi yah, 525

Tan-uth-le-ga, 146

Tan u wa honah, 475, 537

Ta-pa-mis-sto-nah-ho-nah, 376

Ta pa nanechea, 212

Ta-pa-nan-che-ha-bee, 827

R.C. Ta-pa-ni-ah, [R. C. 621,] 788

Ta-pa-sah, 376

Ta-pa-un chea, 139

Ta pa-nan-che-ha-bee, 382

Ta pe ne hubbe, 514

Ta-pe-noon-che-ah, 825

Ta pe oon cheah, 459, 460, 814

Ta pe-um-cheah, 99

Ta-pe-un-che-ah, 138

Ta-peun-cheak, 116

*Tapin, Charles, *264

Tappa non chea, 261, 270

Tappena, 190, 319

Tappe-na-hoo-mah, 28

Ta ram pish te ubbee, 457

*Tarby, Solomon, *72

Tar-ho-ka, 141

Tark-ma-tub-bee, 142

Tar pan a rim bee, 789

Tar-pan-umbee, 715

Tarth Tuner, 701

*Tasaha, *164

*Tasaha Soman, *166

*Tasan tubbe, *12

*Tasha, *318

*Tashambi, *146

*Tashaya, Loman, *170

*Tashico, *104

*Tash ish tabbe, 210

*Tash ish tobi, 150

*Tash kamata fah, *214

*Tash kamai yabbi, *210

*Tash kia kaya, *248

*Tash kia toka et, *2

Tasho yo tubbee, 690

*Tash ubbee, *12

Tas-ka-ho-mah, 143

*Task a pitichi, *186

Tath-le-yo, 385, 570, 817, 827

Tath yo, 469

*Tauampahah, *46

Tau am pish ubbee, 468

Tau-ap-hag-ubbee, 102

Tau-ke-you, 826

*Tau nol thlache, *46

Tau-no-wah-ho-nah, 825

Tau-oon-i-o-cubbee, 816

Tau-pa-na-ish-tan-no-ho-mo, 85

Tau pe nah hubbee, 492

Taw-ap-hag-ubbee, 95, 96

*Tay a, *174

Tay Cubbey, 760

Taylor, Bennone, 76

Taylor, Benone, 77

Taylor, Billy, 425

Taylor, David F., 406

Taylor, Hester A., 406

*Taylor, James, *62, *74, *138, *140, *170

*Taylor, John, *250

*Taylor, Mary, *252

Taylor, Peggy, 406, 450

Taylor, Pirena, 406

*Taylor, Susan, *74

Taylor, William, 78, 82, 142

Tay-yock-ho-mah, 148

Te-ack-ho-mah, 145

Te-ack-hoo-ma, 104

Teah, 532

Teah e min tubbee, 391, 414, 421

Teah ho nah, 551

R.c. Te-ah-hoo-kah, alias How ato nah, R. c. 619

Teah hoyo, 536, 570, 690

Teah pahn tah, 595

R.c. Te ah po le, [R. c. 679,] 1105, 1106

R.c. *Teah tubbee, 380, [R. c. 618,] 761, 781, 788, *142

*Teah tumo, *22

Teah shubbe, 585

Teake-ho-mah, 377, 502

*Teak homah, 476, *62

*Tealla, *256

Tea min tubbee, 185, 190, 197

Tea-ock-homah, 380

Te ock Homer, 704

Tear huyer, 711

Tear Tubbey, 711, 712

Te bah noo kubbe, 531

Te koka, 260, 261

Teballa, 522

Tebulle, 491, 572

Te cum see, 393

Te-ha-cub-bee, 817

Te-ha-kub-bee, 825

Teha Tiner, Elea, 737

Te he cubbe, 267

Te he cubbee, 317

Te-he-gah, 145

Te he kah, 551

*Te hick ubbee, *194

*Tehlayatabi, *162

R.c. Te-ho-ah-cubbe, 598, R. c. 657

Te ho bah tubbe, 535

Te ho mas tubbe, 523

Te-ho-me-stubbee, 383

Te-ho-mus-tub-bee, 817, 828

*Te ho tubbee, *86

*Te ho tubbee, Edmund, *88

*Te-ho-ya, 451, 605, 971, *270

R.c.*Te hoyo, 516, 542, [R. c. 652,] 813, 826, *106

Te-ho-you, 383

Te ho yus, 459

*Tehwihele, *8

Te-in-lubbe, 581

Te i tubbe, 806

Te i tubbee, 805

Teiya, 224

Te lah honah, 537

Tellis, 522

Te loahema, 50

*Te loka, *26

Te loway, 537

Te mache hona, 272

Temah, 484, 517, 518, 521

Te mah he mah, 531

T

Te-mah-ho-ka, 868

Te-mah-ho-kah, 869

Temah la, 452

Te-mah-la-cha, 378

Te-mah-lah, 380, 399, **556, 581**

Te mah lah chee, 555

Temah-me-tubbee, 705

Tema hona, 1038

Te ma ho-tub-bee, 142

Temah tam be, 532

Temaka, 274

Temale, 276

Te-ma-na-ub-bee, 142

Te ma yola, 167, 192, **196, 236**

Te me ah honah, 521

Te me ak ke, 507

Teme hoka, 564

Te mi ah hoyo, 492, 562

Te mi ho ka, 492

Te-mi-yah, 113, 137

Te mi yah tubbee, 396

Te-mi-yea, 383, 461, 516, 824

Te mi yola, 417, 418, 420

Te mola hona, 222

Te-mom-bee, 108

Te mo nah, 515

Te nah, 516

R.C. Te-nam-pa-shubbee, [R. c. 622,] 793

Te-nam-pish-te-ubbee, 382

Teng can she hoka, 930

R.C. Tennessee, 405, [R. c. 672,] 1071, 1072

*Tennesee, *244

Te ock he me lubbee, 401

R.C. Te-ock-ho-mah, [R. c. 616,] 761

Te ock ho mer, 781, 789

Te ok ho mah, 573

Te-ok-ho-nah, 386, 825

Teo-mustubbee, 109

Teo-nah, 388

Teor-Hooker, 715

Teo-tubbee, 112

Terrell, James, 28

*Tesah tonubbe, *260

*Te sam otubbee, *256

*Tesatayubbee, *252

*Tesha hooma, *246

*Tesho ho lah ta, *226

*Te shok chaya, *196

Tethe ubbe, 537

*Teth lela tubbee, *34

Te-wa-na-ha, 96

*Teyea, *98

Tha o hubbe, 501

Tha pe na hubbee, 1096

The-hum-by, 143

The o hah, 1028

Th-la-ho la, 581

Thlak o fache, 540

Thloop-o-tubbee, 375, 442

Thlopo tubbe, 501

Thlopo tubbee, 148

Thlo pulla, 556

Thlo-pulle, 584

Tho-at-ab-bee, 143

Tho-ba, 145

Thock-o fatubbee, or Thock o-tubbee, 401

R.C. Thomas, 224, 233, [R. c. 628,] 834, 835

*Thomas, Amelia, *304

*Thomas, Elias, *108

*Thomas, Juan, *126

*Thomas, Lucy, *222, *230

R.C.*Thompson, 406 [R. C. 673,] *312

*Thompson, Garret, *6, *22

Thompson, Giles, 28

*Thompson, Isom, *6

Thompson, Jacob, 57, 58, 76, 137, 171, 389

*Thompson, Mary, *256

*Thompson, Patty, *22

*Thompson, R., *312

*Thony, Capt., *166

Thoon a poka, 194

*Thopatubbee, *226

*Thopota, Peter, *210

Tho po tubbe, 596

Tho-po-tubbee, 389

Ti ah, 97

Tiambe, 541

Tibbe homah, 574

Tibbe honah, 568, 689

Tib-e-ho-mah, 386, 825

*Tible, Vicey, 206

Tic ba ha ka, 212

Tic ba ho tena, 191

Tic ba hotona, 196

Tic-bah-tubbe, 581

Tic ba pa lubbee, 172, 919

Tic-bone-tah-hubbee, 378

Tic-bo-nub-bee, 839

Tic-but-tah, 394

Tich a bah, 791

Tich-ban-tubbee, 860

*Tick, or Toka, *128

Tick a bah, 702, 761, 775

R.C. Tick-a-bat-tah, alias Tick-a-bo-nah, R. c. 625

Tick-a-bo-nah, 380, 716, 761

R.C. Tick-a-bo-na-te-mah, R. c. 625

Tick-a-but-ab-bee, 143

Tick a hah an timer, 750

Tick ah bat ah, 780, 797

R.C. Tick-ah-boon-tubbee, [R. c. 616,] 789

R.C. Tick-ah-bot-ah, [R. c. 619,] 786

Tick-ah-but-ah, 385

Tick a lin tubbe, 598

Tick a lin tubbee, 405

Tick bafalubbi, 50

Tick bagatubbi, 50

Tick bah, 781

Tick-bah-ha-ga-tub-bee, 139

Tick bah ha kah, 945, 946

Tick-bah-o-nub-bee, 139

Tick bah tubbee, 945, 946

R.C. Tick bam bee, 399, 422, 425, 464, 604, [R. c. 652,] 970

R.C. Tick ban tubbee, 400, R. c. 632

*Tick batoola, *64

R.C Tick-ba-tubbee, R. c. 646

Tick be too lah, 497

Tick-bi-ah, 383

*Tick bone luh gubbee, *82

Tick bone tah yubbe, or Hubbee, 549

Tick buttah, 393, 440

R.C. Tick-collier, or Tikaler, R. c. 614

Tick eah, 436

Tick-e-beab-bee, 138

Ticker bon Tubbey, 706

Tick-lah-tub-bee, 137

Til ba pa lubbee, 178

Till nah, 395

Tieoh, 1031

Tihaya, 200

*Tih lit ambi, Nelson, *176

R.C. Tik-a-bah, R. c. 616

Tik a bah honah, 774

Tik a ba ho tona, 252

Tik a ban timah, 751

Tik-a-bo-nah, 780

Tik-a-bonah, alias Tik a botah, 746

Tik a bonah, or Tik a bottah, 783

Tik a bottah, or Tikabonah, 746, 783

Tik-a-chuf-fah, 144

Tik-ah-bul-tah, 384

Tik ah but tah, 560

Ti kai hona, 219

Tik-a-lee, 808

R.C. Tik a ler, or Tick coller, R. c. 614

Tikaya, 243

*Tik babi, *122

R.C. Tik bahaka, 277, 320, R. c. 646

R.C. Tik-bah-ah-ho-ka, R. c. 673

Tik-bah-ah-o-ka, 381, 581, 1073, 1074

*Tik-bah-ah-onah, *154

Tik-bah-ha-hah, 826

Tik-bah-ha-kah, 383, 459, 813

Tik-bah-ho-nah, 387, 478, 506, 525, 814, 817

Tik-bah-ho-nubbe, 584

Tik bah ne mah, 523

*Tik ba homa, *158

Tik bah oo nah, 525

Tik ba ho tubbe, 559

Tik-ba-ho-tub-bee, 143

Tik bah pa lubbee, 905

R.C. Tik-bah-tubbee, 574, [R. c. 674, R. c. 678,] 1080, 1100, 1101

Tik bah ubbe, 523

*Tik bam bi, *136, *170

*Tik bam bi Silas, *136

*Tik ban tobi, *156

Tik bapa lubbe, 255

R.C.*Tik-ba-pa-lubbee, 319, [R. c. 640,] *232

*Tik bar chi hubbee, Capt., *200

*Tik bar tubbee, *304

Tik ba tubbee, 277

Tik-ba-un-ta-hub-bee, 146

Tik be at lubbe, 256

R.C. Tik-be-a-tubbee, R. c. 642

Tik bech tubbee, 916, 917

*Tik beia, 265, 316, *302

Tik-be ha-gah, 814, 825

Tik be ubbe, or Bumahtahka, 516

*Tik be ubbe, *68

*Tik beyah *96,

Tik-bi-ah, 813, 826

Tik bi yah, 530

Tik bone te mah, 523

Tik bo nubbe, 521, 528

Tik bonubbee, 234, 273

*Tik botobi, *166

Tik-e-bah, 386, 476, 519, 525, 825

R.C. Tik e bah hemah, 525, [R. c. 634,] 868, 869

Tih e be ubbe, 516

Tik-e-be-ubbee, 384, 462, 824

Tik e bone to mah, 750

Tik-e-bon-tubbe, 735

R.C. Tik-e-bon-tubbee, [R. c. 623,] 736

*Tik e kubbee, *122

Tik e timah, 507

Tik ha ho tubbee, 557

Tik-li-e-ho-ge, 143

Tik pa tubbee, 222

Tillemah, 400

Tish-hopia, 80

Tish la tam bee, 1014

Tish-na-tub-bee, 144

*Tish o a homah, *292

Tish o bo nubbee, 982

Tish oche lata, 1027

Tish o che leta, 204

Tish o che teba, 192

Tish o che teta, 198

Tish ochil eta, 223, 264, 316

Tish oc mitta, 194

Tish o e milla, 197

Tish oe mitta, 190, 219

Tish oh aam ba, or **Tishuhamba,** 275

Tish o hamba, 190, 199, 211, 214

Tisho hamba, or Tishpuhamba, 317

Tish-o-ham-bee, 140, 405, 595

Tish-o-has-mittah, 29

*Tish o he cubbee, *98

Tish oh ham bee, 401

Tish o ho cubbe, 516

Tish oh ho ma, 903

*Tish ohomba, *40

Tish-o-hom-bee, 139, 148

*Tish o ho nubbee, 452, *90

Tish ok chia, 515

Tish-ok-chi-ah, 384, 462, 824

*Tish o latah, Capt., *92

Tish-o-li-ah, 141

Tish oma, 192, 216, 903, 904

R.C. Tish omah, 183, 184, 217, 231, 318, [R. C. 640]

Tish omustubbe, 537

Tish-o-mus-tub-bee, 459, 813, 826

*Tish onawa, *10

*Tishonoah, *172

*Tish ononah, *174

*Tish onowa, *12

Tish-o-no-wah-tub-bee, 557, 827

Tish-o-no-wa-tubbee, 385, 469, 817

*Tish oonga lubbee, *284

Tish o peia, 185, 186, 216

Tishopeia, or Elantubbee, 224

Tish opi, 172

*Tish-o-pia, 27, 46, 47, 49, 50, 76, 178, 179, 180, 184, 198, 203, 440, 442, *150

Tisho-pia, or Tish-a-pia, 378

Tish o pia, alias E-lan-tub-bee, 141, 205, 318

Tishopiah, 319, 417, 418, 419, 441, 451, 555, 556, R. c. 642, 916, 918

Tisho pin mitta, 162

Tish-o-tubbe, 517

Tisho tubbee, 142

Tish pu ham ba, or Tishohamba, 317

Tishu, 386, 475, 573, 825

Tish-u-am-ba, 92, 93, 825

Tish-u-a-tubbee, 96

Tish u hamba, or Tishohaamba, 275

Tish u mus tub bee, 472, 473

Tish u mustubbee, or Akwatocubbee, or Hush to mubbee, or Ogleisteia, 275

Tishu no wah tubbee, 475

Tishu-no-wa-tubbee, 386, 524

Tish-wa-ha-gub-bee, 144

Tish-yoh. 141

Tis ly a tubbee, 918

Tis-o-he-chubbe, 581

*Tis onoon tubbee, *264

*Tispamba, *66

Tis-ti-ke-ah, 866

Tocubbee, 211, 214, 378, 452

Tocubbee, or Eocalubbee, 589

Tol-oma-tubbee, 100

Toe-te-homa, 108

Toe-tub-bee, 137

To-ge, 145

Tohah, 468, 598

To-ha-nah, 149

Toh bin gee, 200

To-he-nah, 143

Toh gah, 146

*Toh habi, *164

Toh-la-hu-mah, 100

Toh nola, 1051, 1052

Toh oka, 198

To-hol-la-tub-bee, 140

To hona, 912, 913

Tohonah, 422, 965

To honah temah, 510

*Toh takah, *84

To huam posh ubbee, 468

To hubbe, 508

To hubbee, 385

R.C. To-kah, 388, 575, 599, [R. C. 657,] 984

To-kahago, 212

Tokahajo, 214, 260, 261, 262

To-kah-ho-mah, 813, 826

To kah honah, 383, 459, 516

Tokah-lom-bee, 377

To-ka-ho-na, 138

Tokaia, 190

Tokajo, 212

Tok alam be, 501

Tokalla tubbe, 515

Toke-Hoyno, 139

Tokecha, 197

Toki-ah-carns, 103

Tokiah Carnes, or Tokiah, 451

Tokiah Carnes, 466

Tok ka la too nah, 530

Tok-ho-tam-bee, 145

Tok oh too nah, 747

*Tokola, *230

Tok-o-la-tubbee, 376

R.C. Tok-o-lubbee, [R. C. 626,] 759

To kubbe, 268, 319

To kubbee, or Toka, 484

To-kutch-ee, 386

To-lah-ho-nah, 375, 493, 564, 569, 689, 831

To lah hubbe, 518

To lah tubbe, 515

Tolama, 197

Tolambee, 469

Tol-a-wah, 148

*Tol e humma, *248

*Tole humma, Silas, *248

Tol e wah te mah, 516

*Tolin, *102

Tollo oh ha ma, 906, 907

Tolotah, 602

Tol-o-wa tona, 186

Tol-wah, 387, 478, 532, 827

Tol-wah-ho-nah, 825

Tom, 147, 242

Tom Billy, or La toka, 382

*Tom, Capt., *306

Tom, Jefferson, 147

Tom, Jim, 18, 423, 424, 601

Toma, 380, 404, 498

Toma-ha-Oak-chi-ah, 138

Tom-a-ha-can-tubbee, 854

Tom-a-ha-club-bee, 139

R.C. Tom a-ha-een-lubbee, R. c. 630

*Toma hager, 216

R.C. Tomah heen lah, 541, [R. c. 636,] 880, 881

To-mah-hoke-chiah, 387

Tom-ah-hun-lah, 879

Tomah ko nubbee, 399

Tomah-lacha, 404

Tomah la chah, 424

Toma hoka, 218

Tomahoonah, 148

R.C. *Tomah-tubbee, R. c. 627, *74

Tomal achi, 434

To mam ba, 575

To-man-cha-abbee, 105

R.C. To-man-cha-hubbee, 442, [R. c. 680,] 1114

To-man-che-ab-bee, 145

To-mat-tubbe, 776, 780, 783

Tomat tubbee, 760, 762, 777

*Toma tubbee, 234

To-me-hah-tah, 379

*Tome hattah, 497, *52

Tome heio, 936

Tom-e-hi-yo, 386, 475, 524, 825

Tome hubbe, 523

To-mi-ah, 141

*Tomison, Lemas, *300

Tom-lea-cha, 83

R.C. Tom-ma-tubbee, 280, [R. c. 669,] 320, 1049, 1050

Tommet Tubbee, 701

Tommot, Tubby, 701

*Tommy, Edmund, *42

To-mo-tam-bee, 140

To mot Tubbee, 776

To Mot Tubby, 776

Tom-uh-bee, 139

Tona, 190, 378, 536, 581

Tona-ab-be, 97

*Tona a hager Thompson, *216

*Tonabee, *242

*Tonabbee, *242

*Tona cha, *222

*Tonah, 141, 395, 396, 380, 440, 442, 505, 769, 908, *262

R.C. Tonah, or Tone, 768, 780, 783, R. c. 627

R.C. Tonah hoyo, 396, 407, [R. c. 673,] 1072

R.C. To-nah-te-mah, R. c. 615

R.C. To nah-tim-ah, 561, [R. c. 636,] 884, 885, 886

R.C. Tonah tubbe, 600, R. c. 655

Tonah tubbee, 979

Tona peia, 223

Tona-pi-che, 148

Tonar, 87

To-na-tim-ah, 388

Tonch par tubby, 716

Tone, 378, 546, 569, 690, 829

Tone, or Tonah, 768, 783

R.C. Tonee, or Tonah, 780, R. c. 627

To-ne-he-nah, 148

Toneley, Honer, 702

Toner-Timer, 700, 803

R.C. To-ne-te-mi-ah, 803, R. c. 619

Tone ubbe, 558

Tone-ubbee, 104, 491

Tonia, 531

To-ni-ah, or Ahto-no hambe, 579

To-ni-ga, 142

To-ni-ya, 381, 504, 581

T

Tonk a you, 138

Tonk le, 533

Tonko cubbee, 758

Tonney Timer, 700

Tonney Tiner, 700

Tono, 835

*Tonoh, *256

Tonohoka, 507

Tonomah, 395

To nooncha, 521

*Tonopia humma, *208

Tono temah, 400

*Tonotobi, *184

Tonowah, 440

Tonsh-pah-ho-ca, 797

*Ton-temah, *100, *108

Tonubbe, 547, 590

Tonubbee, 190, 197, 389, 383, 464, 497

Tonubbee, or Tanubbee, 26

Tonuppe hahja, or Okeacha, 953, 954

To-nut-tubbee, 380

Ton-we-che, 380

Too-ah-loop-ka, 375, 690

Too-ga-loo, 83, 142

Toog-la-hona, 108

Toog-lo-stubbee, 1058

Took a chubbe, 525

Took ah lambe, 569

Took-ah-tubbee, 137

Took-alloon-tubbe, 792

R.C. Took-al-loon-tubbe, R. C. 616

Took a lon tubbee, 940

Took a loon-tubbee, 174, 178, 179

Took a loon tubbe, 529, 791

Took a lubbee, 643

Took lah bee, 603

Took lah hemah, 497

*Took la himah, *48, *50

Took la hona, 514

Took la honah, 530

Took lah tubbee, 568, 689

Took le loon tubbee, 799

Took lubbee, 925

Too lah tubbe, 510

Too mah ka, 690

Toonah, 554, 575

Toona lubbe, 256

*Toonlah, Juicy W., *86

Toon lah honah, 521

Toon la honah, 517

Toon nah, 422, 423

Toonsh pah tubbe, 591

*Toontah Doctor, *34

Toosh ba tubbee, 179

Toosh-pah tubbee, 914

R.C. Toosh-pa-tubbee, R. C. 642

*Tootema, *114

Too wah noo hah, 449, 690

Too wak ah, 449

To pah, 400, 440

To-pah-ho-mah, 376, 384, 462, 516, 528, 330

To-pa-homa, 825

To pe lah, 521

To po tubbee, 485

R.C. Toppe-na-no-wa, 253, R. C. 668

Top pe pa noa, 930, 931

*Toppina, *186

Torg-la-ho-na, 137

Tar-mus-tub-bee, 137

Torns, Jack, 18

To she mah, 528

To she nah, 759

To sho ah hoka, 766

To shoah honah, 498

R.C. To-shoo-nah, R. C. 626

To-show ah ho ke, 765

*Tosho yoho, *156

Tosho yo honah, 508

Tosho yotubbe, 449

To-sho-yo-tubbee, 379, 570

*Tosh pabi, Capt., *160

Tosh pah tubbe, 573

Toshu nah, 758

Tota, 269

Totahona, 317

Tota hoyo, 140

To tambee, 385, 540

Tote homa, 273

Tote hoyo, 522

Tote mus tubbe, 520

Tote mus tubbe, 383, 461, 824

To-te-pi-ah, 824

To-te-pi-yah, 384, 461, 521

To-tom-ba, 139, 817

To tom bee, 525, 827

To tubbe, 514

To tubbee, 383, 459, 482, 483, 497, 826

R.C. Toush-pah-hoca, R. C. 619

Towa, 194

Towa-ha, 710

To wah noo wah, 570

To-wa-ka, 29

To-wa-ke, 97

Tow-at-a-ga, 95

Tow-a-tubbee, 788

Towaya, 237

R.C. Tow e cha, 717, 780, 806, R. c. 619

*Towekala tubbe, *14

*Towotah, *166

*Towsh par tubbee, *232

*Tow un tobi, *190

Tow wache, 1058

Trahern, Wesley B., or Train Wesley, 27

Trihopia, 417

Trihopiah, 416

*Truly, H., *170

Tubba fa lubbi, 76

Tubbece, 380, 404, 581

R.C. Tubbee, 403, [R. c. 632,] 701, 861

*Tubbe hake, *44

Tubbey, 711

Tubbey, Yarhen, 713

Tubby, 701

*Tubby, William, *72

Tucha, 199

Tuch-ca-ho-no-ha-ja, 149

Tuch con iah, 789

Tuch-con iarh, 715, 789

Tucherlin, Abbey, 699

R.C. Tuck-ah-lan-tubbee, alias Hock-lan-tubbee, R. c. 623

R.C. Tuck-ah-loon-tubbee, 803, R. c. 617

R.C. Tuck-a-loon-te-mah, R. c. 620

Tuck a loon tubbee, 172

R.C. Tuck-co-niah, R. c. 619

Tuckelan Tubbey, or Hockelan Tubbee, 720

Tucker lan Tubbee, alias Hock e lan, Tubbee, 721

Tuck-er-loon-tubbee, 798

Tuck-ho-la-tubbee, 140, 149

Tuck-ho-lu-tubbee, 89

T

Tucklin, Tubby, 710

Tuc-o-lah, 141

Tug-bit-lee lah, 148

Tui kanchi hoga, 930

Tuk a la ma hona, 271

Tuk a la nubbee, 242

Tuk a loon temah, 799

Tuk a loon tubbee, 170

Tuk a lubbe, 266

Tuke-be-abbee, 112

*Tuk lon-tubbee, *306

*Tuk loon tobi, 170

Tul-luah, 141

*Tuly, *84

Tu-mah, 139

Tu-meen tah honah, 573

Tum-me-la-cha, 115

Tum-u-pish-tinah, 80

Tun-al-up-kah, (Billey McKincey,) 147

Tun am po tubbee, 394

Tuna postaia. 190

Tun-a-wah, or Tunewah, 28

Tun-e-wah, or Tunawah, 28

Tun-e-wak-be, 146

Tun kas he hoka, 253

*Tun nis ser, *252

*Tun nop onubbe, *36

*Tunowa, *130

Tup-a-nah, 148

Tu-pe-na-hoo-ma, 26

*Tuppana homa, *208

Tuppena, 196, 237

Tuppenahoma, or Oklabba, 264, 319

Tuppenanche habbee, 137

Tuppe na nowa, 930

Tur co tick bah, 451

Turnbull, Anthony. 155, 172, 179, 245, 430
1007

Turn bull, Capt., 26, 282

*Turn bull, George, 24, 434, 435, *218

*Turn bull, John, *258

*Turn bull, J. P., *260

Turnbull, Julia, 249

*Turn bull, Lydia, *20, *212, *224

R.c.*Turnbull, Robert, 26, 77, 249, 319, 1006,
1007, R. c. 661, *258, *260

*Turnbull, T. B., *222

*Turnbull, Turner B., *218

Turnbull, William, 179

Tusaha, 50

Tus-ahan-bee, 137

Tus-ah-hah, 140

Tus-ah-pah, 149

Tus-a-hu, 88

*Tusca hemitta, Capt., *288

R.c. Tuscah-ho-mah, 376, 590, 1120, 1121, R. c.
682

R.c. Tus-cah-lo-co-la, R. c., 683

Tus cah min tubbee, 398

Tus cah ho ah, 760

Tus-ca-ho-ca, 92, 142

Tus-ca-ho-ma, 89

Tus ca homah, 415

Tus ca hon che mah tubbe, 763

Tus ca-ho-no-ha-jo, 89

Tus ca how che mah stubbee, or Tus ca mah
stubbee, 734

Tus cah tick lah, or Yock a na homah, 400

Tus ca locola, 1129, 1130

Tusca mah stubbee, or Tus ca how che mah
stubbee, 733, 734

Tusca noah, 781, 788

Tusca nola, 189, 192, 199, 240, 242, 435

Tuscar, 707

Tus-che-ah-chubbee, 380, 761

R.C. Tus-che-ah-chubbee, alias Tus-con-chubbee, R. c. 616

Tus che ah chubbee, or Tus che arch Hubby, 706

Tus che arch hubbey, 709

Tus che arch hubby, 709

Tus che arch hubbey, or Tus con che chubbee, 789

Tus che Arch Hubby, or Tus che ah chubbee, 706

Tus ci aker, 709

Tus-ci-okah, 380, 705

Tus ci oker, 705

Tus co chi ambe, 574

Tus coh homah, 420

R.C. Tus con ah mah tubbee, R. c. 627

Tus con ah mattubbe, 766, 780, 783

Tus-co-nah-mustubbee, 379, 762

Tus cona mallubbe, 767

Tus con che hubbee, 715, 716, 760

Tus con che hubbey, 715, 716

Tuscon chubbee, 781

R.C. Tuscon chubbee, alias Tus-che-ah-chubbee, R. c. 616.

Tuscon chubbee, alias Tusche arch hubbey, 789

Tuscono nahtubbee, 767

Tuscubleha, 224

Tusculle metah, 581

Tuscuppa, or Tuschcubbee, 586

Tuseay tucha, 19

Tush-ca-ho-mo ha jo, 140

Tush-ca-hon-che-mah-tubbe, 736, 780

Tush-ca-hon-che-mah-tubbee, 736

Tush ca hon che mahs tubbee, 732, 761

Tush-ca-hon-che-nahs-tubbee, 379

Tush ca me hah, 985

Tush-co-hon-che-mah-tubbee, 735

Tush-cubbe, or Tush cuppa, 586

Tush-hai-ha, 159

Tush hoker, 758

Tush-honantah, or Kahsoneta, 580

Tush-hoo-nah tah, 381

*Tush-ka-himmittah, *42

Tush kah mahah, 983

Tush-ka-ho-ma, 149

Tush-ka-ho-mah, 140

Tush-kamba, 537

*Tush kanoli, *176

*Tush kanowa, *200, *268

*Tush-kar-kahacho, *304

Tush kato-ka, 139

*Tush kattah, *194

*Tush ka tubby, *240

*Tush kea homa, *16

*Tush kia, *20

*Tush kimastubbee, *246

Tush-ko-na, 581

Tusho Hoker, 757, 758

Tush pah hakah, 746

Tush pah hoka, 515

R.C. Tush-pah-ho-kah, [R. c. 625,] 747

Tush pah oka, 541

Tush pa tubbe, 255, 542

*Tush pa tubbee, 319, *44

Tush Per honer, 739

Tushu tubbee, 492, 539

*Tush wakoya, *174

Tuska, 147

T

Tuska ah tubbe, 567

Tusk-a-ah-wa, 26

Tuska-a-tokah, 386, 470, 520, 817, 827

Tus-ka-a-tub-bee, 147

Tuskal mitta, 237

Tuska hagah, 461

*Tusk a har Jo, *18

Tus-kah-chuch-ah-mah, 376

Tus kah chuckah mah, 588

Tus-kah-ha-kah, 386, 476, 537, 761, 825

Tus kah hoka, 446

Tus-kah-ho-mah, 109

Tusk-ah-hoomah, 142

Tuska hiaker, 704

R.C. Tuskah-no-ah, 380, R. c. 616

Tuskah noah, or Tuskinoar, 705

Tuska homa, 592

*Tuska homer, *160

*Tusk a hom mah, *180

R.C. Tus-ka-hon-che-mah-tubbee, R. c. 623

R.C. Tus-ka-how-che-marsh-tubbee, alias Tus-ka-mah-stubbee, R. c. 623

Tus ka la-meta, 491, 492

R.C. Tus-ka-mah-stubbee, alias Tus-ka-how-che-marsh-tubbee, R. c. 623

Tus-ka-ma-ta, or Tus-kamataha, 28

Tus-ka-ma-ta-ha, or Tus-ka-ma-ta, 28

Tus kam bee, 517

*Tusk an chubbee, *140

*Tusk anowah, *64

Tusk a oh tubbee, 689

Tusk-ca-hon-che-mah-tubbe, 783

Tusk-ca-hon-che-mash-tubbe, 783

Tusk ca howche mah stubbee, alias Tus ca mah stubbee, 733

Tuske ah lick ah, 405

*Tuske akah, *140

Tuske a tubbee, 1003, 1004

Tuskecha, 194

Tusk hoker, 757

R.C. Tus-ki-ah, [R. c. 621,] 788

Tuskia ha, 191, 198, 220, 316

R.C. Tus-ki-a-kah, [R. c. 616,] 710, 760, 781

Tuskiakap, 801

Tuski aken, 700

Tuski aker, 720, 721, 722

R.C. Tuskiatubbee, 225, R. c. 661

Tuskiha, 163

Tuski noar, or Tuskah noah, 705

Tuski okah, 761

Tus-ko-chi-am-bee, 816, 827

Tusko lotto, 560

Tus-mi-ah, 143

Tus-ok-cham-ba, 382, 457

Tus on on cha, 18

Tus-o-tub-bee, 147

*Tus par tubbee, *44

R.C. Tussaha, 218, 255, 912, 913, R. c. 641

Tus-sah-hah, 27, 376, 590

Tussaka, 218

*Tusuk, Saili, *306

Tu-wah-he, 379

Tu-wak-ke, 95, 144

Tu-yah, 103

Tw wah kee, 570

Ty-ah, 145, 1110

*Ty ye, 1080, *40

Ub ah me le, 449

Ub-ah-ni-ah, 380, 539, 584

Ub-ah-ni-ah, alias Bah-ni-ah, 579

U bah wala, 468

Uba-me-lah, 95

U-ba-na-za, 137

U-ba-pis-ubbee, 104

U-ba-we-lah, 144

Ubbachi, 50

*Ub bak kamo, *254

*Ubbanili, *178

*Ub bar hi lo ha, *204

*Ubbe, *312

*Ubbit ton nola, *312

*Ueawak atu bbee, *132

Ug la ubbee, 100

Ug-ly-ub-bee, 146

Uhahnela, or Ah bow wela, 569

Uhah wela, or Ah bow wele, 569

Uh-nah-hombee, 109

*U h wakoh, *190

U-ka, 113, 138

*Uk atubbe, *116

U lan le tubbe, 503

Ula pus abbee, 145

U-lat-to-ho-yo, 147

Ul-te-tarmar, 81

Ul-la-che-mah, 501

*Ullahonubi, *178

Ulmayon, 80

Ulth bo tah, 542

Ulth la honah, 510

Ulth-le-ho-nah, 381

*Ultoko, Capt., *160

Umah, 397

Um me hah to nah, 404

Un-ab-bee, 144, 101

Un-ab-by-ho-gee, 143

Un-ah-che-ha-tub-bee, 144

Unah-che-hoyo, 1086

Unah-haw tu bbee, 553

Unah-he-tub-bee, 144

Unah hool ta, 445

Unah le hoka, 506

Un-ah-lee, 147

U-nah-ta-cha, 142

R.C. U-nah-ta-kah, 615

Unah tim ah, 542

Unah to lubbe, 501

R.C. Un-ah-ton-ah, 377, R. c. 683, 1131

Unah tubbe, 539

R.C. Un ah tubbee, 498, [R. c. 675,] 1084, 1085, 146

Un-an-cha-hub-bee, 143

Unan che, or Nancy, 506

Un-an-che-ah-tubbee, 380

Un-at-ta, or O-nah-ta, 580

Un-at-tee, 144

Una-Tu-nah, 116, 139

Un cha la honah, 1051

Un che le, 508

Un-che-lo, 102

Unch-ho-chub-bee, 146

Un-chi-i-lah, 148

Un chutubbe, 596

R.C. Un-cue-mah, 649

Un-e-po-le-chubbee, 388

Unertaker, 698, 697

Un nah che he mah, 497

R.C. Un noom pi ha mah, 966, 602, R. c. 651

Vol. XXI– 2.

U

Un-no-tam-bee, 147

*Unnuk wia tubbe, Silas, *274

Un num po-le, 104

Un-nump-pola, 144

Unor hooka, 714

Un-ta-che-ah, 148

Un-tah, 394

Un tah ho tim ah, 885, 886

Un-ta-hi-o-che, 379, 538

Un ta ho temah, 498

Untah she mah, 497

Un tah tubbe, 498, 381, 507

Un-tah-tubbe, or Un-tan-tubbe, 581

Un-tan-tub-bee, 144

Un-tan-tubbe, or Un-tah-tubbe, 581

Un te ah, 506

Un te ah tubbe, 502

R.c. Un-te-ah-tubbee, 377, R. c. 679, 1105, 1106

Unte chubbe, 507

Un te cun e ubbe, 503

Un temah honah, 548

Un-te-yah-tubbee, 146

Untimah honah, 569, 690

Un-tu-ka, 148

Un-um-po-le-chubbe, or No pole, 581

*Upehatahbee, *292

Uppa hubbe, 264

Uppasa, 190

Up-pa-tah, 146

Ush cun-ah, 147

Ush-tah uk-le, 381

Usht-tub-bee, 147

Ush wah honah, 551

Ush wat ubbee, 276

Us-ta-he-ah, 389

Ustah hiah, 542

Uth-le-ho-nah, 144

Uth-leip-ok-chi-ah, 143

Uth le ohubbee, 971

Uth-le-pah, 146

Uth-le-pah, Jun'r., 146

Uth-to-va, 146

Utt a tam ba, 205

Uttelemah, 689

Uttutemah, 551, 567

Utubbee, or Hiotubbee, alias Mr. Shoat, 271

U-tubbee, 472, 473, 1101

*U-wah-ah, *120

U-wah-a-tub-bee, 144

U-we-te-mah, 505

Vol. XXII—1.

V

Vaughn, Alexander, 27

Vaughn, Chares, 172,

*Vaughn, Charles, 174, 178, 179, 203, 251, 319, 918, 939, *292

*Vaughn, Geo., *186

*Vaughn, James, *186

Vaughn, Phillip, 172, 178, 179

R.c. Vicey, 50, 403, 407, 425, 428, 432, [R.c 672,] 1069, 1070, 78, 425, 429

*Victor, I. B., *4

Vina, or Malacha, 280

Vina, 1050

*Vin meah honah, *110

Visa, 908

Waahona, 269

*Wa cha sem astubbe, *36

Wack-a-ho-tub-bee, 137

*Wade, Alfred, *174

*Wade, Amos, *92

*Wade, Anna, *206

*Wade, Cuhingham, *94

Wade, Enos, or Eno, 26

Wade, Enos, 171

*Wade, Henry, *182

*Wade, John, *174

*Wade, Susy, *302

*Wade, Vicey B., *214

*Wade, Washington, *88

Wafford, 73

*Wa-hah-ne-yo, 389, 992, 993, *322

R.C. Wa-ha-ne-yo, R. c. 659

Wahatona, alias Mahatona, 220, 316

Wa ha to nah, 158

Wah caya, 198

Wah-cha, 380, 507, 581

Wah ha chah, 403

Wah kah ate mah, 493

Wah kaha tumah, 565

*Wah kah timah, *62

Wah kah tubbe, 550

*Wahkiache, *24

Wah ki ah, 402, 417, 418, 451

Wah-ki-ah-te-ah, 376, 955, 956, 957

Wah ki ah timah, 939

Wah ki ho te mah, 1119

Wah-ki o-nah, 389

Wah kio nubbee, 407

Wah kio tubbe, 544

*Wah kuttubbee, *96

Wahli, 474

Wahli, or Billy, 520

R.C. Wah-sah-pah, R. c. 677

Wah sha pah, 1095, 1096

Wah-tubbe, 518, 570

Wah tubbee, 378, 387, 390, 446, 472, 690, 827

*Waid, Cunningham, *6

*Waid, Capt. John, *6

R.C. Wa-ka-a-ho-ma, R. c. 671

*Wakachi, *120

Wak-a-chi-ho-ge, 143

Wak-ah-che-ho-yo, 381, 507, 581

Wak ah honah, 548

Wak a hok ta, 454

Wak ah o tubbee, 113, 497

*Wak ah timah, *96

Wak ah to na, 471

Wak-ah-tubbe, 581

Wak-ah-tubbee, 375

Wak-ah-tu-nah, 826

Wa kai onubbe, 242

*Wak aiy ona, *8

Wak-a-to-nah, 385, 541

*Wa-ka-Tubbe, *252

Wa-ka-tubbee, 27, 106, 145, 148, 190, 197, 221, 243, 381

Wak a tu nah, 515

*Wakayahokti, *162

*Wak cah tubbee, *58

Wa keia, 185, 223

*Wake tubbee, *274

Wa kia ba, 912

Wa ki ah, 975

Wa ki a hona, 1061

R.C. Wak-i-ah-te-ah, 594, R. c. 649

Vol. XXIII—2.

W

Wak i chubbee, 577

Wak ietu nah, 573

Wak-io-la, 138

Wak i o nubbe, 528

R.C. Wak-i-o-nubbee, [R. C. 629,] 848

Wak i o tubbe, 521, 542

Wak-i-o-tubbee, 138, 384, 385, 462, 824

Wak ka teema, 258

Wak ka teia, 268

R.C. Wak-ka-te-ma, [R. C. 645,] 939

Wak kin, 243

Wakootema, 50

Wa-ko-tah, 147

Wak-ouk-ta, 145

Wak-tub-bee, 142

*Wakuttubbee, *120, *122

*Wak yoho, *2

Wak-yo-tub-bee, 147

R.C.*Wa-la, 592, [R. C. 649,] 957, 958, *296

Wa la honah, 401

Wa-le, 267, 813

*Wale, Sam., *178

*Walea, *54

Wa li, 386, 499, 826

Walis, 237

Waliss, 218

Walk, Johny, alias Ahpaha, 593

R.C. Wal kah ti mah, 385, [R. C. 621,] 717, 780, 786, 791

Walker, Benjamin, 137

*Walker, Charles, *100, *102

Walker, John, 18

*Walker, Richard, *190

*Wall, Dalila, *260

Wall, David W., 27

Wall, D. W., 68

*Wall, James, *64, 140, 144

*Wall, Noah, 18, 27, *236

*Wall, Thomas, *148, 150

Wall, Thomas, alias Thomas Garland, 27

*Wallace, *228

*Wallace, Dickson, *286

*Wallace, Dixon, *146, 148

Wallahaye, 234

*Walle, Selote, *278

Wallee, 520

*Wallis, *178

*Wallitobi, *160

Wansa, 234

Wan-to-sha, 147

Wapotona, 197

Ward, Agnes, 222

*Ward, Catherine, *16

Ward, Eden, 27

*Ward, Edney, *246

Ward, Falissa, 222

*Ward, Jeremiah, *16

Ward, Joel, 222

*Ward, Lizar, *92

*Ward, Logan, *60

Ward, Nelson, 222

Ward, Nicholas, 391

Ward, Silas, 222

Ward, Sophia, 977

*Ward, Stephen, *104

Ward, Syllin, 222

*Ward, Tobias, 118, 191, 197, 222, 415, 433, 482, *230

*Ward, Turner, 27, 433, *246

*Ward, William, *184

*Ward, Willie, *38

Ware, or Weir, Andrew, alias Ah toke co la, 503

*Warhey, Lucy, *260

*Warkahche. Jackson, *36

Warkache, *36

*Wark ary oemah, *172

*Warren, James, *258

*Wasah pah, *302

Wash co mab, 457

Wash co mak, 525

Wash co make, 382

Washington, 50, 243, 279

*Washington, Martha, *298

Washita, 221

Wash-ko-mok, 816, 827

Waskin, 221

Was-koo muk, 90, 91, 137

Was-ma-la-tubbee, 137

Wa ta hoyo, 221

Wa teer, 141

Wa te mah, 518, 542

Wa ti mah, 141

R.C. Wa to nah, 389, 591, [R. c. 658,] 991, 992

*Watson, *78

*Watson, Jonas, *162

*Watson, Nancy, *128

*Watson, Widow, *190

*Wattice, *40

Wat tubbee, 94, 141

*Wattuce, *80

Wa tubbe, 538

Watubbe, or Oon wah tubbe, 565

R.C *Wa-tubbee, 86, 139 [R. c. 627,] 779, 814, 826, *92, 274

Wa tubbee, or Oon wa tubbee, 493

Way la ho nah, 391

*Way oki, *162

Way te mah, 391

R.C. Way Tubbee, 28, 440, 594, [R. c. 614,] 808

We ah ho ka, 987

We ah honah, 520

We ah ish to nah, 503

We-ah-ish-ton-ah, 377

Wea Tubbey, 694

*Weaver, Auston, *292

Weaver, The, 142

*Webster, Jackson, *10, 12

Weenee, 601

Wee shock sehoma, 241

Wee shock shehoma, 240, 319

Wee shock shehoma, Capt., 282, 287

Wee shoc shee homa, 297, 299, 300

Wehatona, 191

R.C. We-hat-teo, 379, [R. c. 615,] 700, 781, 803

We hat to, 762

*Wehayoke, *72

We-hi-cha, 147

We-lah-ka, 142

*Welis sa, *204

*Welsey, John, *66

R.C. We nah ka, 465, 601, [R. c. 655,] 979

We-nok-ha, 147

R.C. We-shoc-cha-ho-mah, R. c. 618

We shoc che ho mah, 761, 800

We shoc che ho man, 713

We shochshe homah, Captain, 975, 976

We shock che ho mah, 781

*We shock che huna, *148

We shock she homa, 242, 411

We shock she homah, 426, 427, 434, 438, 467, 581

We shoc she homa, 192, 193, 199, 295, 296, 297, 433

We-shoc-ske-ho-mah, 380

Wesley, 279

*Wesley, Benj., *264, 302

Wesley, Charles, 223

*Wesley, Daniel, *306

*Wesley, Mrs. E., *314

*Wesley, Jackson, *300

*Wesley, Pahle, *300

*Wesley, Tandy, *10

*Westly, Benj., *288

*Wetabi, *156

*Whatner, James, *186

Whi-shoc-che-homa, 103

*White, Byrd, Capt , *314

*White, Jerry, *38

*White, Jonas, *36

*White, Lewis, 26. *36

*White, Sarah, *86

*White, Susan, *76

Whit-e-he-na, 107

*Whitibird, Tomme, *198

R.C. Wi ah to nah, [R. C. 676,] 1088, 1089

Wi a tubbee, 1005

*Wilkins, Morris, *32

Willah ka, 140

Willee, 601

*Willey, *76

William, 397, 405, 591, 889

*William, Billy, *306

*William, Byington, *14

*William, Gilbert, *154

*William, McNut, *158

*William, Sylvester, *146

*Williams, Amanda, *4

*Williams, Jack, *26

*Williams, James, *32

R.C. Willis, 492, 564, 606, [R. c. 653,] 1073

*Willis, Abel, *286

*Willis, Josiah, *6

*Willis, Juicy, *118

*Willis, L., *258

*Willis, Levi, *102

*Willis, S. P., *160

W

Wilson, 398

R.C. Wilson, Hannah, 602, [R. c. 651,] 966

*Wilson, Jonas, *256

*Wilson, Kanah, *200

Wilson, Levi,

Wilson, Lewe, 432

*Wilson, Lona, *244

*Wilson, Melinda, *216

Wilson, Mrs., 27

*Wilson, Nancy, *244

Wilson, Sue, 26

*Wilson, Tom, 404, 465, 975, *244

Winchester, 50, 253

*Winlock, Bazil, *42, 84, 86

*Winlock, Selina, *42

*Winlock, Silis, *76

*Winlock, Thos., *42, 84

Winna, 223, 597

Winne, 567

Winney, 407

Winny, 689

Wish-a-moon-tubbee, 163

*Witubbee, *120

Wiz-y, 567, 689

Wok oy o, 1031

*Woodridge, Rhody, *120

*Woodridge, William, *120

*Worcester, Samuel, *278

Wo sho ha, 1054

*Wright, Alfred, *208

*Wright, Allen, *214

*Wright, Dixon, *110

Wright, Judge, 191, 208, 408

*Wright, Simon, *118

*Wright, Sophy, *112

*Wright, Susan, *208

Wy-ha-cha, 140

Yacatona, 235

Yaccomma, 234

Ya chok pia, 178

*Yachubbee, 420, *6

Yacotamba, 275

Yacotattubbee, 169

Yacotima, 197

Yacotona, 220

R.C. Yacowatubbee, 667

R.C. Yah hah lubbee, 618

Ya ha mah, 567, 689

Yaha po na, 137

Ya hap pa, 276

Yah atchie, 1051

Yah ho ka tonah, 532

Ya hi o ka, 148

Yahk, 497

*Yahk atah, 62

Yahk ubbe, 542

Yah mak in tubbe, 512

R.C. Ya ho to na, 643

Ya ho yo, 79

Yah tubbee, 377

Yai ho ka, 109

*Yakacha, 64

Yak ah to nah, 816

Yak ah tubbee, 997, 999

Yake o to nah, 396

Yak it te tubbee, 137

*Yak meh tubbee, 304

*Yak na kin tubbee, 6

*Yak ne homa, 80

*Yak no to to bi, 186

*Yak oh ti ma, 128

*Yak o me, 136

Yak o me tim ah, 492

Yak o me too nah, 509

Yak on tubbee, 316

*Yam be, 318

Ya min ta ho nah, 377

*Ya mo nubbee, Sim, 282

Yan-ish-lok-na, 461

*Yan ish lok nah, 523, 824, 383, *86

Yan moon tubbee, 567

Yan oon i o cubbee, 457

Ya pa nam che habee, 457

*Ya pul lak, 20

Yar ho tubbey, 713

Yar ke chub bee, 142

Yatah, 589

*Yatake, 16

*Yatoka, 8, 22

Ya wa to cah, 148

*Yaw wa, 6

*Yay a chabi, 158

Ya zoo ho pia, 378, 689, 568

Yea cutch a, 781, 800

R.C. Yea cutch ah, 616

Yea ha lubbee, 800

R.C. Yeah bee, 613, 614, 780, 807, 808

Yeah by, 695, 697

R.C. Yeah ho tubbee, 800, R. c. 618

Yeah otchey, 708

Yea me tuner, 708

Yea min tar, 789

Yea min ter holey, 704

Year bey, 691, 692, 694, 785

Year-buy, 785

R.C. Year by, 695, 808, R. c. 613, 614

Yee ah bee, 807

Y

Ye hen a le tubbee, 145

Yeh lu a let ubbee, 96, 101

Yehome stubbee, 457

Yel lah, 1032

Yem a hoka, 493, 565

Yem ak ah tubbe, 516

Yem e chubbe, 521, 827

Yem e ho nah, 525, 868

Yem e tiah, 548

Yem e tubbe, 517, 540, 574

Yem e tubbee, 139, 375, 385, 567, 689, 826

Yem in tah, 145

Yem in ta bo ka, 923

R.C. Yem in ta ho ka, 668

Yem ish lok nah, 584

Yem ma, 378, 497

Yemma chubbee, 178

Yemma ho nubbe, 599

Yemma hubbe, 567, 689

Yem me, 808

*Yem me chubbee, 250

R.C. Yemme ho nah, 634

Yem mo nubbee, 379

Yem o honah, 547

Yem o nubbe, 499

Yem o ti ah, 502

Ye nim tah ho nah, 498

Yeo cutcha, 380, 706, 760

Yeoka, 707

Yeo pah tah, 141

Yeo pa tah, 83

Yeo poh tah, 88

*Yeorhfu, 146

Yeota, 252, 319

R.C. Yeotah, 83, 141, R. c. 667, 921

Yerbey, 379

*Yerorly, 146

Yime chubbee, 469, 817

*Yim ei tubbee, 80

*Yim e tiah, 78

*Yim in ta hona, 16

*Yim in to na, 8

Yimma, 197, 391, 414, 415

R.C. Yimma chubbee, 180, 255, 252, 319, R. c. 641, 668, 906, 1047

*Yimmah, 74

Yimma hoka, 273

Yimma ho na, 236

Yimma ho nah, 393

R.C. Yimma ho nubbe, 657

Yimma ho nubbee, 982

Yimmanola, 272

R.C. Yimma to nah, 592, 649, 957, 958, 959

Yimma tubbe, 263

Yimmeak a go, 317

Yimme akyo, 271

*Yim me chubbee, 386, *260

Yim mee, 185

Yimme too nah, 378

Yimmetubbee, 222

*Yimmihona, 134

Yim min tah, 392

Yim min tubbee, 393

*Yimmi tonah, 220

Yimmo nubbee, 553

Yimmo tiah, 377, 442

Yim mubbee, 442

Yioka, 403

*Yiotah, 254

Yoah tam bee, 566

Yoba, 499

Yo tah che mah, 547

Yo tah tubbee, 378, 552

Yocache, 193

Yo ca con tu nah, 147

Yo ca ma tubbee, 190

Yo ca ta, 235, 316

Yocka ta, 191

Yock ha tah, 788

Yock o te mah, 140

Yocita, 83

Yock ah, 463, 403

Yock ah tim ah, 394

Yock ah to nah, 862

R.C. Yock ah tubbe, 659

Yock ah tubbee, 989, 990

Yock a ma tubbee, 398, 451, 400

Yock a na homah, 400

R.C. Yock a te mah, 615, 806

Yock a to nah, 399

Yock a tubbee, 395

Yock e ma tubbee, 147

Yock euny ho nubbee, 190

R.C. Yock hah tah, 380, R. c. 619

Yock ha tah, 464, 760, 781

Yock ha tel, 772

Yock ha ter, 780

Yock ho toba, 142

Yock i hater, 716

Yock ki oh chah honah, 395

Yock ma chubbee, 392

Yock nah tah, 716

Yock o tah lubbee, 405

Yock, o tah nubbee, 400

Yock o tee mah, 721

R.c. Yock o te mah, 623, 722

Yoc mah, 148

Yoc o toma, 190

Yo cubbee, 376

Yoc un tubbee, 140

R.C. Yoc un tu nah, 281, R. c. 670

Yoh hun nubbee, 422

Yo ho to nah, 916

Yo hubbe, 515, 530

Yoka, 574

*Yoka chubbe, 595, *92

Yo ka ha jo, 317

Yok a haw tubbee, 144

Yok ah ham be, 499

Yok ah honah, 526

Yok a hona, 117

Yok ah sho, 581

Yok ah to nah, 457, 522, 827

Yok ah tubbee, 484, 596, 575

Yok a ma tubbee, 421

Yok a mit im mah, 143

Yok a na la, 137

Yok an tubbee, 143

Yok an tu nah, 1059, 1060

Yok ash e mah, 384

Yok a tam bee, 378, 554

Yok a te mah, 145

R.C. Yok a to nah, 382, R. c. 633

Yok a tubbee, 388, 520, 872

Yok ha, 105

R.c.*Yok hah tah, R. c. 627, *190

Yok bat ter, 783

Yok i ah, 516

Yok io tahimah, 559

Yok io teim ah, 492

Yok ish ah, 143

Yok ka, 145

Yok kah tubbe, 581

Yok ke oh, 100

Vol. XXV— 4.

Yokko, 508
Yokko mah, 399
Yok lona, 516
Yok me tam be, 515
Yok me tiah, 514
Yok me tubbee, 569, 690
*Yok no la, 383, 459, 813, *96
Yok no lah, 460, 826
Yok nu la, 459
Yoko, 400
Yoko ho tubbee, 251
Yok o ma tubbee, 1043, 1044
Yok o me cha honah, 510
Yok o me che honah, 584
Yok o me che hon nah, 382
Yok o me timah, 558
Yok on tubbee, 223
Yok o nubbee, 1051
*Yok o tah, 122
Yo ko ta hah chubbe, 533
Yok o tam be, 528
Yok o te mah, 523
Yok o tim ah, 498
Yok o tom bee, 378
Yok o toon tubbee, 243
Yok o tubbe, 505
R.C. Yok o tubbee, 148, 499, 872, R. c. 635
Yok un lubbee, 1030
Yok un tubbee, 207
Yo kut che, 825
Yo kut chee, 475
Yo mo tam ba, 149
Yo mo tam bee, 85
Yo nah, 459, 762, 845
Yo na ho ka, 191
Yon ah tah, 459

Yon ah te kah, 448
Yon at e ga, 146
Yon e la, 1029
*Yoner, 310
*Yonlthe, 256
Yo pollah, 523
Yo po na, 147
Yo pul lah ho nah, 513
*Yo ta, 172
Yo tah, 140, 203, 926
*Yo tah, Capt., 286
Yo tubbee, 147, 813
You ah, 380, 383, 531, 783, 813, 826
You ah tah, 383, 532, 813, 826
You ah te kah, 377, 497
Young, A. F., 191
Young Alexander, 408
You poo kubbee, 116
*You theya, 284
You wa, 197
You wah, 519
R.C.*Yow ah, 190, 754, 780, R. c. 626, *102
Yowa hoka, 198, 219
Yow ah to nah, 464, 417, 418
Yow a to nah, 141
Yow er, 400
Yow wah to nah, 400
Yow wa to nah, 463
Yuck er lan tubbe, 783
Yum ah to nah, 560
*Yume tubbee, 118
Yum mach ubbee, 922
R.C. Yum mo nubbee, 674, 1077, 1078
Yun ish lok nah, 505
R.C. Yun ok in tubbee, 678, 1103, 1104
Yu quah ham bee, 588

Vol. XXVI—1.

Zemetubbee, 417

Zochata, 196

Y

Z

Key to Symbols

R.C. means Person Rejected as a 14th Article Claimant

* means that the case was adjudicated by the Atoka Revisory Board

R'd means Record of Court of Claims

The Numbers refer to Pages of Record of Court of Claims, and where numbers are preceeded by * they refer to the pages of the Record of Cases adjudicated by the Atoka Board.

www.ingramcontent.com/pod-product-compliance
Lightning Source LLC
Chambersburg PA
CBHW051318020426
42333CB00031B/3399